T0183574

Pro Cloud Native Java EE Apps

DevOps with MicroProfile, Jakarta EE 10 APIs, and Kubernetes

Luqman Saeed
Ghazy Abdallah

Apress®

Pro Cloud Native Java EE Apps: DevOps with MicroProfile, Jakarta EE 10 APIs, and Kubernetes

Luqman Saeed
Cantonments, Accra, Ghana

Ghazy Abdallah
Alwakra, Qatar

ISBN-13 (pbk): 978-1-4842-8899-3
https://doi.org/10.1007/978-1-4842-8900-6

ISBN-13 (electronic): 978-1-4842-8900-6

Managing Director, Apress Media LLC: Welmoed Spahr
Acquisitions Editor: Steve Anglin
Development Editor: Laura Berendson
Coordinating Editor: Gryffin Winkler

Cover designed by eStudioCalamar

Cover image by Bhupesh Talwar on Unsplash (www.unsplash.com)

Distributed to the book trade worldwide by Apress Media, LLC, 1 New York Plaza, New York, NY 10004, U.S.A. Phone 1-800-SPRINGER, fax (201) 348-4505, e-mail orders-ny@springer-sbm.com, or visit www.springeronline.com. Apress Media, LLC is a California LLC and the sole member (owner) is Springer Science + Business Media Finance Inc (SSBM Finance Inc). SSBM Finance Inc is a **Delaware** corporation.

For information on translations, please e-mail booktranslations@springernature.com; for reprint, paperback, or audio rights, please e-mail bookpermissions@springernature.com.

Apress titles may be purchased in bulk for academic, corporate, or promotional use. eBook versions and licenses are also available for most titles. For more information, reference our Print and eBook Bulk Sales web page at http://www.apress.com/bulk-sales.

Any source code or other supplementary material referenced by the author in this book is available to readers on GitHub (https://github.com/Apress). For more detailed information, please visit http://www.apress.com/source-code.

Printed on acid-free paper

I dedicate this book to my wife, for her patience. And to my boys, for never giving me the space to write this book.

—Luqman Saeed

To Luqman Saeed for encouraging, supporting, and giving me the honor to co-author this book, and my parents, wife, and siblings for supporting me throughout.

—Ghazy Abdallah

Table of Contents

About the Authors

Luqman Saeed is currently an enterprise Java developer and independent software development trainer. His almost two decades of industrial experience spans management and leadership positions across various sectors, including software development and teaching. He started with PHP as a hobby and now does enterprise Java development full time. He is currently in the production process of the second edition of the much popular Java Enterprise Edition 8 for Beginners course on Udemy, this time updated and revised for Jakarta EE. His passion is helping software development teams get productive with the powerful, modern, intuitive, and easy-to-use Jakarta EE enterprise development platform.

Ghazy Abdallah is a passionate enterprise Java developer, founder of the Java User Group Sudan (SudanJUG), and a tinkerer. He enjoys the use of modern cloud infrastructure to deliver enterprise applications and site reliability engineering. He spends his time learning and teaching the latest in cloud-native development.

About the Technical Reviewer

Josh Juneau has been developing software and database systems for several years. Database application development and sophisticated web apps have been the focus of his career since the beginning. Early in his career, he became an Oracle database administrator and adopted the PL/SQL language for performing administrative tasks and developing applications for Oracle database. In an effort to build more complex solutions, he began to incorporate Java into his PL/SQL applications and later developed stand-alone and web applications with Java. Josh wrote his early Java web applications utilizing JDBC to work with back-end databases. Later, he incorporated frameworks into his enterprise solutions, including Java EE, Spring, and JBoss Seam. Today, he primarily develops enterprise web solutions utilizing Java EE.

He extended his knowledge of the JVM by developing applications with other JVM languages such as Jython and Groovy. In 2006, Josh became the editor and publisher for the *Jython Monthly* newsletter. In late 2008, he began a podcast dedicated to the Jython programming language. Josh was the lead author for *The Definitive Guide to Jython, Oracle PL/SQL Recipes*, and *Java 7 Recipes*, which were published by Apress. Since then, he has continued to author Java-related books for Apress, including his most recent work entitled *Java 9 Recipes*. He is an avid contributor to Oracle's *Java Magazine*, and he speaks at Java User Groups and conferences when he has the opportunity.

He works as an application developer and systems analyst, and he is a contributor to the Chicago Java Users Group. Josh is an Apache NetBeans committer and a Java Champion. He participates in the JCP and has been a part of the Jakarta Faces expert group for the development of Java EE 8. Josh has a wonderful wife and five children with whom he loves to spend time. To hear more from Josh, follow his blog, which can be found at `http://jj-blogger.blogspot.com`. You can also follow him on Twitter via @javajuneau.

Acknowledgments

We'd like to acknowledge the excellent work that has been and still being done in the Jakarta EE and MicroProfile communities. The transition from Java EE to Jakarta EE and the smooth incorporation of cloud-native standards on top of a stable base via MicroProfile for a platform of such scale and reach can only be described as incredible. The work done so far is a testament to the power of the platform and its ecosystem.

Introduction

Thank you very much for picking up this book. The Jakarta EE platform has gone through a major milestone over the last couple of years. This started with the stagnation of Java EE 8 and culminated in the transfer of the entire platform to the Eclipse Foundation and the eventual release of Jakarta EE 10. The current Jakarta EE platform is a remarkable departure from its earlier J2EE versions. Unfortunately, the bad experiences that developers had with the then platform have always created confusion in the minds of new and upcoming enterprise Java developers. Our goal with this book is to help you become a Jakarta EE developer by distilling the core of the platform in the various chapters of this book.

Our goal is not to teach you everything you need to know about Jakarta EE. For that, you can take a look at the various specifications that make up the platform. Our goal is to teach you how "little" you need to know to get productive with the platform. We distilled 80% of the everyday Jakarta EE we do in our practice into the concise chapters of this book so you can finish all of it in two or so weeks. Throughout this book, we focused on keeping things concise and to the point.

We cover both the oft-neglected theory and history of the platform alongside the core APIs that you will use in every single application you write on the platform. We also cover the use of the Eclipse MicroProfile APIs and how they interweave with the Jakarta EE platform to provide you a cohesive platform for application development. By the end of this book, you will have a firm theoretical and practical foundation in enterprise Java development using Jakarta EE. You will also understand much better the various acronyms that abound in its nomenclature.

Chapter 1 sets the context for the book by exploring the theoretical foundations and history of the Jakarta EE platform. Chapter 2 follows by taking a look at general Java enterprise development in a cloud-native microservices era. Chapter 3 then introduces the sample code that forms the centerpiece of discussions throughout the book. Chapter 4 sets off the rest of the book by taking a deeper look at the Jakarta Contexts and Dependency Injection API. This API is single-handedly the most important on the platform because it weaves together the disparate parts into one cohesive whole. The chapter discusses the practical aspects of the specification that you will use in your everyday development.

Chapter 5 follows with another discussion on the Jakarta Persistence API, the standard object-relational mapping API for the platform. Chapter 6 covers creating and consuming RESTful resources with the Jakarta REST API. Chapters 7 through 11 cover the Eclipse MicroProfile Config, Fault Tolerance, Metrics, Health Check, and JWT Propagation APIs, respectively. Chapter 12 takes a look at testing Jakarta EE applications using the TestContainers Java library, while Chapter 13 steps back to take a bird's-eye view of everything discussed so far in the book within the context of the sample code. The final chapter, Chapter 14, discusses breaking down a monolith into microservices ready for cloud deployment. Throughout the book, we discuss the use of containers to make Jakarta EE development much more productive and faster. The sample code of the application is set up for deployment with Kubernetes. You can use it as a template for your own projects.

To make the most of this book, you should be comfortable with Java SE, ideally have at least Java 11 installed. Some familiarity with enterprise Java development (doesn't really matter if it is Spring based) should be helpful but not required. You also will need to have Apache Maven, since that is the build tool we use for the book code. You can use any modern Java IDE that supports Maven. You should be able to import the code into your IDE of choice as long as it has Maven support. We hope this book shows you how concise, modern, intuitive, easy, and productive the Jakarta EE platform has evolved to be from the days of J2EE.

Feel free to reach out to us on LinkedIn (Luqman Ghazy) at any time with any feedback you have. Once again, thank you for picking up this book. We hope it helps in solidifying your Jakarta EE development career.

Source Code

All code used in this book can be found at github.com/apress/pro-cloud-native-java-ee-apps.

CHAPTER 1

The Theory of Jakarta EE and MicroProfile

Jakarta EE (formerly Java EE) is a set of community-developed, abstract specifications that together form a platform for developing end-to-end, multitier enterprise applications. Jakarta EE is built on the Java Standard Edition and aims to provide a stable, reliable, and vendor-neutral platform on which to develop cloud-native applications.

This chapter discusses the general theory surrounding the Java Enterprise Development platform. Enterprise Java–related nomenclature comprises a lot of technical words that might not be so clear. This chapter breaks down Java EE – now Jakarta EE – into its theoretical form such that by the end of this chapter, you will become familiar with the large number of Enterprise Java–related terminologies.

What Is a Specification?

Jakarta EE is made up of individual specifications, each specification covering a specific API, for example, Jakarta WebSocket, responsible for providing an API for writing applications that support communicating via a WebSocket protocol on the platform. These individual specifications are grouped into a single "umbrella" specification for a given Jakarta EE release. For example, the latest release, Jakarta EE 10,[1] is released under umbrella specification 10.

A specification is a document that outlines the functions of a given set of APIs. This document outlines what the expected behavior should be for various scenarios and invocations of the given API. The specification itself can be thought of as a blueprint for the API. The counterpart to a Jakarta EE specification is the implementation of that

[1] Jakarta EE Platform 10 | The Eclipse Foundation

L. Saeed and G. Abdallah, *Pro Cloud Native Java EE Apps*, https://doi.org/10.1007/978-1-4842-8900-6_1

specification. As the specification only states what the expectations and functions of an API are, the implementation of that specification is what does the job of actualizing those expectations and functions when any given API in that specification is invoked by a developer.

The specifications and their corresponding implementations are generally separated. This, for you as a developer, means you can simply code against the "abstract" specification (blueprint) and run your code using different implementations. This implies the freedom to pick an implementation that suits your needs without having to rewrite your code. For implementation vendors, this means more competition and, ultimately, better and faster innovations atop the base specifications.

In the past, the various (Java EE) specification releases happened under the Java Community Process (JCP[2]) Java Specification Request (JSR). The JSR is a process where any interested person (individual or registered entity) submits a document to the project management office of the JCP, proposing the development of a new or significant revision to an existing specification. The entire process, from the proposal of the specification document to the final release and a reference implementation, all happened as part of the JSR.

As an umbrella JSR, Java EE itself had a reference implementation in the form of GlassFish Application Server. This implementation was the "reference" that acted as the base for other umbrella spec implementations. Over the years, a number of Java EE full implementations have come out, including WildFly, Open Liberty, and Payara, among others.

From version 8 of Java EE, the specification process moved from the JCP to the Eclipse Foundation along with the GlassFish project. The concept of reference implementations also changed to compatible implementations, to better reflect the focus on cross-vendor neutrality and compatibility. However, to better understand what Jakarta EE is and how it came to be, a historical tour of Java EE releases is needed to get a better understanding of the context and objectives of Jakarta EE as a platform today and how the release process differs from what it was under the JCP.

[2] Java Community Process

Java EE Release History

Java 2 Platform, Enterprise Edition (J2EE 1.2)

The first release of the platform was on December 12, 1999, and was called Java 2 Enterprise Edition or J2EE for short. It featured the initial specification release of the platform, in the form of version 1.2. One of the key features of this novel (at the time) platform was the concept of Enterprise JavaBeans. The EJB API was intended to make it easy to encapsulate complex business logic in a component that was managed by a specialized runtime. This runtime provided EJB components with ancillary services like transactions, security, and scalability.

Java 2 Platform, Enterprise Edition (J2EE 1.3)

The next version of the Enterprise Java Platform was 1.3, released on September 24, 2001. This was contained in the umbrella JSR 58. The key features of this release were the introduction of new Java Connector Architecture (JCA) and the Java Message Service (JMS) APIs. The EJB API also saw improvements.

Java 2 Platform, Enterprise Edition (J2EE 1.4)

The next version of the platform, J2EE 1.4, was released on November 11, 2003. This version was contained under the umbrella JSR 151. The key feature of this release was the "adherence to the Web Services Interoperability Organization's (WS-I's) Basic Profile 1.0 document for implementing interoperable Web services."[3]

Java Platform, Enterprise Edition (Java EE) 5

The next release of the platform saw a rebranding of the name from Java 2 Enterprise Edition to Java Platform, Enterprise Edition. This would have been J2EE 1.5, so, naturally, this saw the rebranded version becoming Java EE 5. This release, under the umbrella JSR 244, featured Java annotations and came out on May 11, 2006.

[3] J2EE 1.4 spec certified | InfoWorld

Java Platform, Enterprise Edition (Java EE) 6

Java EE 6 was released on December 10, 2009, under the umbrella JSR 316. This release was the last major one under Sun Microsystems, before its takeover by Oracle a year later. Its main features were the introduction of CDI-managed security and the introduction of REST APIs.

Java Platform, Enterprise Edition (Java EE) 7

Almost four years after the release of Java EE 6, Java EE 7 was released on May 28, 2013, under the umbrella JSR 342. This release featured the introduction of the WebSocket and JSON processing APIs, as well as enhancements to HTML5 support in the JSF API. This release was also monumental because it was the first major Java EE release after Oracle acquired Sun Microsystems, the company that hitherto had been the trademark owner of the Java Platform.

Java Platform, Enterprise Edition (Java EE) 8

More than four years after the release of Java EE 7, Java EE 8 was released on August 31, 2017, under the umbrella JSR 366. Key features of this version were HTTP/2 and CDI-based security. Java EE 8 was a very important release because it was partly the result of a lot of pressure from grassroots community groups like the Jakarta EE Ambassadors (formerly Java EE Guardians[4]) that was brought to bear on Oracle to complete the release. This resulted in the scope of the release being reduced.

From Java EE to Jakarta EE

As you can see from the preceding chronological release history, the number of years between each release kept getting longer and longer, culminating in a more than four-year gap between the release of Java EE 7 and 8. In a fast-paced ecosystem like that of the Java Platform, four years between releases[5] was a significant gap. This necessitated

[4] The Java EE Guardians Rebrand as the Jakarta EE Ambassadors

[5] Lack of Java EE 8 Progress l Jakarta EE Ambassadors

calls by the community for Oracle to come clear[6] on its intentions for the Enterprise Java Platform, having inherited it as part of its purchase of Sun Microsystems. To the community, it seemed Oracle had abandoned Java EE. With a wide-reaching set of APIs that even non-Java EE products build upon, the death of Java EE would be catastrophic to the entire ecosystem. Essentially, Java EE formed the foundation of a large part of the enterprise development market in the Java space.

Later in 2017 however, after the release of Java EE 8, Oracle decided to move the Java EE Platform to an open source foundation to make it a full community-driven development platform. This transfer comprised the Java EE platform specs, complete with the Test Compatibility Kit (TCK). After consultations with key Java EE players RedHat and IBM, the Eclipse Foundation was chosen as the new home of the Java EE platform.

At this point, the Java EE platform was almost two decades old, and the implication was that the task of transferring such a massive platform from a proprietary entity to an open source foundation was monumental. One noteworthy hurdle had to do with intellectual property and trademark rights. To make the transfer as manageable as possible, the process was broken down into three main stages,[7] namely:

1. Transfer API and implementation code
2. Transfer Test Compatibility Kit (TCK) code, new specification process
3. Refactor API package name, transfer and update specification documents

Transfer API and Implementation Code

As discussed in the preceding sections, Jakarta EE is made up of individual specs, and each spec could have N number of releases in the past up to the point of transfer to Eclipse Foundation. It was decided to transfer only the latest released versions of each spec to the Eclipse Foundation. The top-level Eclipse Project, Eclipse Enterprise for Java

[6] Stagnation with Java EE 8: Can the Java Community Make a Difference?

[7] Transition from Java EE to Jakarta EE

(EE4J[8]), was created with the corresponding GitHub organization eclipse-ee4j[9] to act as the home of the specs and their implementations.

With a new home at the Eclipse Foundation, the transferred code was built using Eclipse Foundation's servers and infrastructure, the result staged to a Maven repository with the groupId changed from javax.* to jakarta.*. This change of groupId was significant because the Eclipse Foundation could not use the javax namespace due to legal restrictions. A new build of the reference implementation, GlassFish now called Eclipse GlassFish, was produced from these new artifacts and ran against the Java EE 8 TCK.

With the Eclipse GlassFish build passing the TCK, it was released as version 5 on January 29, 2019. This release under the jakarta.* package and jakarta groupId was technically still Java EE, because it was Java EE 8 certified. This only marked the release of the Java EE platform released from the new Eclipse Foundation's EE4J project on GitHub rather than the Java EE project. Also note that all the earlier versions of the various specifications that make up the Java EE platform are not managed nor maintained by the Eclipse Foundation as part of the platform.

Transfer Test Compatibility Kit (TCK) Code, New Specification Process

This stage involved the transfer of the TCK from which new binaries were built for the new Jakarta EE version specification. This stage also saw the introduction of the new Jakarta EE Specification Process (JESP).[10] The new JESP itself adopts the existing Eclipse Foundation Specification Process (EFSP) v1.2[11] with some few modifications. Along with the JESP, the Eclipse Foundation Technology Compatibility Kit license[12] was also released.

Together, these two legal frameworks now guide the development of Jakarta EE specifications and the release of compatible implementations, the whole process, managed end to end by the Eclipse Foundation. New Jakarta EE implementations must pass the TCK to be certified as compatible implementations of the platform and be

[8] Eclipse EE4J

[9] Eclipse EE4J Top-level Project and community related issues

[10] Jakarta EE Specification Process | The Eclipse Foundation

[11] Eclipse Foundation Specification Process

[12] Eclipse Foundation Technology Compatibility Kit License – v1.0

eligible[13] for enlistment on the Eclipse Foundation page for Jakarta EE downloads.[14] The goal of the JESP is to be as lightweight as possible, encouraging a "code first" approach to developing the platform, thus allowing for more experimentation and faster iteration.

Note that within the context of the Eclipse Foundation, we have been using the term "compatible implementation," while hitherto, with Java EE at the JCP, we used the term "reference implementation." This is because at the Eclipse Foundation, the concept of a "reference" implementation was scrapped in favor of compatible implementations. The goal is to make the certification process as easy and fast as possible and also to create a more level-playing field, thus advancing innovation in the implementation ecosystem.

The next steps in this process entailed updating the Javadoc of the various APIs, relicensing the resulting JAR files and testing same against the GlassFish 5.1 version, using the binaries built from the newly transferred TCK. The result of all these was the first release of Java EE as the newly transferred Jakarta EE, version 8. The official date for this release was September 10, 2019. Note that the release of Jakarta EE 8 still had GlassFish 5.1 as the compatible implementation. Also, this release did not feature any new APIs. It was solely "under-the-hood" changes that marked the first full release of the platform under the stewardship of the Eclipse Foundation.

This stage of the transfer of Java EE to the Eclipse Foundation also saw the revision and renaming of the various APIs to a more consistent naming convention. For example, the Java Persistence API (JPA) was renamed to Jakarta Persistence. The Java Authentication SPI for Containers (JASPIC) became Jakarta Authentication, and its counterpart, the Java Authorization Contract for Containers (JACC), became Jakarta Authorization. The Contexts and Dependency Injection (CDI) API became the Jakarta Contexts and Dependency Injection. This simplified naming convention made it easy to grasp the myriad APIs of the platform by just their names.

Up to this stage of the transfer, to develop applications on the platform, you needed to use the dependency shown in Figure 1-1.

[13] `https://jakarta.ee/compatibility/get-listed/`

[14] Jakarta EE Compatible Products | Enterprise Java Application and Web Servers | The Eclipse Foundation

```
<dependency>
    <groupid>javax</groupid>
    <artifactid>javaee-api</artifactid>
    <version>8.0</version>
    <scope>provided</scope>
</dependency>
```

***Figure 1-1.** Java EE dependency*

After the release of Jakarta EE 8, the maven coordinates changed to the dependency shown in Figure 1-2.

```
<dependency>
    <groupid>jakarta.platform</groupid>
    <artifactid>jakarta.jakartaee-api</artifactid>
    <version>8.0.0</version>
    <scope>provided</scope>
</dependency>
```

***Figure 1-2.** Jakarta EE dependency*

Jakarta EE 8 was a drop-in replacement for Java EE, meaning you could switch without any form of refactoring in your code or API change, because the various APIs were still within the javax.* package. Changing these to jakarta.* leads us to the final step of the transfer process.

Refactor API Package Name, Transfer and Update Specification Documents

This stage of the transfer process entailed renaming all the API packages to jakarta.* namespace. For example, the Entity Manager in Jakarta Persistence moves from javax.persistence.EntityManager to jakarta.persistence.EntityManager. The resulting release from this step was Jakarta EE 9,[15] followed five months later by Jakarta EE 9.1. This release was almost identical with the previous version, 8, the notable exception being the change in package names and baseline support for Java 11.

Given the wide use of Java 8 in most production systems, the APIs were still compilable with JDK 8, but implementations were required to pass the TCK running JDK 11. Some specifications that were moved from Java EE to Java SE and were again removed in JDK 11 were added back, some as mandatory, others as optional specs. For example, Jakarta Activation and Jakarta XML Binding were added as mandatory and optional specs, respectively. Eclipse GlassFish version 6 was also released as the first compatible implementation for Jakarta EE 9.

Also, in this step of the transfer process, the code of the specification docs were transferred, marking the final remaining artifact to be transferred to the Eclipse Foundation and signaling the completion of the transfer process. This final step, and its culmination in the release of Jakarta EE 9, was aimed mostly at the tooling ecosystem, to have them ready, updated, and extended to support the new platform. For you as a developer, Jakarta EE 9 is identical to Jakarta and Java EE 8. Upgrading from the previous versions of the platform to Jakarta EE 9, though, will result in nontrivial refactoring of your code because of the package change. Thankfully, there are tools[16] that can automate that migration for you, making it as smooth and easy as possible.

Jakarta EE 10 and Beyond

On August 24, 2021, the Jakarta EE Specification Committee[17] approved the Jakarta EE 10 Release Plan[18] through an official ballot. This plan had been created, discussed,

[15] Jakarta EE 9 Released! | The Eclipse Foundation

[16] Using IntelliJ IDEA's migration tool

[17] Specification Committee | The Eclipse Foundation

[18] Jakarta EE 10 Release Plan

reviewed, and amended by the Jakarta EE Community between June and August of the same year. The Release Plan outlines the details of the release timeline, scope, deliverables, and individual specification expectations. The expected release date for version 10 is the second quarter of 2022.

Jakarta EE 10 is expected to continue the evolution of the platform into a cloud-native platform for modern enterprise application development. One of the notable features of this release will be support for Java 17, the current LTS of the base Java SE platform. Even though Java 11 is the minimum required version, compatible implementations will be required to pass the TCK executed with Java 17.

This will significantly make it easy for enterprises to adopt the latest JDK and thus benefit from the faster iteration of features on the Java Platform overall. You as a developer will also be able to use new features in application development without having to worry about compatibility with your chosen Jakarta EE–compatible implementation.

Another possible notable highlight of this release will be the introduction of the Jakarta Core Profile. Jakarta EE (and Java EE before it) has always had "profiles," where a subset of the specifications that make up the full platform are grouped together to serve a narrow, common development purpose. These profiles are as follows:

- Web – This profile contains a subset of the platform APIs and technologies geared toward the development of mostly web applications like Jakarta Faces. This profile is for developers who do not desire the full set of APIs available on the platform. You only need a servlet container like Apache Tomcat to run this profile.
- Full – This profile contains the entire gamut of APIs and technologies available on the platform. It is geared toward developers in enterprise settings that develop multitier applications. A fully compatible implementation of the platform like WildFly[19] is needed to run this profile.

Jakarta EE 10 aims to possibly release the core profile alongside the existing two. What is the core profile? It is another subset of the platform APIs that contains "core" APIs aimed at developing modern, cloud-native, microservices applications to be

[19] WildFly

deployed through container platforms like docker to cloud application orchestration platforms like Kubernetes. The list of APIs expected to be part of the core profile are

- Jakarta EE Core Profile
- Jakarta Annotations
- Jakarta Contexts and Dependency Injection Lite
- Jakarta Dependency Injection
- Jakarta Expression Language
- Jakarta Interceptors
- Jakarta JSON Binding
- Jakarta JSON Processing
- Jakarta RESTful Web Services

These APIs, when paired with the Eclipse MicroProfile[20] project, form the basis for developing cloud-native enterprise Java applications. This profile, however, is still tentative for Jakarta EE 10 and will only be included if the release plan[21] of the core profile specification gets approved in time.

Jakarta EE and Eclipse MicroProfile

Jakarta EE (and Java EE before it) is a very critical platform in the Java ecosystem and, indeed, in the entire software development industry. Given the sheer number of projects, frameworks, and libraries that owe their existence and evolution to the Jakarta EE (and its "ancestor" J2EE) platform, there is no gainsaying the fact that Jakarta EE is an important tool in the arsenal of any Java developer.

Software development has evolved over the last few decades, from single massive, centralized applications to the current distributed, containerized, cloud-native microservices paradigm. Jakarta EE started in an era where the dominating software development paradigm was the monolith architecture. As such, its evolution had always

[20] MicroProfile

[21] Jakarta EE 10 Core Profile Release Plan

been much more optimized for developing monolith applications. That is not to say you cannot use Jakarta EE alone in developing microservices. You definitely can.

As we have discussed in previous sections, Jakarta EE was developed through the Java Community Process (JCP). This process wasn't entirely optimized to keep up with the pace at which software development was evolving. As you have seen in the release history of Jakarta EE (or more correctly, Java EE in that context), the duration between each release kept getting longer, while the pace of change in the software development industry kept getting faster. The natural consequence of this is that at some point, Jakarta EE had a lot more changes to catch up on in the industry with each release.

Even though you could use the standard Jakarta EE APIs to develop microservices, there was no clear, standardized support defined for the various platform runtimes. This meant that each application server implemented support for using Jakarta EE for microservices in a nonportable, nonvendor-neutral way. This could result in fragmented, noncoherent support for developing cloud-native, microservices applications on the platform. Oracle's unclear strategy for the platform between Java EE 7 and 8 did not help in keeping confidence in the platform as well.

It is within this context that application server vendors and various Java User Groups came together to find a way to augment the existing Jakarta EE platform with a separate set of specifications geared at developing cloud-native, microservices enterprise Java applications. At JavaOne 2016, the Eclipse MicroProfile project was announced as a new collaborative project for providing a set of APIs that are needed in a typical microservices application.

The Eclipse MicroProfile project is built on the Jakarta EE platform as a set of standardized specifications, containing a subset of the platform APIs, in addition to individually developed specs, that aims at providing a standard, portable, vendor-neutral way to build modern, cloud-first microservices applications. Version 1.0 of the project comprised the CDI, JAX-RS, and JSON-P APIs. Eclipse MicroProfile therefore came into existence as a way to extend the Jakarta EE (or, again, more correctly Java EE in that context) platform for a modern application development paradigm.

At the time Eclipse MicroProfile was announced, the Jakarta EE platform was still developed through the JCP. In this regard, one of the key objectives of the EMP was to eventually create JSRs at the JCP with developed EMP (Eclipse MicroProfile) specs, having the Eclipse Foundation act as the proposed spec lead. The project was designed to move fast and allow for a much more rapid and frequent release cadence to keep pace with an ever-evolving industry. There is practically no barrier to contributing. All you have to do is to fork the sandbox repository[22] on GitHub, implement your idea, and submit it as a pull request for feedback and iterations.

Another major goal of the EMP is to dispel the notion that Jakarta EE is "heavy" in the sense that you need a full-blown compatible application server to run it. Even though modern full JEE (Jakarta EE) compatible runtimes are very lean and lightweight, the past experiences with the major pain points of earlier releases of the platform (the J2EE era) and its accompanying application servers at that time still lingered on. Thus, EMP aimed to give vendors much smaller implementation requirements to help make running it as fast and lightweight as possible.

A year after the unveiling of the EMP, Oracle announced the transfer of Java EE to the Eclipse Foundation. The result of this is that the parent platform of the EMP found its way back to the same entity. Even though both projects are now managed by the same foundation, they are kept as separately evolved specifications. JEE is now going to evolve at a much faster pace relative to its time at the JCP, but slower than EMP. The goal is to have the JEE platform remain the matured, stable, and reliable development platform that enterprises of all sizes have come to trust while still incorporating tested and industry-accepted modern paradigms quicker.

The current release of Eclipse MicroProfile is version 5, summarized in Figure 1-3, is made up of 18 total APIs: 13 core and 5 stand-alone, as shown in the image below.

[22] GitHub - eclipse/microprofile-sandbox

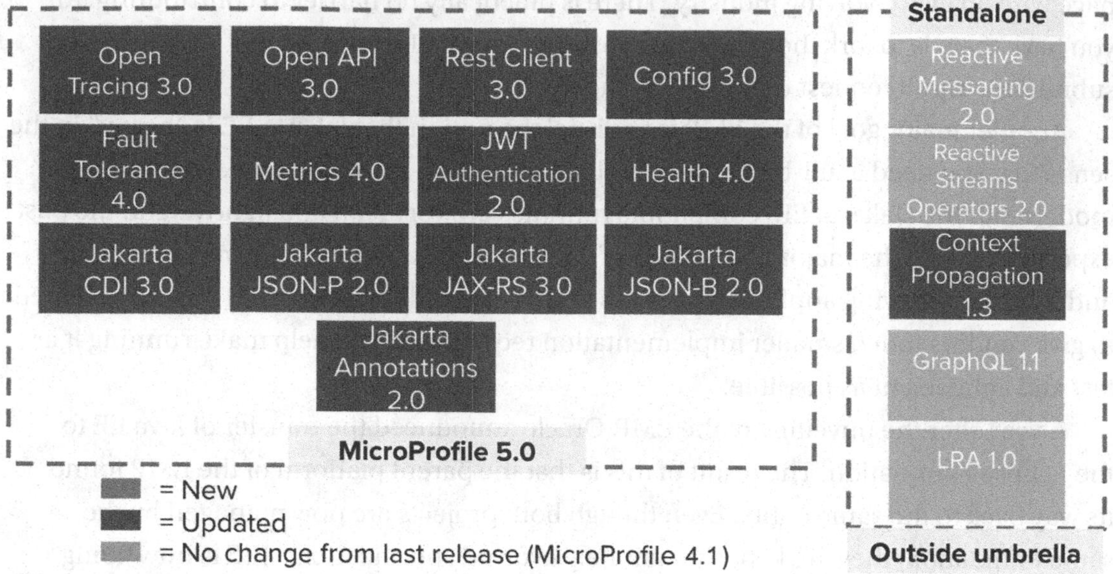

***Figure 1-3.** Eclipse MicroProfile specs*

As you can see, the EMP contains APIs geared at developing microservices. Let us take a brief look at each. The rest of this book covers both JEE and EMP in detail.

OpenTracing[23]

The OpenTracing API provides an API for tracing the flow of requests across various service boundaries. In a typical microservice environment, you are going to have a given number of individual interdependent services all acting in unison to fulfill a given application objective. The OpenTracing API of EMP adheres to the OpenTelemetry[24] (a super set of the now archived OpenTracing) specification.

[23] MicroProfile OpenTracing 3.0 Specification

[24] Migrating from OpenTracing | OpenTelemetry

OpenAPI[25]

The OpenAPI specification of the EMP aims at providing a unified, vendor-neutral Java API for the OpenAPI specification. The OpenAPI specification (v3[26]) describes how application developers can publish application API documentation for use by their clients.

Rest Client[27]

The EMP Rest Client is an API that provides a typesafe way to invoke REST services. It abstracts you from having to handle the underlying, low-level work needed to translate calls to and from RESTful web services into their respective Java types.

Config[28]

The EMP Config API provides a flexible, easy, and extensible way to manage application configuration. It gives you a way to manage various sources of configuration variables and mapping different sources to different deployment scenarios.

Fault Tolerance[29]

The EMP Fault Tolerance specification defines a flexible, easy-to-use system for building resilient microservices. It provides API constructs for managing timeout, retry, fallback, circuit breaking, and bulkheads in a microservices application.

[25] MicroProfile OpenAPI 3.0 Specification
[26] OpenAPI-Specification/3.0.0.md at main
[27] MicroProfile Rest Client 3.0 Specification
[28] MicroProfile Config 3.0 Specification
[29] MicroProfile Fault Tolerance 4.0 Specification

Metrics[30]

The Metrics specification provides a way to expose application and system metrics through well-defined endpoints. The Metrics API isn't a replacement for the JMX[31] API. Its objective is to provide an easy way to gather and monitor application metrics in a polyglot environment.

JWT Auth/Propagation[32]

The JWT specification gives you a way to use OpenID Connect–based JSON Web Tokens for role-based access control of microservices endpoints. With services using the RESTful architecture being stateless, there is the need to always pass some form of security context to every called endpoint so a security context can be created and verified. The JWT specification aims to help you achieve that in a standard, portable, and predictable way.

Health[33]

The EMP Health specification provides a simple mechanism for machine-to-machine mechanism for validating the availability or otherwise of a microservice. It provides a way for services to be able to answer the simple question: Are you available and ready to accept requests? This is especially critical in containerized cloud environments where you have orchestrators like kubernetes responsible for destroying and provisioning services.

CDI[34]

The EMP project ships the Jakarta Contexts and Dependency Injection specification as the default dependency injection mechanism. CDI provides you a way to build loosely

---

[30] MicroProfile Metrics 4.0 Specification

[31] Getting Started with Java Management Extensions (JMX): Developing Management and Monitoring Solutions

[32] MicroProfile JWT 2.0 Specification

[33] MicroProfile Health 4.0 Specification

[34] Jakarta Contexts and Dependency Injection 3.0 Specification

coupled applications, by abstracting you from managing the various interdependencies between your application components.

JSON-P[35]

The Jakarta JSON Processing specification provides a vendor-neutral set of APIs for parsing, generating, transforming, and querying JSON data using a streaming or object model. JSON-P is one of the Jakarta EE platform specifications that EMP implementations are required to support.

JAX-RS[36]

The Jakarta RESTful Web Services is another of the Jakarta EE specifications that is shipped with the EMP project. The JAX-RS specification defines a set of APIs for developing RESTful web services as defined by the REST architectural style by Dr. Roy Fielding.[37]

JSON-B[38]

The Jakarta JSON Binding is another of the specifications that EMP implementations are mandated to support. JSON-B provides a set of APIs for automatically binding Java objects to JSON documents in a transparent way, with the option to customize according to your needs.

Annotations[39]

Jakarta Annotations is another of the Jakarta EE APIs that is shipped with each implementation of EMP. This specification defines annotations for use within the wider component technologies on the Jakarta EE platform. Being a mostly annotation/metadata-driven platform, this specification aims at providing a unified base

[35] Overview (JSON Processing API documentation)

[36] Jakarta RESTful Web Services

[37] Architectural Styles and the Design of Network-based Software Architectures

[38] Jakarta JSON Binding

[39] Jakarta Annotations

specification around which various other annotation-driven specifications on the platform can create their own annotations.

Together, the preceding set of specifications form the full EMP suite of APIs for creating cloud-native applications. These specifications are supported by all implementations of the EMP. There are other optional specifications that implementations are not mandated to support, as shown in the "Outside umbrella" in the previous image. Together with the larger Jakarta EE platform, developing enterprise, vendor-neutral applications on the Java platform has become exciting again. For you as a developer, mastering application development with Jakarta EE will equip you with skills that can easily be transferred to other platforms like the Spring Framework.

Jakarta EE and the Spring Framework

A discussion of the theory and history of Jakarta EE will not be complete without a look at the Spring Framework.[40] Jakarta EE (or more correctly its ancestor J2EE) was not the most productive or easy-to-use development platform in its early history. It required a lot of manual configurations through XML files and required your components to extend artifacts in the platform, among others. As a result, the platform acquired the fame for being arcane, only used by big companies that had a lot of money to spend on developers.

Naturally, a lot of books got published on how to develop on the platform. One that stood out was *Expert One-on-One J2EE Design and Development*[41] by Rod Johnson, published in October 2002. In the book, Rod postulated the idea of increased use of dependency injection and Plain Old Java Objects (POJOs), as opposed to the J2EE way of manually configuring, managing, and mixing application dependencies with infrastructure code. He demonstrated this in the sample application built throughout the book: an online seat reservation app built with over 30K[42] lines of infrastructure code. A significant part of the application code was an implementation of his ideas for a clean separation of application and infrastructure code.

[40] Spring

[41] Expert One-on-One J2EE Design and Development

[42] History of Spring Framework and Spring Boot

The publisher of the book, Wrox, had a page[43] for it, with the sample code available for download, complete with errata and a user forum. The book was a success. The ideas propounded in it resonated with a lot of J2EE developers of the time. People started using parts of the released code in their personal projects. In early 2003, fellow developers Juergen Hoeller and Yann Caroff joined hands with Rod to create an open source project from the infrastructure code developed in the book. This project would be called Spring, an aphorism connoting a fresh start after a J2EE "winter."

Version 0.9 of this new, alternative enterprise Java development framework was released in June 2003. In March the following year, Spring 1.0 was released. The new framework was an instant hit and, to a large extent, a breath of fresh air as J2EE was the only credible way of developing nontrivial enterprise applications on the Java platform. It is fair to say the Spring Framework owes its existence to the limitations of the then J2EE platform.

Over the following years, as J2EE became Java EE, it started getting better. Taking inspiration from the Spring Framework, the platform increasingly became metadata driven, relying heavily on the use of annotations for various configurations and defaulting to much predictable defaults in the absence of any explicit directive by the developer. By the release of Java EE 7, the platform was completely different in terms of developer productivity relative to the J2EE era. The advent of specifications like the Contexts and Dependency Injection, the pruning and "defattening" of the EJB API, and the less reliance on XML configuration files in a way realized the patterns originally proposed in Rod's book.

The Spring Framework, in the meanwhile, had grown to become a much bigger development platform than its original release. It had gone beyond its original function of an inversion of control[44] (IoC) container to comprise APIs that covered the gamut of end-to-end application development. As it grew in breadth, so did the need to configure its various components. Gradually, the need for XML configuration files started to creep in, up to a point where it had become not so dissimilar to the earlier J2EE.

While Java EE had become an almost fully metadata-driven platform, where you needed just one dependency to have everything automatically configured and available, Spring had become much more reliant on the developer to configure its various components, mostly through XML config files. To be fair, Spring was originally based on the Java Servlet specification, and that meant a typical Spring developer would need to

[43] Expert One-on-One J2EE Design and Development Sample Code

[44] Inversion of Control Containers and the Dependency Injection pattern

have knowledge of servlet and Spring configurations. In effect, application development with Spring had become almost as complex[45] as it was on J2EE.

In October 2012, Mike Youngstrom raised an issue[46] on the Spring Jira board, discussing how Spring configuration could be made easier. He wrote, "I think that Spring's web application architecture can be significantly simplified if it were to [be] provided tools and a reference architecture that leverages the Spring component and configuration model from top to bottom. Embedding and unifying the configuration of those common web container services within a Spring Container bootstrapped from a simple main() method." It was in this thread that Spring Boot was mentioned[47] as a then nascent project to address the complexity Mike raised. Spring Boot, a subproject of the Spring Framework, therefore, itself came to address the shortcomings of its parent project, just as the parent project was born to address the challenges developers faced in using the then J2EE.

Today, both Jakarta EE and Spring are equally good and productive enterprise Java application development platforms that exist to make your life easier. Both platforms have a history of influencing each other to innovate and become better with each release. The ultimate winner in this "innovation contest" is you, the developer. There is really no need for some of the intense, flame wars in some corners about which is better or worse. Both platforms trace their roots back to the J2EE platform and as such are more complementary than competing platforms. As a Java developer, your knowledge of Jakarta EE can easily be transferred to the Spring platform with minimal effort. Having an informed history of both platforms is essential in knowing how similar, rather than different, they are. As this book is about Jakarta EE, let us take a brief look at why you would want to learn about application development on the platform.

Why Jakarta EE?

You have so far taken a historical tour of Jakarta EE and how it relates to Eclipse MicroProfile. You have also looked at Spring from the perspective of Jakarta EE. Together, these two platforms form the dominant options for enterprises in the Java ecosystem. The Java Platform still does have even more frameworks out there for developing all kinds of applications.

---

[45] Why I hate Spring

[46] Improved support for container-less web application architectures

[47] Spring Boot initial idea

As a Java developer, CTO, or the platform architect of an enterprise, you are spoiled for choice when it comes to frameworks and platforms for software development. A question you might be asking yourself is: Why should I choose Jakarta EE as my primary software development platform? What makes it a better choice?

There are number of reasons to at least give Jakarta EE a try, key among them being

- Standardization
- Openness
- Stability
- Ease of development
- Portability
- Pick and choose – tank or pistol
- Amazing documentation

Standardization

Every single specification on the platform, before the transfer to Eclipse Foundation, went through a rigorous process of both public and the JSR Expert Group scrutiny before finally being voted on by the JCP EC. New specification releases at the Eclipse Foundation equally go through a similar peer-reviewed mechanism.[48] This ensures all specifications that form part of the platform have been weighed in terms of backward compatibility, benefit to the Java Platform as a whole, and that they meet well-defined technical criteria. You can rely on the fact that Jakarta EE specifications are going to be available and reliable for a long time. This is especially crucial for long-lived enterprise applications. You can also be sure any given API invocation will act the same predictably across different compatible implementations of the platform.

Openness

Jakarta EE specifications are developed in a code first approach through the Jakarta EE Specification Process. This process is a simple and open one where anyone interested in advancing the platform can contribute in the form of a specification. Being code

[48] Guide to the Jakarta EE Specification Process | The Eclipse Foundation

first means you start with the actual code of the proposal, get it reviewed, and receive feedback in time. This ensures you don't invest resources in going through the contribution process only to not have your contributions/specification accepted.

Stability

Jakarta EE being a standard means the Eclipse Foundation will only accept and standardize industry tried and tested technology. For long-lived apps that will require maintenance, no room for using fad tech that will vanish tomorrow. Every Jakarta EE technology is industry tried and tested (both against the TCK and in production) and here for the long haul. Newer, less mature, and rapidly evolving technologies on the other hand are the perfect candidates for the MicroProfile project, which builds and integrates very well on top of Jakarta EE platform. So if your application requires it, you still have access to cutting-edge APIs available that you can rely on.

Ease of Development

Application development with Jakarta EE and Eclipse MicroProfile is effortless. All that's needed is an application server or Jakarta EE–compliant runtime and one (or two) maven dependency Minimal configuration, convention over configuration, minimal to no XML and predictable, reliable defaults are all benefits that come out of the box with developing on the Jakarta EE Platform. For example, for quick prototyping, the JEE specification provides for a default datasource that you can get right to using without needing to configure anything.

Portability

Jakarta EE as a standard means that your application should work with minimal to no configuration change across various compatible implementations of the standard, as long as the developer codes against the standard. This is compelling because you don't get locked into any given Jakarta EE application runtime vendor. Your code is portable across various application servers as long as you use the standard Jakarta EE APIs.

Pick and Choose – Tank or Pistol

Jakarta EE, combined with the Eclipse MicroProfile project, is a huge platform that may appear intimidating. But you can pick and choose whatever API in the group your application requires. You can use the platform as a tank or pistol - you decide. All the various APIs are integrated as a whole if you choose to use the whole platform or can stand alone individually if you choose to nitpick. As a set of abstract specifications, the compatible implementation provides all that is needed to run your application; you only ship your code. As such, you end up with much lighter deployment artifacts, made up mostly of your code.

Amazing Documentation

Jakarta EE is a well-organized community project that has an amazing amount of documentation. Notable is the Jakarta EE Tutorials,[49] the official Jakarta EE handbook. There are also lots of community and corporate organized conferences like Devoxx and Oracle JavaOne[50] that place a lot of emphasis on server-side Java development. There are also books written by individual developers like this one you are reading, all focused on helping you become a well-grounded enterprise Java software developer.

Summary

We have taken a long tour of the history of Jakarta EE, from its early iteration as J2EE to the present-day Jakarta EE, in this chapter. The Jakarta EE platform of today is remarkably different from its J2EE ancestor. Combined with Eclipse MicroProfile, the JEE platform is a modern, powerful, productive, and easy-to-use enterprise, cloud-native application development platform that is worth the investment to learn. Now that you have the theoretical foundations, the rest of this book will teach you the practical skills needed to become a professional enterprise, cloud-native Java application developer using the tried and tested Jakarta EE platform. See you in Chapter 2.

---

[49] The Jakarta® EE Tutorial

[50] JavaOne 2022

CHAPTER 2

Enterprise Java, Microservices, and the Cloud

Software application development has changed significantly over the years. The entire process of writing, testing, shipping, and deploying code has seen rapid changes, culminating in the current cloud-native era of software engineering. The Java Platform has also over the years evolved into a capable platform for modern application development.

This chapter introduces you to cloud-native application development by looking at the history of Jakarta EE application deployment, some factors that accelerated the rise in cloud adoption, an introduction to cloud-native software development through the 12-factor app, and finally a look at Jakarta EE within in a cloud-native software application development world.

The Birth of Java 2 Enterprise Edition (J2EE)

The Java Programming Language, originally named Oak, was publicly released in May 1995 by then Sun Microsystems. The promise of "Write Once, Run Anywhere" immediately appealed to developers, coupled with the then Netscape announcing support for this new language in its browser of the same name gave the language the push it needed to start its journey to application development dominance. At that time, web browsers had started making the Internet accessible to more people, and companies had started looking for ways to offer more interactivity to users of their websites.

Java, the programming language, was originally developed for creating applications for household devices like handheld entertainment controllers. However, that didn't

L. Saeed and G. Abdallah, *Pro Cloud Native Java EE Apps*, https://doi.org/10.1007/978-1-4842-8900-6_2

go quite well to expectations, and with built-in support by the then Netscape browser, the language gradually pivoted toward being a client-side development language with the applets and JavaBeans constructs. As time went on, the database connectivity API, Java Database Connectivity (JDBC), was added to address the need for data access in applications.

Ease of use, being web enabled, and automatic garbage collection were some critical factors that pushed the Java adoption momentum across companies. Realizing that the language could be used on the server for server-side application development, Sun decided to capitalize on this and the other nascent, emerging application server market by introducing the Servlet specification. The idea of the Servlet specification was to have a Java application on the server, where clients could make calls to and, in return, receive processed data. This data could be HTML or anything else the browser could handle.

Along the line, IBM[1] released the Enterprise JavaBeans specification as an independent project to simplify Java server–side development with the automatic provision of general-purpose services that are common to most enterprise applications like security, transactions, scalability, and remote invocation capabilities. The EJB specification also provided support for the remote invocation of a business method through remote interfaces. With these disparate capabilities, Java became a great language for developing n-tier architecture applications, adopted by a lot of large enterprises.

In 1999, Sun finally introduced a new, cohesive platform fully targeted at developing large-scale, distributed enterprise applications. This platform brought together all the disparate specifications that had been developed as part of transitioning Java to a server-side programming language into one "umbrella" specification. The EJB spec originally released by IBM was also included in this new platform as EJB 1.0. This new platform was called the Java 2 Platform, Enterprise Edition, or J2EE. The initial version was 1.2.

Built on the Java Platform, J2EE was designed to run on application servers that implemented the specification. This meant you could theoretically write your application once and run it on any server that implemented the specification. The platform was also inspired by previous work in the distributed enterprise systems arena like the Common Object Request Broker Architecture (CORBA[2]). To ensure that application servers adhered to the specification and could call themselves certified J2EE

[1] A Detailed Guide to Enterprise Java Beans (EJB) with Code Examples

[2] Common Object Request Broker Architecture (CORBA)

runtimes, Sun introduced a licensing scheme, part of which required application servers to pass a compatibility test suite (CTS).

The application server market, as we mentioned earlier, was nascent at that point, with analysts predicting it to develop into a multibillion-dollar industry. This spurred a rush of vendors into the market. And with the release of J2EE, a lot of these vendors went in for J2EE certification. Some of these vendors are BEA Systems, Nokia, Compaq, IBM, Oracle, SAP, Sybase, Macromedia, Hitachi, and TIBCO Software. All these companies offered application servers on which J2EE applications could be deployed. All these servers were also proprietary, on-premise deployments. It is worthy of note that Sun itself had an application server, originally called iPlanet, but later renamed Sun ONE. The two dominant vendors in this market, however, were IBM's WebSphere and WebLogic from BEA.

There was another open source budding project called the Enterprise JavaBeans Open Source Software (EJB-OSS) that implemented the EJB application programming interface (API) from the J2EE specification. This project gradually implemented the specification, but was not J2EE certified. The name of the project was also eventually changed to JBoss. This open source application server made significant inroads into the enterprise environments of the time.

Monoliths

The dominant application development model at this time was the monolith. This development paradigm is where applications are built as one giant "bundle," with all layers and components forming one giant cohesive deployment artifact. This paradigm has its advantages and disadvantages. Changing any part of the application meant having to redeploy the whole application.

A typical J2EE application would be deployed as a Web Application Archive (WAR) or Enterprise Application Archive (EAR). The WAR file format was used for deploying J2EE applications developed using the web profile of the specification. WAR archives could be deployed to servlet containers or any runtime that implemented the web profile spec of the larger J2EE specification. EAR archives were used to deploy fully fledged J2EE applications that were developed using the gamut of the J2EE specification.

The J2EE platform was very much suited to developing monolithic applications. This is mostly due to the fact that at the time the platform was developed and released, and years after that, the monolithic architecture was the most dominant and popular application development paradigm available. Consequently, the platform evolved to meet the needs of enterprises that were developing their software using this paradigm.

Among the advantages of the monolithic application development architecture are as follows.

Development Speed

Given that every component of the application is in a single codebase, it is simple to have teams of developers working on it, implementing different features and functions at any point in time. With the addition of version control systems like Git, monolithic application development is simple and straightforward.

Simpler to Onboard

It is simple to onboard a new developer onto a project that uses a monolithic architecture. Because everything is unified in a cohesive, singular codebase, it is easy for new developers to get productive as soon as possible.

Simplified Testing

With everything in a single deployment artifact, it is generally easier to write unit and integration tests for the various components of any given monolithic application.

Simplified Deployment

As everything needed to run a monolithic application is bundled into a single archive (WAR or EAR), it is relatively simple to deploy: drop the generated archive into the deployment folder of any given runtime.

Simplified Scaling

With a simpler deployment model where everything is bundled together, it is relatively simple to scale a given monolith application by running multiple copies on different servers, routing traffic to same with a load balancer.

These, among others, made monolithic architecture a straightforward choice for most enterprises. Features could be added at a much more measured pace, development teams could be scaled, and the application itself could be easily deployed with new changes with minimal effort.

A Changing Development Landscape

However, with the upsurge in Internet-connected devices, a general shift in software consumption from local installation to cloud hosting, the rise in popularity of web applications like Gmail, the rise in popularity of third-party hosted deployment infrastructure (e.g., AWS), the rise in popularity of the REST architecture, the rise of the API ecosystem, the increasingly lower cost of outsourcing deployment infrastructure, a boom in the number of companies offering competitive products and services, and an increasingly interconnected world meant that software development could not be as it was. Let us take a cursory look at these critical factors.

Rise of Internet-Connected Devices

The general popularity of the Internet, starting in the early 2000s, and a general expansion of Internet accessibility, was followed by an increase in Internet-connected devices. Brands like BlackBerry and Nokia pioneered the use of the Internet on mobile phones, with the introduction of the iPhone greatly popularizing the concept of "the Internet in your pocket."

General Shift in Software Consumption

The rise of Internet-connected devices also signalled a change in how software was consumed by users. In the early days of computing, the software was built into the hardware of the computer. This paradigm kept evolving to the point of the rise of connected devices. The natural nature of the Internet meant that software didn't have to be necessarily installed on the consuming device for it to be used.

Rise in Popularity of Web Applications

Consequent to the rise of connected devices and a shift in the general pattern of software consumption is the rise in popularity of web applications. Massively popular applications like Gmail ushered in an era where web applications would become the default means of consuming software. This shift was very significant because it meant that enterprises would need to pivot how they got their software to final end users.

Rise in Popularity of Third-Party Hosted Infrastructure

The rise in popularity of third-party hosted infrastructure around the same time as the abovementioned points were taking place signalled a new era of application development for both established and startup enterprises alike. The advent of Amazon Web Services (AWS), with its offering of massive cloud infrastructure, meant that enterprises could now fully outsource all that is needed to create, test, and continuously deploy applications to an external service provider. This, consequently, entailed a shift in how applications were developed.

Rise in Popularity of the REST Architecture

The Representational State architecture, as pioneered by Dr. Roy Fielding in his PhD thesis,[3] started gaining popularity around this time. This architecture proposed a way for applications to expose and consume information through predictable interfaces in the form of endpoints.

Rise of the API Ecosystem

The API ecosystem also started flourishing around this time. This ecosystem is where other companies offer specialized services in the form of APIs over the Internet, for instance, an API service for managing currency exchange rates. Enterprises could now outsource orthogonal functions to third-party companies specializing in that particular area. All these are consumed through RESTful endpoints.

[3] Architectural Styles and the Design of Network-based Software Architectures

Lower Cost of Outsourcing Infrastructure

The rise in firms specializing in hosted infrastructure meant it generally was cheaper to outsource the entire stack needed from development to deployment rather than host in house.

Boom in Competitive Firms

The preceding listed factors all combined in one way or the other to give rise to the number of competitors in any given market. A larger pool of potential users, an almost equal level playing field for delivering software over the Internet, and relatively cheaper infrastructure hosting services all combined to create an even footing for more firms to enter into any given market.

The Rise of Microservices

The abovementioned points are all factors in one way or another that caused the software development industry to take another look at the way software was developed, tested, and deployed. Enterprises deployed their applications to servers that they principally owned and managed. Most had fully dedicated in-house teams that were responsible for managing the entire server stack needed for the full application development lifecycle. This meant that enterprises needed to concern themselves with procuring, installing, and managing server stacks for their applications. This proved quite expensive for smaller firms and startups.

The advantages of the monolithic architecture also created other consequent challenges when a given application grew in size and complexity. A given application could grow so large and complex such that adding the most minute of change would require a lot of automated and manual tests to ensure there is no negative, unintended side effect. The simplest of changes also meant rerunning the entire application deployment pipeline. Because everything is in one bundle, the simplest of bugs could also bring down the entire application.

As a result of varying combinations of all the factors mentioned so far, the software development industry started taking a look at another software development paradigm.

This paradigm, called microservices,[4] proposed a way of developing software that took all the preceding factors into consideration. This idea was inspired by the Unix philosophy of writing a full application by breaking it down into individually siloed units, all communicating through a well-established, predictable interface.

The microservices paradigm proposes writing software by breaking it down into smaller services, where each service is responsible for a single function or feature of the overall application, with each service being independent of the other, and all services communicating over the HTTP protocol through RESTful endpoints. These services could be independently deployed and managed by orchestration services across a given cluster of servers. Also implicit in the microservices architecture is the fact that the application and the entire development process is carried out in the "cloud."

The microservices architecture became an instant hit, because it addressed a number of the pain points of very large monoliths. Among its advantages are as follows.

Managing Complexity Through Decomposition

Because each unit of the application is developed as a separate sub-application, it is relatively easier to manage the overall application development as it grows more complex.

Easier to Maintain

Because the overall application consists of individual, independent units, it is easy to add new features and fix bugs without the risk of breaking the entire application. Any problem in a given service is restricted to that service.

Faster Development

Because developers don't need to have knowledge of the full application, it is relatively faster to develop using the microservices architecture because each development team will mostly need to know about the service they are working on. As a result, applications could be released faster.

[4] 33rd Degree – Conference for Java Masters – Micro services – Java, the Unix Way

Scalability

An application built through the microservices architecture can be scaled relatively easily because resources can be directed to scaling only those parts or services that need scaling.

Resilience

In a production environment, an application developed as a suite of microservices would not go down when one service goes down. It is also easier to build targeted resilience into services that are critical to the overall application.

Easier Adoption of New Technologies

The core feature of the microservices architecture of services exposing their features through RESTful interfaces means that the implementation of those features is completely separated from the client-facing interface. This means that individual services can adopt new technologies faster, only needing to deal with the implementation detail without necessarily affecting the client-facing interface.

Cloud-Native Development

Implicit in the microservices architecture is the concept of cloud-native application development. The Cloud Native[5] Computing Foundation (CNCF) defines[6] it as "Cloud native [are] technologies [that] empower organisations to build and run scalable applications in modern, dynamic environments such as public, private, and hybrid clouds. Containers, service meshes, microservices, immutable infrastructure, and declarative APIs exemplify this approach. These techniques enable loosely coupled systems that are resilient, manageable, and observable. Combined with robust automation, they allow engineers to make high-impact changes frequently and predictably with minimal toil."

[5] Cloud Native Computing Foundation

[6] Cloud Native Foundation Charter

The CNCF definition gives an overview of how modern software development is done. It aims at optimizing the entire development process to be as efficient as possible and to be able to deliver as much value to customers as possible. The cloud-native principles aim at helping enterprises manage the complexity of modern application development. In an era where any given application can be consumed by and through a myriad of devices and means, a set of adaptable patterns that increases the chances of a successful development process is needed.

The idea behind cloud-native development is to be able to deliver resilient applications to customers faster and cheaper. As users demand more from applications, enterprises must find an efficient way of delivering value to users at reduced cost. Cloud-native development is a way for enterprises to realize an agile development process that results in resilient, healthy, secure, and reliable applications to users.

Cloud-native applications rely on cloud service providers. As mentioned in the definition of the cloud native by the CNCF, there are three kinds of cloud services that an enterprise could make use of.

Public Cloud

A public cloud is a set of computing services that are managed by a third-party provider, with these services accessible via the Internet to different customers. A typical example is the general-purpose suite of compute services from Amazon Web Services (AWS).

Private Cloud

A private cloud refers to a set of computing services that are owned by a single enterprise, either managed by that enterprise in their own data center or by a third-party service provider for a fee. This was the dominant mode of application deployment before the popularity of cloud-hosted compute services. Enterprises would set up their own compute infrastructure, managed by in-house staff. There are now many third-party private cloud providers out there, such as AWS Virtual Private Cloud.

Hybrid Cloud

A hybrid cloud is a cross between a public and private cloud. It often provides much greater flexibility and options.

The 12-Factor Application[7]

The 12-factor application is a widely accepted set of guidelines for developing cloud-native applications. It proposes factors that can help developers create applications that are highly optimized for cloud environments. These factors are as follows.

Codebase

This factor entails having a separate codebase for each service or component of the application. Common functionality or shared services should be put in libraries that can be dropped into each codebase through a dependency management system (e.g., Maven). A given codebase can be deployed to different stages of the deployment pipeline.

Dependencies

Each microservice should declare, bundle, and separate its dependencies from the other services. No two services should have common dependencies such that a change in the dependency of one service has an impact on the other service. All services should be fully siloed in terms of their dependencies.

Configuration

Microservices should have their configurations stored in an external environment such that those configurations can change between the various deployment stages without having to change code.

Backing Services

A backing service is any service a given microservice needs and consumes over the network as part of its normal operation. A 12-factor app should treat backing services as resources accessible via addressable URLs. The goal is to decouple the application from the backing service such that the backing service can be interchanged with another without any impact to the microservice.

[7] The Twelve-Factor App

Build, Release, Run

The build, release, and run stages should be fully separated. Each stage should be tagged with a unique identifier that makes it possible to be able to roll back to that particular point. Modern release tools like Jenkins[8] help with this.

Processes

12-factor applications should be run as independent, stateless processes that share nothing. No service should operate based on the assumption of the existence of some data outside of what that service will generate at runtime.

Port Binding

Each microservice should be bound to a specific port from which it will listen for requests. No two services should be bound to the same port.

Concurrency

When the need for scaling arrives, each microservice should be scaled out horizontally rather than vertically. When each service is run as a stateless process, it is easy to scale out horizontally.

Disposability

Each microservice should be disposable. A given service should be disposable at a moment's notice without loss of data. Creating microservices as stateless processes means they can be destroyed at any time without any side effects.

[8] Jenkins

Dev/Prod Parity

Development, staging, and production environments should be as similar as possible, without sharing any data. Because a 12-factor application is designed to be continuously deployed, it is important to reduce the friction between the various stages as much as possible.

Logs

Logs give a glimpse into the internals of each running microservice. As such, each service should only concern itself with writing logs to the default output stream available. Log aggregator tools can then be used to collect and analyze these logs for corrective actions, if any.

Admin Processes

One-off administrations like database migrations should be run as one-off processes, preferably in an identical environment as the application runs.

Containers and the Cloud

The crux of cloud-native applications is the ability to package applications into images and run them as containers. Containerization tools like Docker and orchestration tools like Kubernetes make it easy to package an application with its runtime and deploy it to server stacks where they are automatically provisioned to service requests. This abstraction makes it possible to run any given Java application anywhere you can run the packaged image as containers.

As discussed earlier in this chapter, enterprise Java applications are deployed to runtimes that implement the enterprise Java specification. Containerization has increasingly made it possible to run enterprise Java applications in public, private, and hybrid clouds as containerized apps. Application server vendors now have to compete on how easy it is for their runtimes to be packaged and run as cloud-native artifacts.

Enterprise Java and Cloud-Native Development

J2EE and its successor Java EE, even though originally designed for developing multitier, large, monolithic applications, could be used to develop microservices as well. As discussed in the previous chapter, a decline in the development pace of the platform along the line when the popularity of microservices began to rise meant that the platform fell behind in adopting some of the changes needed to position itself as a suitable platform for cloud-native development.

This development, however, did not stop the Java community from starting projects to fill in the void. Notable among these is the Eclipse MicroProfile project. There are other projects equally geared toward building cloud-native enterprise Java applications such as Dropwizard,[9] Helidon,[10] Micronaut,[11] and Quarkus.[12] All these frameworks provide APIs for developing applications that are resilient, fault tolerant, configurable, stateless, containerizable, and portable across cloud environments.

Summary

The standardization of the Eclipse MicroProfile project and its positioning as an independent subset of the larger Jakarta EE platform provide a mature, dependable, predictable, and reliable platform for enterprise cloud-native application development.

Throughout the rest of this book, you are going to learn how the various APIs on the Jakarta EE platform, augmented by others from the Eclipse MicroProfile project, can be used to develop modern, cloud-native, testable, resilient, fault-tolerant, configurable, portable, and secure enterprise applications. You will learn how developing enterprise applications using a mature platform like Jakarta EE will help you develop long-lived, maintainable Java applications. See you in the next chapter.

[9] Dropwizard

[10] Helidon

[11] Micronaut Framework

[12] Quarkus

CHAPTER 3

Enterprise Applications – Architecture

Modern enterprise applications have evolved over the years to become cloud native, resilient, fault tolerant, and reliable. Users of such applications have come to expect the application to always be available, irrespective of network latency and other possible failures that could occur during the runtime of an application.

In order to meet such expectations, a number of application development patterns have evolved to help application developers craft applications that meet current deployment standards and the needs of modern users. The goal of this chapter is to explore a number of such patterns, namely, dependency injection, REST web services, data persistence, and cloud-native functionalities and constructs within the context of the reference application for this book.

Enterprise Applications – What Are They?

An enterprise software application can be defined as a nontrivial, relatively complex, multitier application developed by an organization to solve a specific problem for a given target market. Different types of organizations have different expectations from the provision of any given enterprise application to a market. A for-profit enterprise would expect revenue in return; a nonprofit would expect some form of advancement of some ideology. Whatever the organization and type of software provided, all enterprise applications do have some common traits that make them nontrivial to develop.

A typical application would have three tiers – the user interface, the middle layer, and the data storage. The UI is where the end users actually interact with the application. The middle layer is the "orchestration" part that handles interactions between the UI

L. Saeed and G. Abdallah, *Pro Cloud Native Java EE Apps*, https://doi.org/10.1007/978-1-4842-8900-6_3

and the data warehouse. The data warehouse refers to the database management system used to store application-generated data into a permanent storage mechanism. Whether an application is a monolith or microservice, these tiers generally run through the full application.

The UI could be a traditional HTML page, for applications developed for human interaction. Or it could be RESTful endpoints, for applications designed for other applications to consume. The term "user interface" has evolved to include the point at which final clients of a given application interact with that application. The middle or service layer typically contains artifacts that handle security, data warehouse transactions, and interactions with other services (internally and/or externally), among others.

From an engineering perspective, all nontrivial applications need certain core functionalities from the platform on which they are developed. The extent to which a platform will provide any of the functions enumerated as follows depends on maintainers, community, and target market of the platform. However, these functions can generally be expected to be available in any platform geared at developing enterprise applications.

Dependency Management

Whether an application is a monolith or a collection of microservices, each component of the application will have dependencies that need to be managed. For a nontrivial application, a given component would have dependencies on other components, which would in turn have other dependencies on yet other components. The chosen software development platform should provide a mechanism for automating this kind of complex dependency management. For the Jakarta EE platform, the Jakarta Contexts and Dependency Injection API is the primary way of managing application dependency. CDI not only helps you automate dependency management, it also provides other add-on functionality that helps you create loosely coupled, extensible, and maintainable applications.

RESTful Web Service

Modern enterprise applications are generally exposed as a set of RESTful web services to be consumed by clients. The primary client could be a purely JavaScript application that is part of the microservices of the overall application. Other clients could be third-party applications. Whatever the application development paradigm, the development platform should have a solid API for developing modern RESTful services. For Jakarta EE, the Jakarta RESTful Web Services API is the standard API for developing REST web services on the platform.

Data Persistence

Every application will generate and store data in one way or the other. The generated data could be from the application itself or retrieved from some external service. It could yet be user-created data. However the data gets created, almost all enterprise applications will have a need to store such data into a durable data store. The database management system could be a traditional RDBMS database or a NoSQL data store. The development platform must provide API constructs for the creation, reading, updating, and deletion of such data. It should also have some form of transaction management built into such API constructs. For the Jakarta EE platform, the Jakarta Persistence API provides the needed API constructs for transforming and mapping Java objects into RDBMS database table records, persisting, retrieving, updating, and deleting those records.

Ancillary Cloud Features

These are the three core, traditional functionalities that cut across the majority of enterprise applications. In addition to these core platform functions, a modern, cloud-native application also needs some ancillary functionalities to allow it to be deployed and automatically managed on cloud environments. The most popular of these cloud-native ancillary features are outlined in the following sections.

Health Check

For a cloud-native application deployed to and managed by an orchestration tool like Kubernetes, an application needs to be able to answer two simple questions: Are you live? If yes, are you ready to accept requests? The responses to these questions will determine if the orchestration tool routes requests to the application instance or not. The Eclipse MicroProfile project provides the Health Check API for creating readiness and liveness endpoints that can be queried for responses to the abovementioned questions.

Fault Tolerance

Every application will fail at some point. A cloud-native application should be able to recover from any such failure gracefully. The Eclipse MicroProfile Fault Tolerance API provides all the constructs needed to develop such fault-tolerant cloud-native applications.

Configuration

A cloud-native application should have its configuration externalized such that the configuration values can be changed and targeted at different environments without having to change the application code. The Eclipse MicroProfile Config API provides the API for managing application configuration.

Metrics

Application metrics provide insight into the state of an application. Cloud-native applications should be able to generate meaningful metrics that can be collected and analyzed in order to take any corrective measures if necessary. The Metrics API of the Eclipse MicroProfile provides a set of APIs for generating application metrics available at predictable endpoints.

Introduction to JWallet

The case study application for this book is called JWallet, a cloud-native microservices financial application for storing and carrying out transactions on money, built on the Jakarta EE platform that showcases the various APIs and how to use them together. In this chapter, we are going to take an overall tour of the application within the context of the core and ancillary functionalities discussed to this point in the chapter. Subsequent chapters will then go into detail for each API.

JWallet – Setup

The Apache Maven[1] dependency resolution and build management system is the most popular dependency and build management tool for developing Jakarta EE applications. JWallet is set up as a multimodule Maven application, with three microservices (account, wallet, and rate) and one general-purpose module (core), as shown in Figure 3-1.

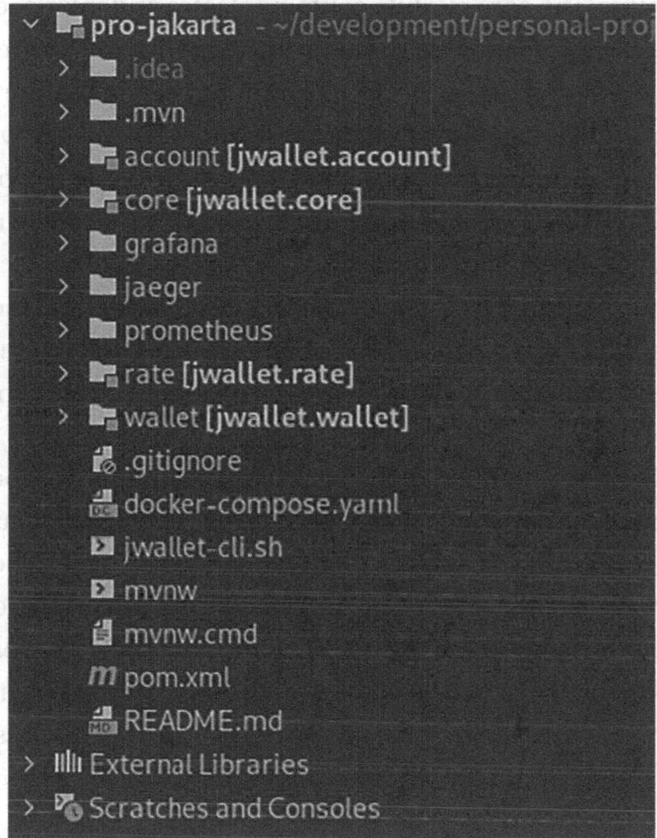

***Figure 3-1.** JWallet project structure*

A Note on IDE

The IDE used for the screenshots and writing the reference code for this book is the IntelliJ IDE. However, you do not need to use the same IDE. Any Java IDE that supports Apache Maven should be sufficient.

[1] Apache Maven

The grafana, jaeger, and prometheus folders contain configuration files for the Grafana, Prometheus, and Jaeger projects. Grafana[2] and Prometheus[3] are open source projects that scrape, organize, and display metrics exposed by an application through Eclipse MicroProfile metrics, while Jaeger[4] is a project that implements the open tracing[5] specification.

The account module contains the account microservice that is responsible for handling user accounts. The core module contains classes and interfaces common to all the other services. The rate module contains the exchange rate microservice. This service is in charge of making external calls to a currency exchange rate service for converting between various currencies in the application. Finally, the wallet module is the central place where transactions take place. It is the module responsible for creating wallets and debit and credit transactions. It is also the module responsible for implementing querying for wallets, transactions, and balances.

The application is managed by a single Project Object Model xml file (pom.xml[6]) in the root folder. This pom file is where the base dependencies and modules are declared. The main dependencies for this application are the Jakarta EE and Eclipse MicroProfile dependencies.

Listing 3-1 shows the declaration of the Jakarta EE full platform dependency. Line 5 sets the scope of the dependency to provided. This means that our application is not going to ship any Jakarta EE jar files on the produced artifacts. The full platform implementation is expected to be provided by the underlying compatible implementation that the application will be run with. Our application only declares its dependency on the platform and leaves the provision of the actual implementation of the various Jakarta EE APIs to the server. Maven will add it to the classpath used for compilation and testing, but not the runtime classpath.

[2] Grafana

[3] Prometheus

[4] Jaeger

[5] What Is OpenTracing? Everything You Need to Get Started | Scalyr

[6] Maven - Introduction to the POM

Listing 3-1. Jakarta EE dependency

```
<dependency>
      <groupId>jakarta.platform</groupId>
      <artifactId>jakarta.jakartaee-api</artifactId>
      <version>9.1.0</version>
      <scope>provided</scope>
</dependency>
```

Listing 3-2 shows the declaration of the Eclipse MicroProfile dependency. Similar to the Jakarta EE dependency, the EMP dependency also has its scope set to provided, again, meaning that the application expects the underlying compatible runtime implementation to provide the EMP implementations.

This kind of separation of application and platform dependency is one of the key reasons why Jakarta EE platform is well suited for developing modern applications. The separation results in the shipment of minimal application deployment artifacts. In a cloud-native environment where continuous development, testing, and deployment[7] are the standard, the smaller the deployment artifacts, the faster and cheaper that turnaround becomes.

Listing 3-2. MicroProfile 5 dependency

```
<dependency>
      <groupId>org.eclipse.microprofile</groupId>
      <artifactId>microprofile</artifactId>
      <version>5.0</version>
      <type>pom</type>
      <scope>provided</scope>
</dependency>
```

Listing 3-3 shows the declaration of the various maven modules that make up the application. From the perspective of maven, you can have as many modules as your application desires. Each module can be a fully functional application, as is the case in our project with the rate, wallet, and account modules. You can also create dependencies between the modules. Again, in JWallet, the three other modules have a dependency on the core module.

[7] Continuous integration vs. delivery vs. deployment

Listing 3-3. JWallet modules

```
<modules>
    <module>core</module>
    <module>wallet</module>
    <module>rate</module>
    <module>account</module>
</modules>
```

Listing 3-4 shows the declaration of dependencies used for application tests. Every application should have automated testing. Because we are only interested in these dependencies for testing, they are scoped to the test phase. This means that they will only be available for the test compilation and execution phase.

Listing 3-4. Test dependencies

```
<!--JUnit-->
<dependency>
    <groupId>org.junit.jupiter</groupId>
    <artifactId>junit-jupiter</artifactId>
    <version>5.8.1</version>
    <scope>test</scope>
</dependency>
<!--Testcontainers-->
<dependency>
    <groupId>org.testcontainers</groupId>
    <artifactId>testcontainers</artifactId>
    <version>1.16.3</version>
    <scope>test</scope>
</dependency>
<dependency>
    <groupId>org.testcontainers</groupId>
    <artifactId>junit-jupiter</artifactId>
    <version>1.16.3</version>
    <scope>test</scope>
</dependency>
```

```
<!--JAX-RS client-->
<dependency>
      <groupId>org.glassfish.jersey.core</groupId>
      <artifactId>jersey-client</artifactId>
      <version>3.0.4</version>
      <scope>test</scope>
</dependency>
<dependency>
      <groupId>org.glassfish.jersey.inject</groupId>
      <artifactId>jersey-hk2</artifactId>
      <version>3.0.4</version>
      <scope>test</scope>
</dependency>
<dependency>
      <groupId>org.glassfish.jersey.media</groupId>
      <artifactId>jersey-media-json-binding</artifactId>
      <version>3.0.4</version>
      <scope>test</scope>
</dependency>
<dependency>
      <groupId>org.glassfish.jersey.media</groupId>
      <artifactId>jersey-media-json-processing</artifactId>
      <version>3.0.4</version>
      <scope>test</scope>
</dependency>
```

The application declares three plugins in the build element of the pom file as shown in Listing 3-5. The first one is the OpenLiberty[8] maven plugin. OpenLiberty is an open source Jakarta EE–compatible implementation from IBM. It is one of many available implementations that you can choose from to run your Jakarta EE applications. This plugin allows us to run our application through maven without having to set up the server manually. The other two plugins are the maven war[9] and failsafe plugins[10] for

[8] Open Liberty

[9] Apache Maven WAR Plugin

[10] Apache Maven Failsafe Plugin

packaging and running integration tests, respectively. Because these dependencies are declared in the base pom file, they are available to all the modules declared in the modules element.

Listing 3-5. JWallet build section of the root pom.xml

```
<build>
    <plugins>
        <plugin>
            <groupId>io.openliberty.tools</groupId>
            <artifactId>liberty-maven-plugin</artifactId>
            <version>3.5</version>
            <configuration>
                <libertyRuntimeVersion>22.0.0.3</libertyRuntimeVersion>
                <copyDependencies>
                    <location>${project.build.directory}/liberty/wlp/usr/
                    shared/resources</location>
                    <dependency>
                        <groupId>org.apache.derby</groupId>
                        <artifactId>derby</artifactId>
                    </dependency>
                </copyDependencies>
            </configuration>
        </plugin>
        <plugin>
            <groupId>org.apache.maven.plugins</groupId>
            <artifactId>maven-war-plugin</artifactId>
            <version>3.3.2</version>
        </plugin>
        <plugin>
            <groupId>org.apache.maven.plugins</groupId>
            <artifactId>maven-failsafe-plugin</artifactId>
            <version>3.0.0-M6</version>
            <executions>
                <execution>
```

```
                <goals>
                    <goal>integration-test</goal>
                    <goal>verify</goal>
                </goals>
            </execution>
        </executions>
      </plugin>
    </plugins>
</build>
```

The pom file for the core module shown in Listing 3-6 is very minimal with no additional dependencies and a notable exception being it is packaged as a jar file. This is because the core module will be depended upon by the other three modules for common functionality, but itself isn't a microservice that is deployable, hence packaged as a jar to be included in the other modules/microservices. This core module will act as the orchestration module through which the other modules communicate with each other.

Listing 3-6. Core module pom.xml

```
<?xml version="1.0" encoding="UTF-8" ?>
<project xmlns="http://maven.apache.org/POM/4.0.0"
    xmlns:xsi="http://www.w3.org/2001/XMLSchema-instance"
    xsi:schemaLocation="http://maven.apache.org/POM/4.0.0
    http://maven.apache.org/xsd/maven-4.0.0.xsd">
      <modelVersion>4.0.0</modelVersion>

      <parent>
            <groupId>com.example</groupId>
            <artifactId>jwallet</artifactId>
            <version>1.0-SNAPSHOT</version>
      </parent>

      <artifactId>jwallet.core</artifactId>
      <packaging>jar</packaging>

      <build><finalName>core</finalName></build>
</project>
```

The pom.xml files of the account and rate microservices are similar to that of the wallet microservice as shown in Listing 3-7. They are very minimal with the only dependency being that of the core module. Any dependency that is exclusive to any given module can be declared in that module's pom file. Also note that their packaging format is war. This means they can be deployed as stand-alone applications to an application server. In our case, the OpenLiberty server will be used to run everything.

Listing 3-7. Wallet module pom.xml

```
<?xml version="1.0" encoding="UTF-8" ?>
<project xmlns="http://maven.apache.org/POM/4.0.0"
    xmlns:xsi="http://www.w3.org/2001/XMLSchema-instance"
    xsi:schemaLocation="http://maven.apache.org/POM/4.0.0
    http://maven.apache.org/xsd/maven-4.0.0.xsd">
    <modelVersion>4.0.0</modelVersion>

      <parent>
            <groupId>com.example</groupId>
            <artifactId>jwallet</artifactId>
            <version>1.0-SNAPSHOT</version>
      </parent>

      <artifactId>jwallet.wallet</artifactId>
      <packaging>war</packaging>

      <dependencies>
            <dependency>
                  <groupId>${project.groupId}</groupId>
                  <artifactId>jwallet.core</artifactId>
                  <version>${project.version}</version>
            </dependency>
      </dependencies>

      <build><finalName>wallet</finalName></build>
</project>
```

The application is bundled as a collection of container images that can be deployed and managed by docker, docker compose, and Kubernetes. The entry point for creating the container images is a Dockerfile file in each module folder. The Dockerfile of the wallet microservice is shown in Listing 3-8.

Listing 3-8. Wallet module Dockerfile

```
FROM icr.io/appcafe/open-liberty:22.0.0.3-full-java11-openj9-ubi

COPY --chown=1001:0 src/main/liberty/config /config
COPY --chown=1001:0 src/main/liberty/derby-10.14.2.0.jar /opt/ol/wlp/usr/
shared/resources
COPY --chown=1001:0 target/*.war /config/apps

EXPOSE 3001

RUN configure.sh
```

Line 1 defines that our image is based on an OpenLiberty full image which contains full support for Jakarta EE and MicroProfile. Lines 3–5 copy the OpenLiberty config file, Apache Derby embedded database JDBC drivers, and our application artifact (.war) files to the created image so it gets autodeployed upon server startup. Line 7 exposes port 3001 the app is expected to listen on. Finally, line 9 runs the OpenLiberty configure.sh file to preconfigure and activate required features.

In the root folder, we have a docker-compose.yaml file that serves as the entry point to run the application using docker compose which declares six services, the wallet, rate, and account services corresponding to the three microservices of the application and the jaeger, prometheus, and grafana services. These services do have interdependencies among themselves.

The wallet service is built from the Dockerfile found in the wallet folder of the wallet module and exposes port 3001 as shown in Listing 3-9, the rate from the Dockerfile in the rate folder and exposes port 3002 as shown in Listing 3-10, and the account service from the account folder Dockerfile and exposes port 3003 as shown in Listing 3-11. Of interest is the health check[11] done for each of these three services. A simple curl call is made to the default Eclipse MicroProfile health check endpoint for each of them. This is used to tell docker the readiness of the containers to start accepting requests. And also

[11] Docker Health Check

have some environment variables to configure the tracing agent to connect to our tracing server Jaeger.

Listing 3-9. Wallet docker compose service

```
wallet:
  image: jwallet/wallet:latest
  ports:
    - "3001:3001"
  environment:
    JAEGER_AGENT_HOST: jaeger
    JAEGER_AGENT_PORT: 6831
    JAEGER_SAMPLER_TYPE: const
    JAEGER_SAMPLER_PARAM: 1
  healthcheck:
    test: curl --fail http://localhost:9080/health || exit 1
  build:
    context: wallet
    dockerfile: Dockerfile
```

Listing 3-10. Rate docker compose service

```
rate:
  image: jwallet/rate:latest
  ports:
    - "3002:3002"
  environment:
    JAEGER_AGENT_HOST: jaeger
    JAEGER_AGENT_PORT: 6831
    JAEGER_SAMPLER_TYPE: const
    JAEGER_SAMPLER_PARAM: 1
  healthcheck:
    test: curl --fail http://localhost:9080/health || exit 1
  build:
    context: rate
    dockerfile: Dockerfile
```

Listing 3-11. Account docker compose service

```
account:
  image: jwallet/account:latest
  ports:
    - "3003:3003"
  environment:
    JAEGER_AGENT_HOST: jaeger
    JAEGER_AGENT_PORT: 6831
    JAEGER_SAMPLER_TYPE: const
    JAEGER_SAMPLER_PARAM: 1
  healthcheck:
    test: curl --fail http://localhost:9080/health || exit 1
  build:
    context: account
    dockerfile: Dockerfile
```

The jaeger service is based on the jaeger docker image as pulled from Docker Hub. This service declares a dependency on the wallet, rate, and account services, so docker compose will start the jaeger service after them. Since jaeger is a request tracing application, it needs to have something to trace. And the wallet container, being the root container, is one on which jaeger depends as shown in Listing 3-12.

Listing 3-12. Jaeger docker compose service

```
jaeger:
  image: docker.io/jaegertracing/all-in-one:1.31
  ports:
    - "5775:5775/udp"
    - "6831:6831/udp"
    - "6832:6832/udp"
    - "5778:5778"
    - "16686:16686"
    - "14268:14268"
  depends_on:
    - wallet
    - rate
    - account
```

The prometheus service is based on the prometheus docker image pulled from Docker Hub. This service also declares a dependency on the wallet, rate, and account services; on the volume section of the service declaration, a copy of the bundled prometheus.yml file is bundled into the created container. This file configures the endpoints where prometheus will scrape for metrics on wallet, rate, and account services and other related configurations such as scrape intervals as shown in Listing 3-13.

Listing 3-13. Prometheus docker compose service

```
prometheus:
  image: docker.io/prom/prometheus:v2.34.0
  volumes:
    - ./prometheus/prometheus.yaml:/etc/prometheus/prometheus.yml
  ports:
    - "9090:9090"
  depends_on:
    - wallet
    - rate
    - account
```

The final service, grafana, based on the image pulled from Docker Hub, declares a dependency on prometheus. Both grafana and prometheus are applications for displaying application metrics. However, grafana is a much more user-friendly and configurable monitoring application than prometheus. So the general practice in the observability space is to configure grafana to consume the metrics scraped from the application by prometheus. This way, you get the best of both worlds - prometheus being good at scraping the metrics and grafana being good at displaying them. On the volume section of the service declaration, a copy of some preconfigured dashboards is bundled, taking advantage of grafana provisioning feature as shown in Listing 3-14.

Listing 3-14. Grafana docker compose service

```
grafana:
  image: docker.io/grafana/grafana-oss:8.4.4
  ports:
    - "3000:3000"
  environment:
    GF_AUTH_ANONYMOUS_ENABLED: 'true'
```

```
volumes:
  - ./grafana/provisioning/datasources:/etc/grafana/provisioning/
    datasources
  - ./grafana/provisioning/dashboards:/etc/grafana/provisioning/
    dashboards
depends_on:
  - prometheus
```

Hello, World!

Subsequent relevant chapters will be going into detail for each of the mentioned ancillary services declared in the docker file. For now, as we have seen the setup of the application, before taking a peek at the code, let us run the traditional hello world. Since the application is packaged and run as docker containers, the jwallet-cli.sh script in the root folder is a shell script that supports getting the application up and running through docker compose or kubernetes. The various supported commands are available through the help command as shown in Listing 3-15.

Listing 3-15. jwallet-cli.sh help command output

```
~> ./jwallet-cli.sh help

Usage:
  jwallet-cli.sh <command>
Commands:
  build       : build docker images
  up-compose : run jwallet on docker-compose
  down-compose: stop jwallet running on docker-compose
  up-kube     : run jwallet on kubernetes (using k3d)
  down-kube   : stop jwallet running on kubernetes (using k3d)
```

For our hello world, we are going to first build the images and everything with the build command followed by the up-compose command. The initial building of the various images and application artifacts could take some time depending on the speed of your network and computer. Running the up-compose command after should get the application up and running. For ease of reference, the README.md file has a summary of the endpoints for accessing the various services of the application as shown in Listing 3-16.

Listing 3-16. README.md entry for running and accessing the JWallet service

```
Running JWallet
1. Docker compose
Requires
 - docker-compose
Start / Stop
- start ./jwallet-cli.sh up-compose
- stop ./jwallet-cli.sh down-compose
Access service
- Wallet module http://localhost:3001/wallet
- Rate module http://localhost:3002/rate
- Account module http://localhost:3003/account
- Jaeger tracing http://localhost:16686
- Prometheus http://localhost:9090
- Grafana http://localhost:3000
```

Accessing the Hello endpoint on the wallet service, we get a message indicating the service is up and running as shown in Listing 3-17. It's also the same for rate and account services as shown in Listings 3-18 and 3-19, respectively.

Listing 3-17. Accessing the wallet service Hello endpoint

```
~> curl http://localhost:3001/wallet/api/hello
Hello wallet module
```

Listing 3-18. Accessing the rate service Hello endpoint

```
~> curl http://localhost:3002/rate/api/hello
Hello rate module
```

Listing 3-19. Accessing the account service Hello endpoint

```
~> curl http://localhost:3003/account/api/hello
Hello account module
```

We can also check if our microservices are up and ready by querying their health check endpoints. For the wallet microservice, a call to http://localhost:3001/health should give us the status as shown in Listing 3-20.

Listing 3-20. Accessing the wallet service health endpoint

```
~> curl http://localhost:3001/health
{
  "checks": [
    {
      "data": {},
      "name": "wallet-liveness",
      "status": "UP"
    },
    {
      "data": {},
      "name": "wallet-readiness",
      "status": "UP"
    }
  ],
  "status": "UP"
}
```

For the rate service, a call to http://localhost:3002/health should give us its health status as shown in Listing 3-21.

Listing 3-21. Accessing the rate service health endpoint

```
~> curl http://localhost:3002/health
{
  "checks": [
    {
      "data": {},
      "name": "rate-liveness",
      "status": "UP"
    },
    {
      "data": {},
      "name": "rate-readiness",
      "status": "UP"
    }
```

```
  ],
  "status": "UP"
}
```

And for the account service, http://localhost:3003/health should equally give us the health check status of the account microservice as shown in Listing 3-22.

Listing 3-22. Accessing the account service health endpoint

```
~> curl http://localhost:3003/health
{
  "checks": [
    {
      "data": {},
      "name": "account-liveness",
      "status": "UP"
    },
    {
      "data": {},
      "name": "account-readiness",
      "status": "UP"
    }
  ],
  "status": "UP"
}
```

Application Architecture Overview

Microservices as an application development paradigm is well known and understood. However, there is no single definition of how it is realized. Contrasting with monoliths, where it is clear all application code is developed as a single unit, microservices do not lend itself to such straightforward realization. One microservices application could be made up of physically separate services, that is, each microservice of the application is a separate maven project in its own codebase, and all the services orchestrated with some form of orchestration tool like BPM.[12]

[12] Business Process Management

Another could be a set of separate services developed in a common codebase, with each service acting as a module in the project. There are other variations of the way microservices can be realized in a given application. Whichever implementation style that is chosen, the microservices application should generally meet the descriptions of microservices as discussed in the previous chapter.

JWallet

JWallet, the reference application for this book, starts off as a set of microservices developed in a common project where each service is a maven module in the project. In a later chapter, we will refactor the application into physically separate services to realize the other form of microservices development. Table 3-1 shows the endpoints for accessing the various services in the application.

Table 3-1. *showing the endpoints in jwallet*

Module	URL
Wallet	http://localhost:3001/wallet
Rate	http://localhost:3002/rate
Account	http://localhost:3003/account
Jaeger	http://localhost:16686
Prometheus	http://localhost:9090
Grafana	http://localhost:3000

The application, as discussed in the previous section, is a maven multimodule application. The primary UI of the application is the various endpoints for creating and carrying out transactions in a given wallet. The REST endpoints are developed with the Jakarta RESTful API (JAX-RS). The root entry point of the application is the CONTEXT_PATH/api endpoint. Every JAX-RS application must have a root entry point that acts as the base path for all REST endpoints for that given application. This root REST endpoint is declared as shown in Listing 3-23 on the core module.

Listing 3-23. Root JAX-RS entry point

```
@ApplicationPath("api")
public class JaxrsConfigurations extends Application {
}
```

The annotation `@ApplicationPath("api")` on line 1 tells the JAX-RS runtime that we want to host all REST endpoints in this application under the base path "api." The class JaxrsConfigurations then extends the Application class from the JAX-RS API. With this configuration in place, all REST endpoints can be accessed as subpaths of the api path. So, for example, the hello path of the wallet service is http://localhost:3003/wallet/api/hello.

The hello resource in the wallet module is declared in the class HelloResource as shown in Listing 3-24.

Listing 3-24. Hello endpoint

```
@Path("hello")
public class HelloResource {

    @GET
    @SimplyTimed
    @Traced
    String hello {
        return "Hello account module";
    }

}
```

JAX-RS resources are hosted as Java classes and resource endpoints hosted as methods of that class. In the HelloResource example earlier, line 1 declares that this class and all resources contained within it are hosted on under the /hello path. The @Path annotation is from the JAX-RS API. What this means is that any REST endpoint that we wish to expose in this class will be accessed as a subpath of the /hello path. Line 4 uses the @GET annotation to define the method hello declared on line 6 as an HTTP GET method. Because this method has no other path defined, it will be the default GET method called by the JAX-RS runtime when the path /wallet/api/hello is accessed.

The return type of the method is the value that is returned to the client. In this example, the simple String message "Hello wallet module" is returned when a GET call to /hello is made. JAX-RS supports the return of many different types. Because the HelloResource class does not explicitly specify the content types it consumes and produces, the runtime defaults to using simple types. We will shortly see how we can declare the MIME[13] type a given JAX-RS resource consumes and produces.

Line 5 also annotates the hello method with the @SimplyTimed annotation from the Eclipse MicroProfile metrics API. This annotation tracks elapsed time and count of the method invocation. Simply by annotating the hello method with this @SimplyTimed, the MicroProfile runtime is going to expose a metric for invocations of this method that tracks the number and duration of each call. The exposed metrics can be consumed by any number of applications. In the case of JWallet, we can see the metric through the bundled Prometheus (accessible at http://localhost:9090) and Grafana (accessible at http://localhost:3000) observability applications, as shown in Figure 3-2.

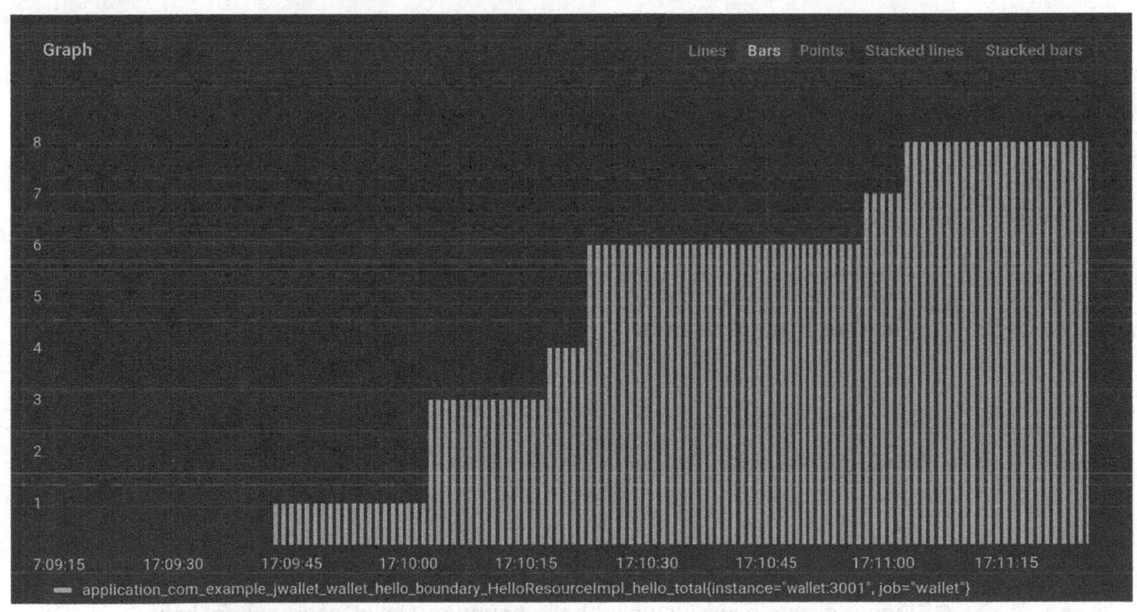

***Figure 3-2.** Grafana metric explorer*

Line 6 also annotates the hello method with the @Traced annotation from the Eclipse MicroProfile metrics API. This annotation tracks incoming requests to the service and also subsequent requests to other services.

[13] MIME types

In my sample deployment, the Hello resource of the wallet module (accessible at http://localhost:3001/wallet) has been called eight times, with each call listed in the list as shown in Figure 3-3 (accessible at http://localhost:16686). Clicking one of the calls takes us to the detail page for the tracing as shown in Figure 3-4.

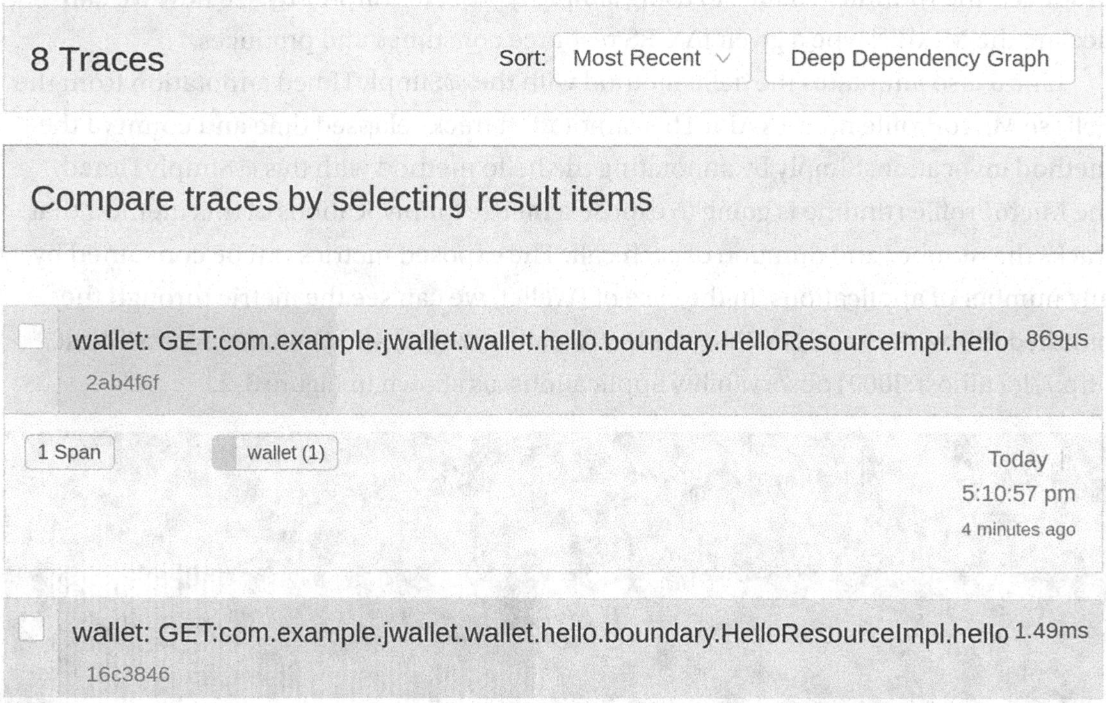

8 Traces
Sort: Most Recent
Deep Dependency Graph

Compare traces by selecting result items

wallet: GET:com.example.jwallet.wallet.hello.boundary.HelloResourceImpl.hello 869μs
2ab4f6f
1 Span
wallet (1)
Today
5:10:57 pm
4 minutes ago

wallet: GET:com.example.jwallet.wallet.hello.boundary.HelloResourceImpl.hello 1.49ms
16c3846

***Figure 3-3.** Jaeger tracing – trace list*

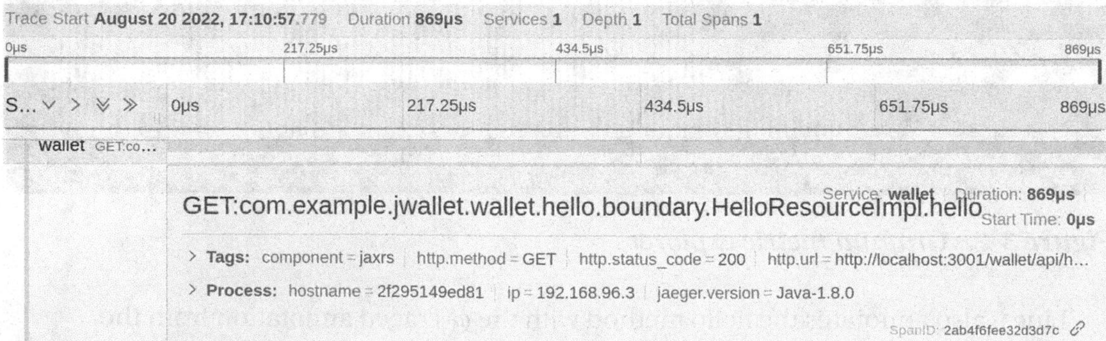

***Figure 3-4.** Jaeger tracing – trace details*

The detailed list of one of the traced calls shows the date and time of the call (1), the service in which the called resource is and the duration (2), and some details of the traced call, including the full resource endpoint (3). All of this detail is handled by the MicroProfile metrics runtime. All we had to do was to declare our hello resource method as timed. Chapter 6 goes into detail about the Jakarta RESTful Web Services API. For now, let us take a cursory look at the WalletResource.

The Wallet resource is the root entry point into the application. It hosts the various methods for creating, debiting, crediting, and querying wallets. It is declared as shown in Listing 3-25.

Listing 3-25. Wallet module endpoints

```
@Consumes(MediaType.APPLICATION_JSON)
@Produces(MediaType.APPLICATION_JSON)
@Path("wallets")
public class WalletResource {

      @Inject
      WalletService walletService;
      ...
}
```

The Wallet resource is defined in class WalletResource.java. Lines 1 and 2 use the @Consumes and @Produces annotations to declare the MIME types that the resource methods of this resource class can consume and produce, respectively. Because the JSON[14] data format is the most popular format for RESTful web services, all the resource endpoints in JWallet consume and produce JSON data in the JSON format. For the WalletResource, the constant MediaType.APPLICATION_JSON passed to the two annotations tells the JAX-RS runtime that all resource methods declared in this class consume and produce JSON. What this implies is that clients can make calls to resource methods in this class, passing in any requisite data in JSON format. The runtime will handle the conversion between the passed JSON data and the corresponding Java type. The same thing goes for the returned type.

[14] JSON

Line 3 declares that this class is hosted at the wallets resource path. Similar to the hello resource, all resource endpoints in this class can be accessed as subpaths of the /wallets path. Line 6 uses the @Inject annotation from the Jakarta Contexts and Dependency Injection API to declare a dependency on the WalletService.java class. This is a declarative way of asking for component dependencies in Jakarta EE. Chapter 4 will discuss the CDI API in detail. For now, let us take a look at the first resource method for creating a wallet as shown in Listing 3-26.

Listing 3-26. WalletResource create wallet method

```
@POST
@Traced(operationName = "create-wallet")
@SimplyTimed(name = "create_wallet_timer")
public BalanceResponse createWallet(CreateWalletRequest
createWalletRequest) {
        return walletService.createWallet(createWalletRequest);
}
```

The first line uses the @POST annotation to declare that method createWallet, declared on line 4, is a POST resource. In the absence of any explicit path using the @Path annotation on this method, a POST request to the resource path /api/wallets will be routed to this method. The method takes as a parameter the CreateWalletRequest and returns the BalanceResponse types. Because the resource class declares that it both consumes and produces the JSON type, the JAX-RS runtime takes care of the conversion from and to JSON on our behalf. From your perspective as a Java developer, you're writing Java methods.

Line 2 declares the method as @Traced, passing in a name for the trace operation name. This annotation is from the Eclipse MicroProfile OpenTracing API. The use of this annotation exposes metrics about calls to this method that can be consumed by observability applications. In JWallet, the bundled Jaeger application consumes and shows the create-wallet trace as in Figure 3-5.

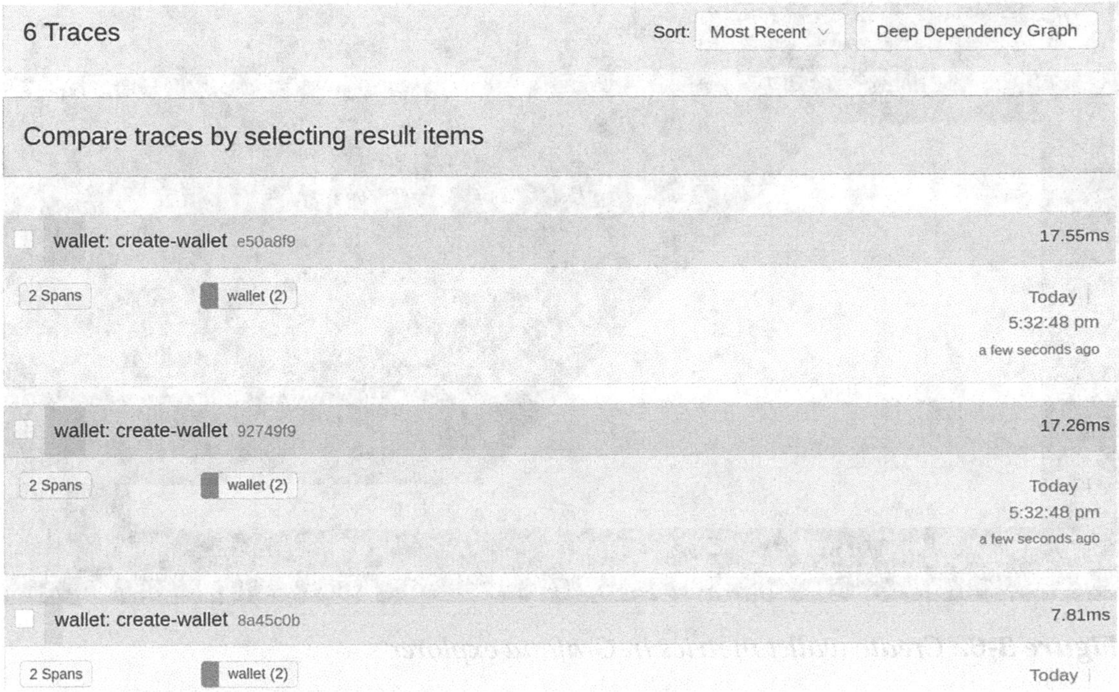

Figure 3-5. *Create wallet trace list*

As Figure 3-5 shows, our create-wallet trace shows that the method has been called a total of six times for my sample deployment. Each trace in the list, similar to what we saw with the HelloResource, will show the date, time, duration, and other relevant information about the trace. One noticeable difference between this trace and that of the HelloResource we looked at earlier is that this metric has been explicitly named, unlike the HelloResource trace which used the fully qualified class name as the name of the metric because we did not pass in an explicit name.

Line 11 also declares the method as @SimplyTimed, but this time around, passing in an explicit name for the timer. The metric exposed by this annotation can be observed in the bundle Grafana application as shown in Figure 3-6.

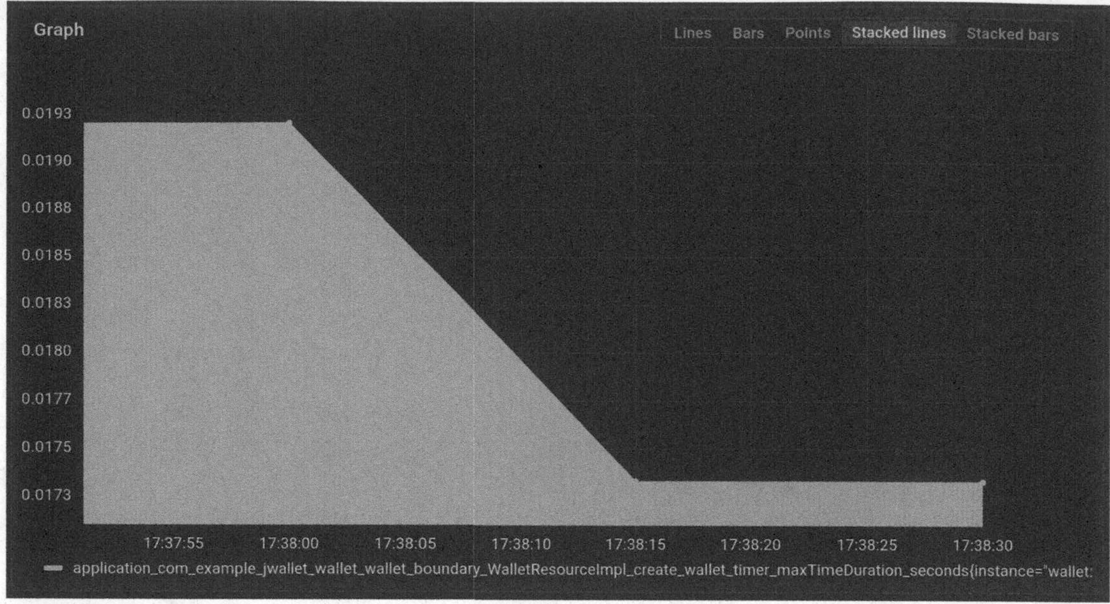

***Figure 3-6.** Create wallet metrics in Grafana explorer*

Figure 3-6 shows one metric from the list of metrics exposed by our @SimplyTimed method. This metric shows the maximum time duration of each call. The Grafana application is displaying this information as received from the bundled Prometheus application. The Eclipse MicroProfile Metrics API exposes base, vendor, application, and other custom metrics that can be consumed and displayed for observation. For example, the Grafana metrics browser shows some of the list of metrics that Eclipse MicroProfile generates for our application as shown in Figure 3-7.

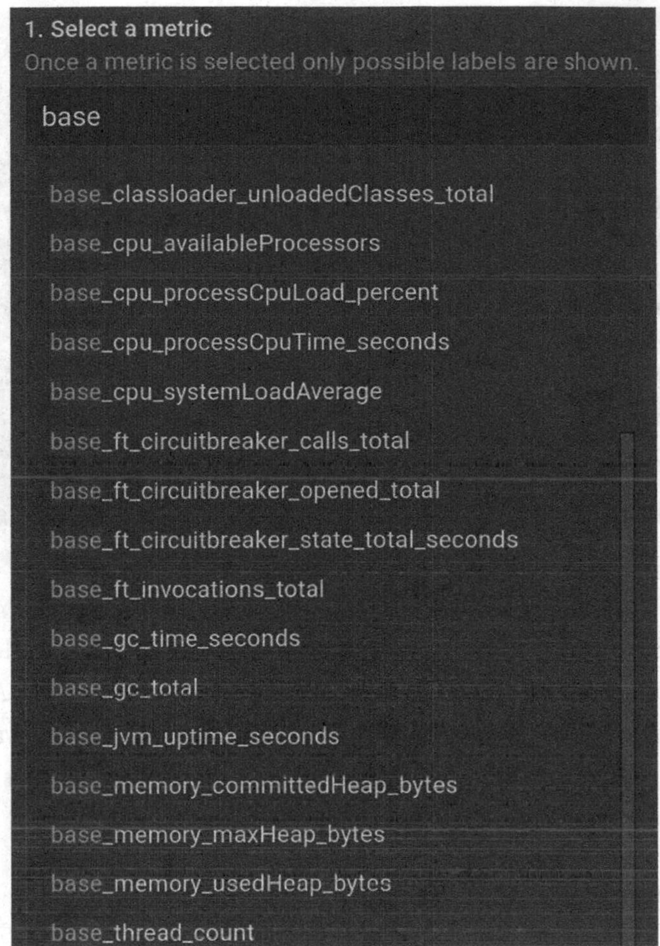

***Figure 3-7.** Grafana metrics browser*

Chapter 9 goes into detail about exposing and displaying various metrics using the Eclipse MicroProfile Metrics API.

With our resource method in place, we can now make a sample REST call to it using any REST client. The client could be another service in JWallet, a JavaScript client, another application written in Python, for instance, or any other tool that can make REST calls. For our sample call, we use the Insomnia REST client. Let us create a wallet with a call to our createWallet resource method in WalletResource as shown in Figure 3-8.

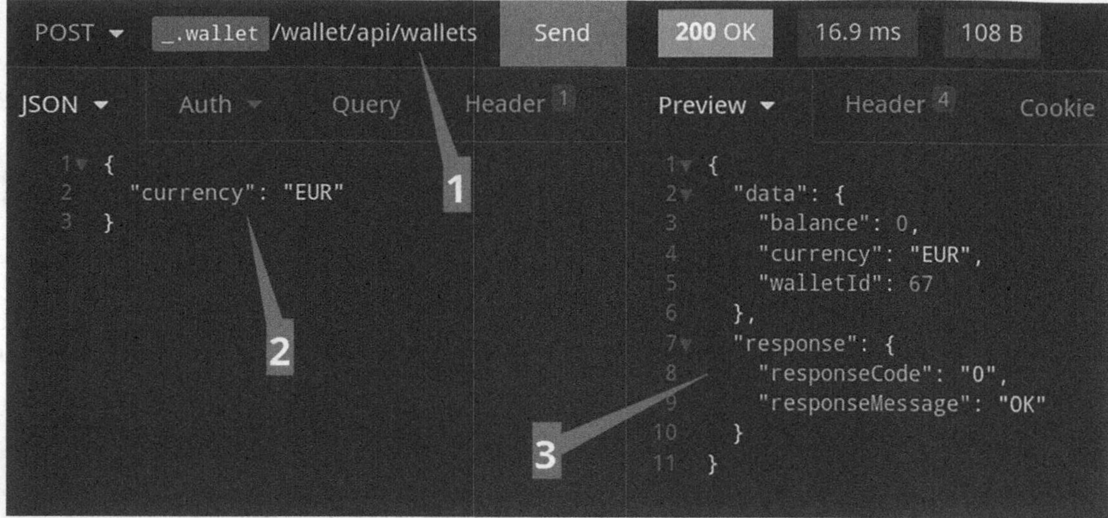

Figure 3-8. *Create wallet API call in Insomnia*

We make a POST request to the resource http://localhost:3001/wallet/api/wallets (1) with the JSON representation of the CreateWalletRequest Java type (2). A successful call results in the returned JSON representation of the BalanceResponse Java type (3). The CreateWalletRequest.java and BalanceResponse.java classes are shown in Listings 3-27 and 3-28, respectively.

Listing 3-27. CreateWalletRequest class

```
public class CreateWalletRequest {

    private String currency;

    public String getCurrency() {
        return currency;
    }

    public void setCurrency(String currency) {
        this.currency = currency;
    }
}
```

Listing 3-28. BalanceResponse class

```
public class BalanceResponse extends Response<BalanceResponse.
BalanceResponseData> {

      public static BalanceResponse of(BalanceResponseData data) {
            BalanceResponse response = new BalanceResponse();
            response.setData(data);
            return response;
      }

      public static class BalanceResponseData {
            private long walletId;
            private BigDecimal balance;
            private String currency;

            public long getWalletId() {
                  return walletId;
            }

            public void setWalletId(long walletId) {
                  this.walletId = walletId;
            }
            public BigDecimal getBalance() {
                  return balance;
            }

            public void setBalance(BigDecimal balance) {
                  this.balance = balance;
            }

            public String getCurrency() {
                  return currency;
            }

            public void setCurrency(String currency) {
                  this.currency = currency;
            }
      }
}
```

These two types were transparently converted from and to JSON, respectively, when we made the REST call by the JAX-RS runtime. Chapter 6 goes into much detail about JAX-RS. For now, let us take a look at the createWallet method on the WalletService that the REST createWallet resource method delegated to for the creation of the wallet as shown in Listing 3-29.

Listing 3-29. WalletService create wallet method

```
@Stateless
public class WalletService {

    @Inject
    WalletRepository walletRepository;
    @Inject
    TransactionRepository transactionRepository;
    @Inject
    RateService rateService;

    public BalanceResponse getBalance(final long walletId) {
        Wallet wallet = walletRepository.findById(walletId);

        BalanceResponseData data = new BalanceResponseData();
        data.setWalletId(wallet.getId());
        data.setBalance(wallet.getBalance());
        data.setCurrency(wallet.getCurrency());

        return BalanceResponse.of(data);
    }

    public BalanceResponse createWallet(final CreateWalletRequest
    createWalletRequest) {
        Wallet wallet = new Wallet();

        wallet.setBalance(BigDecimal.ZERO);
        wallet.setCurrency(createWalletRequest.getCurrency());
        wallet = walletRepository.save(wallet);

        return getBalance(wallet.getId());
    }
}
```

Line 1 uses the @Stateless annotation from the Enterprise JavaBeans (EJB) API to declare class WalletService as a stateless bean. This singular annotation transforms this class into a pooled, transactional, and secure bean that is fully managed on our behalf by the EJB runtime. By being transactional, every method that is invoked on WalletService will be called in a transactional context, meaning the EJB runtime will create and commit transactions for each call. Chapter 5 goes into detail about using the EJB API in connection with JPA.

WalletService also declares dependencies on WalletRepository, TransactionRepository, and RateService. All these dependencies are declared using the @Inject annotation, delegating the creation, injection, and destruction of these dependencies to the Contexts and Dependency Injection runtime (much more on this in Chapter 4).

WalletService declares a method createWallet that takes a CreateWalletRequest type as the parameter. The method then does some basic initialization of the Wallet.java type and then delegates the rest of the work to the WalletRepository. The Wallet.java is the entity[15] being used to represent a wallet or bank account. In the Jakarta Persistence API, database tables are modelled as Java classes, with instances of those Java classes mapped to database table records.

The Wallet entity, as shown in Listing 3-30, is a simple Java class that is declaratively marked as an entity using the @Entity annotation from the JPA API.

Listing 3-30. Wallet entity class

```
@Entity
public class Wallet extends AbstractEntity {

    private Long userId;

    private String currency;
    private BigDecimal balance;

    @OneToMany(mappedBy = "wallet")
    private Set<Transaction> transactions;

    // Getters & Setters
}
```

[15] Entity, attribute, and entity type

Line 1 uses the @Entity annotation to declare this class a JPA entity. What this translates to is that a database table will be created with the name Wallet, and each field of the Java class mapped to columns in the created table. The Wallet entity has four fields; three of them are simple types and one a collection type. The simple types (Long, String, and BigDecimal) will be mapped directly to columns in the Wallet database table. The java.util.Set collection type declared in the field transactions is going to be mapped specially based on the declarative relationship between the Wallet type and the Transaction type. In this case, one wallet instance can have many transactions.

The Wallet class, as shown in Listing 3-30, extends the AbstractEntity. When using JPA to model entities, you will find yourself having very common fields across most of the entities. It is good practice to abstract these common fields into a superclass that will be inherited by all subclasses that need these common fields. The Jakarta Persistence API gives you different ways of modelling this parent-child inheritance relationship. In this example, the AbstractEntity, as shown in Listing 3-31, will not have any database table of its own. All the fields in the AbstractEntity will be put in inheriting subclasses. We are opting for the "single table per inheritance" strategy.

Listing 3-31. AbstractEntity class

```
@MappedSuperclass
@EntityListeners({ AbstractEntityEntityListener.class })
public abstract class AbstractEntity implements Serializable {
  @Id
  @GeneratedValue(strategy = GenerationType.AUTO)
  protected long id;

  protected LocalDateTime created;
  protected LocalDateTime updated;

  protected String createdBy;
  protected String editedBy;

  // Getters & Setters
}
```

AbstractEntity is declared as an abstract class that is serializable. It is declared as a `@MappedSuperclass` to tell the JPA runtime that we want the mapping information of this class applied to its subclasses. JPA will not create a separate database table for this class. All the fields declared in it will be mapped to inheriting subclasses.

Line 4 uses the `@Id` annotation to declare the field id of type Long as the unique table identifier or primary key[16] for this class. Line 5 uses the `@GeneratedValue` to tell the runtime how this unique field should be generated. In our example, we are opting to let the JPA runtime handle the automatic creation of the primary key. Because the Wallet entity inherits from the AbstractEntity, all these are automatically and transparently mapped to the Wallet table as shown in Figure 3-9.

id	balance	created	createdby	currency	editedby	updated	userid
51	0	2022-08-2…	Dummy User	EUR	<null>	<null>	<null>
52	0	2022-08-2…	Dummy User	EUR	<null>	<null>	<null>
1	150	2022-08-2…	Dummy User	EUR	Dummy User	2022-08-2…	<null>
59	0	2022-08-2…	Dummy User	EUR	<null>	<null>	<null>
60	0	2022-08-2…	Dummy User	EUR	<null>	<null>	<null>
61	0	2022-08-2…	Dummy User	EUR	<null>	<null>	<null>
62	0	2022-08-2…	Dummy User	EUR	<null>	<null>	<null>
63	0	2022-08-2…	Dummy User	EUR	<null>	<null>	<null>
64	0	2022-08-2…	Dummy User	EUR	<null>	<null>	<null>
65	0	2022-08-2…	Dummy User	EUR	<null>	<null>	<null>
66	0	2022-08-2…	Dummy User	EUR	<null>	<null>	<null>
67	0	2022-08-2…	Dummy User	EUR	<null>	<null>	<null>

Figure 3-9. *Wallet database table*

The Wallet database table shown in Figure 3-9 is mapped from the Wallet entity. The id, created, createdBy, editedBy, and updated fields correspond to the respective fields in the AbstractEntity class. These fields were created because of the Wallet entity inheriting the AbstractEntity. In the database, there is no separate table for the AbstractEntity.

The WalletRepository implements the repository pattern[17] for managing instances of the Wallet entity as shown in Listing 3-32.

[16] Primary Key

[17] Designing the infrastructure persistence layer | Microsoft Docs

Listing 3-32. WalletRepository class

```
@RequestScoped
public class WalletRepository extends BaseRepository<Wallet, Long> {

  public WalletRepository() {
    super(Wallet.class);
  }

  @Override
  public Wallet findById(final Long id) {
    final Wallet wallet = super.findById(id);
    if (wallet == null) {
      throw new WalletNotFoundException();
    }
    return wallet;
  }
}
```

It extends the BaseRepository, passing in the entity and primary key types. The BaseRepository has common methods that correspond to the create, read, update, and delete operations common to all database tables. The only method that WalletRepository overrides is the findById method. The save method that was called on the WalletRepository in the WalletService is simply inherited from the BaseRepository, as shown in Listing 3-33.

Listing 3-33. BaseRepository class

```
public abstract class BaseRepository<E, K> {

  @PersistenceContext
  EntityManager em;
  Class<E> clazz;

  public BaseRepository() {}
  public BaseRepository(Class<E> clazz) {
    this.clazz = clazz;
  }
```

```
  public E findById(K id) {
    return em.find(clazz, id);
  }

  List<E> findAll(String querName) {
    return em.createNamedQuery(querName, clazz).getResultList();
  }

  public E save(E entity) {
    em.persist(entity);
    return entity;
  }

  public E merge(E entity) {
    return em.merge(entity);
  }

  public E refresh(E entity) {
    em.refresh(entity);
    return entity;
  }

  public void remove(E entity) {
    E mergedEntity = merge(entity);
    em.remove(mergedEntity);
  }

}
```

The BaseRepository, as shown in Listing 3-33, uses Java generics[18] to create flexible, generified CRUD[19] methods. The BaseRepository itself also depends upon the EntityManager[20] interface to interact with the JPA runtime. The EntityManager is injected into the BaseRepository on line 4 using the `@PersistenceContext`[21] annotation. This annotation tells the JPA runtime that we need an instance of the EntityManager injected

[18] Java Generic Types
[19] CRUD
[20] JPA Entity Manager
[21] JPA Persistence Context

into the annotated field for us. It also tells the runtime to manage the injected instance for us. With this injection, we can then call various methods on the EntityManager interface to carry out operations on our entities. Chapter 5 will go into in-depth detail about the EntityManager.

Testing

Every application should have some form of testing, preferably a combination of unit, component, integration, and manual testing. Every Maven project has a default testing folder for creating tests. JWallet has separate tests for each microservice that test the various functionalities of the application. Because there is no universally accepted definition of how to write tests, all applications implement tests in different ways. Because the primary UI of JWallet is the REST endpoints, the integration tests consist of firing requests to those endpoints and making JUnit assertions on the responses.

In the Java space, there are a myriad of testing frameworks and libraries that you can choose from. The combination of libraries chosen will mostly depend on the application being developed. As a Jakarta EE application, JWallet needs an implementation to run. Consequently, to run the tests, we need to have the application deployed even in a testing context. One library that makes managing the testing infrastructure for Jakarta applications easy is the TestContainers[22] project. JWallet bundles the TestContainers library, making it easy to run the full, end-to-end integration tests using the Maven command mvn verify -Dtc.

The entry point for the tests in the wallet microservice is the AbstractWalletIT as shown in Listing 3-34 .

Listing 3-34. AbstractWalletIT class

```
public class AbstractWalletIT {

  protected static final String walletServiceUrl;
  protected static final WebTarget target;
  static {
```

[22] Testcontainers

```
    boolean testInContainer = System.getProperties().containsKey("tc");
    String walletServiceUrlTemplate = "http://%s:%d/wallet/api";

    if (testInContainer) {
      final DockerComposeContainer composeContainer = new
      DockerComposeContainer(new File("docker-compose.yaml"))
          .withExposedService("wallet", 3001);
      composeContainer.start();

      walletServiceUrl = String.format(walletServiceUrlTemplate,
          composeContainer.getServiceHost("wallet", 3001),
          composeContainer.getServicePort("wallet", 3001));
    } else {
      walletServiceUrl = String.format(walletServiceUrlTemplate,
      "localhost", 3001);
    }

    target = ClientBuilder.newClient().target(walletServiceUrl);
  }
}
```

This does some initialization in a static block starting, checking if you passed in the tc property as part of running mvn verify. If you did, then a new instance of a DockerComposeContainer is created and started using the docker-compose.yaml file in the root of the wallet module as shown in Figure 3-10.

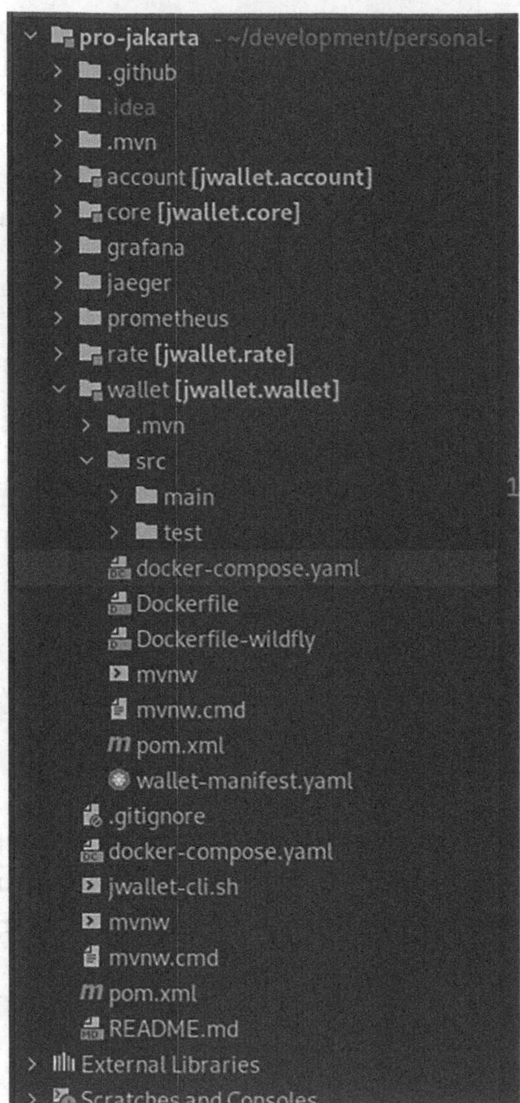

***Figure 3-10.** Docker-compose.yaml file in the project structure*

The created DockerComposeContainer instance is used to get the host and port of the deployed wallet microservice and then instantiate the walletServiceUrl variable. If no tc property is passed, then the walletServiceUrl is instantiated using localhost. Then a new WebTarget object is created using the JAX-RS ClientBuilder. With this setup in place, the test subclasses that extend the AbstractWalletIT can use this target object to fire REST calls to various resources in the wallet microservice.

For example, the HelloResourceIT fires a call to the HelloResource endpoint and makes a simple assertion on the received response as shown in Listing 3-35.

Listing 3-35. HelloResourceIT class

```
class HelloResourceIT extends AbstractWalletIT {
  @Test
  void hello() {
    String response = target.path("hello").request().get(String.class);
    assertEquals("Hello wallet module", response);
  }
}
```

Line 4 makes a GET call to our HelloResource and reads the String Java type from the response, because we know our HelloResource method returns a string. Line 5 then uses the assertEquals method from the JUnit assertions API to test if the received response is equal to what we expect.

The WalletResourceIT also extends the AbstractWalletIT as shown in Listing 3-36. Line 3 declares a createWallet JUnit test (line 2 using the `@Test` annotation). Similar to the hello test discussed earlier, the createWallet test constructs a CreateWalletRequest object and makes a POST request, passing in the created object to the Entity.json method to convert it to JSON to be sent to the resource method. The second parameter to the .post method (line 9) is the class type of the expected return type from the resource. Because our createWallet resource method returns a BalanceResponse, we pass in BalanceResponse.class. We then assigned the returned value to a variable of type BalanceResponse and then proceeded to make some assertions on it.

Listing 3-36. WalletResourceIT class

```
class WalletResourceIT extends AbstractWalletIT {
    @Test
    void createWallet() {
        CreateWalletRequest createWalletRequest = new
         CreateWalletRequest();
        createWalletRequest.setCurrency("USD");

        BalanceResponse balanceResponse = target.path("wallets").request()
                .post(Entity.json(createWalletRequest),
                BalanceResponse.class);

        assertEquals("0", balanceResponse.getResponse().getResponseCode());
```

```
        assertEquals("OK", balanceResponse.getResponse().
        getResponseMessage());

        assertEquals(createWalletRequest.getCurrency(), balanceResponse.
        getData().getCurrency());
        assertEquals(BigDecimal.ZERO, balanceResponse.getData().
        getBalance());
        assertNotNull(balanceResponse.getData().getWalletId());
    }
    // More tests
}
```

In Chapter 6, you will see in much more detail how the JAX-RS client API can be used to make REST calls to other resource methods both within and outside of JWallet.

Summary

This chapter introduced the case study application of this book, a Jakarta EE and Eclipse MicroProfile application called JWallet. We looked at the setup through the various Maven pom.xml files and discussed the architecture. We discussed how the application is deployed and took a look at the various container declaration files. We briefly looked at the use of the Jakarta Persistence, Contexts and Dependency Injection, and RESTful Web Services APIs in the application. We then made REST requests to the application and used both Grafana and Jaeger to see some of the application metrics as exposed by the Eclipse MicroProfile Metrics API. Finally, we took a brief look at the test setup.

The next chapter takes a detailed look at the Jakarta Contexts and Dependency Injection API. This API is a standard way of gluing disparate parts of a given Jakarta EE application together in a clear, extensible, and maintainable way. Chapter 5 after that goes into the detail of the Jakarta Persistence API followed by Chapter 6, which then gives you a solid grounding in developing modern RESTful web services with JAX-RS. Together, these three APIs form the core of every modern Jakarta EE application. Let's get going!

CHAPTER 4

Managing Dependencies with CDI

Every nontrivial application will be made up of different components working together to fulfill the objectives of the application. These components will have intricate dependencies on each other. Managing this complex interdependence manually can be a very daunting task. The Jakarta EE platform provides the Jakarta Contexts and Dependency Injection API that you can use to automate the process of managing application component dependencies.

You can think of the CDI API as a black box that you make invocations to and "magically" get instances of your application components with a well-defined lifecycle and other added features. Jakarta CDI is analogous to the kitchen in a restaurant. Most of the time, you simply walk into a restaurant, peruse the menu, make an order, and after a brief moment have your order prepared and served with cutlery and other ancillary stuff. The CDI runtime is quite similar except your "order" is delivered instantaneously.

With CDI, your various application components declare their dependencies and have the runtime manage the creation, injection, and destruction of the created instances. You invert the control of dependency management. Dependency injection is effectively a form of the inversion of control[1] pattern of application development. In this chapter, and the rest of this book, we loosely use the term component to refer to any piece of an application that can be encapsulated in a Java class.

By the end of this chapter, you will learn how the CDI API bean management (we will extensively see what a bean is), producer, interceptor, and event mechanisms help you write maintainable, loosely coupled applications that will live for the foreseeable future. You will also learn how these constructs transparently allow you to implement tried and tested design patterns with minimal effort.

---

[1] InversionOfControl

L. Saeed and G. Abdallah, *Pro Cloud Native Java EE Apps*, https://doi.org/10.1007/978-1-4842-8900-6_4

An Overview of CDI in Jakarta EE 10

The latest version of the CDI specification being shipped with Jakarta EE 10 is CDI 4.0.[2] This release features a split of the core CDI API into Lite and Full. CDI Lite is designed to run in more restricted environments and features a subset of the original features. CDI Full contains the Lite and all other features that were in core CDI in previous Jakarta EE releases. This chapter and the rest of the book focus on CDI Full, which is what is shipped with the full Jakarta EE 10 release.

Key Features of CDI

The CDI API gives you a set of features that help in developing loosely coupled, complex enterprise applications. Having a loosely coupled application means that the various components of your application aren't rigidly tied to each other. This way, it is easy to substitute one component for another without having to significantly rewrite the application. The following are the core features that the CDI API has available for helping you achieve that.

Typesafe Dependency Resolution Mechanism

CDI uses Java types to resolve dependencies. Unlike other dependency injection implementations that are string based, CDI uses Java types through a combination of metadata and Java beans to resolve dependencies that you declare. This is achieved through a sophisticated resolution mechanism that allows you to select dependencies at development or deployment time.

Well-Defined Lifecycle Contexts

CDI allows you to bind stateful objects to a well-defined, extensible lifecycle context. Each instance of a bean that you request from the runtime has a predictable lifecycle, complete with callbacks that you can hook into.

[2] Jakarta Context Dependency Injection 4.0 | The Eclipse Foundation

Integration with the Web Tier

Through integration with the Jakarta Unified Expression Language (EL), contextual objects like Jakarta Enterprise Beans can be accessed directly from a Jakarta Server Faces page.

Interceptors

CDI interceptors allow you to associate interceptors with Java objects through typesafe interceptor bindings. You can use these interceptors to implement features that are orthogonal to the core of any given bean.

Events

CDI events are a powerful, typesafe way to have completely separate components of your application communicate in a fully decoupled way through the use of event notifications. One component can fire an event, and any registered listeners of that event will be notified or called by the CDI runtime, passing in the requisite event object automatically.

An SPI for Creating Extensions

CDI provides a service provider interface for the creation of portable extensions that integrate with the container. An example of a CDI portable extension is the Apache DeltaSpike[3] project.

These are the main features provided by CDI for enterprise application development on the Jakarta EE platform. The rest of this chapter goes into detail about how to take advantage of these features in application development. Let us start by seeing how to activate CDI in a Jakarta EE application.

CDI Activation

Bean Discovery Modes

To understand how CDI is activated in an application, we first need to discuss the concept of bean discovery modes. A bean discovery mode determines how the CDI runtime treats possible CDI components in an application. There are three bean discovery modes as follows.

[3] Apache DeltaSpike

None

This mode tells the CDI runtime to not scan for any beans during application boot time. Setting the bean discovery mode to this is effectively disabling CDI in the application. You will rarely ever use this option.

Annotated

The annotated bean discovery mode tells the CDI runtime to only scan for components annotated with CDI bean defining annotations. Bean defining annotations are CDI constructs that can be used to define a bean in one way or the other. A bean defined using any of these CDI constructs in an annotated bean discovery mode is an implicit bean. The annotated bean discovery mode is the default in the absence of an explicit setting or CDI configuration file. This means that if you do not explicitly set the bean discovery mode, CDI will only scan for implicit beans in your application.

All

The all bean discovery mode tells the CDI runtime to scan for all beans in an application, irrespective of whether the bean has an explicit CDI bean defining annotation or not. This mode explicitly enables CDI. Setting the bean discovery mode to all means you can inject a POJO with no explicit CDI annotation, and the runtime will still be able to create instances for you. The reference application for this book will use this bean discovery mode. All further discussions in this chapter and the rest of the book assume an explicit, bean discovery mode set to all.

The beans.xml File

The main configuration file for CDI is the beans.xml file. It is a simple file that can be used to set the bean discovery mode explicitly and register other CDI components. A typical example of the beans file is shown in Listing 4-1.

Listing 4-1. The beans.xml file used in jwallet

```
<?xml version="1.0" encoding="UTF-8"?>
<beans xmlns="https://jakarta.ee/xml/ns/jakartaee"
       xmlns:xsi="http://www.w3.org/2001/XMLSchema-instance"
```

```
    xsi:schemaLocation="https://jakarta.ee/xml/ns/jakartaee
    https://jakarta.ee/xml/ns/jakartaee/beans_4_0.xsd"
    version="4.0" bean-discovery-mode="all">
</beans>
```

Listing 4-1 shows the beans.xml file using the new 4.0 schema file. The bean discovery mode value is set to all. By this beans.xml file, we have explicitly enabled CDI in jwallet, and by setting the value of the discovery mode to all, every bean/POJO in our application is automatically a CDI bean and will be scanned at application boot time.

The CDI Container

The word container is often associated with inversion of control. It refers to the central piece of software that is responsible for creating, injecting, and destroying instances of dependencies as requested by their dependents. The CDI container, on the Jakarta EE platform, is the runtime responsible for managing the relationships between the various, disparate components of an application. Dependencies between different parts of an application can get very complex and unwieldy to manage manually.

The CDI container is responsible for scanning and validating your application at boot time to ensure there is no CDI violation. A violation of the CDI constructs will prevent an application from starting because the CDI container will throw an error when it scans and discovers a violation. You will rarely get a runtime CDI error because of this startup scan and validation by the container.

The CDI container is also responsible for creating contextual instances of your beans, adding relevant CDI enrichment to those created instances, assigning them to relevant contexts, and finally destroying those instances when the contexts they're bound to get destroyed. You can think of the CDI container as a black box that only appears to answer your requests and disappears into the shadows when not needed. You as a developer will mostly not need to think much about the CDI container however, you just have to know it's there in the background and ready to answer your requests.

Beans and Contextual Instances

What Is a CDI Bean?

A bean is the most atomic component in CDI. A bean in CDI is any Java class that has either a no-arg constructor or at least one injectable constructor. It can optionally be explicitly annotated with one or more CDI annotations. The few restrictions on a CDI bean are that it cannot be an inner or abstract class. A CDI bean isn't very different from a JavaBean.[4] In fact, any JavaBean is automatically a CDI bean. Technically, this kind of bean is called a managed bean - managed in the sense that the creation and destruction of such bean instances are fully managed by the CDI container.

The other technical kind of CDI bean is session beans. Session beans are components annotated with any of the bean defining metadata from the EJB[5] spec, namely, @Stateless, @Stateful, and @Singleton. Any bean annotated with any of these annotations is automatically a CDI bean in addition to being an EJB and has the features and services provided by both specifications. We will talk about EJB in a section later in this chapter.

You implement your application logic in a bean class and optionally add CDI features to it using one or more CDI metadata. You can then declare dependencies on your beans in other components, which are also beans. An example of a CDI bean is shown in Listing 4-2.

Listing 4-2. showing the WalletService as a CDI bean

```
public class WalletService {
}
```

Listing 4-2 shows a simple POJO called WalletService. This class is a fully valid CDI bean that can be injected into other beans. Even though WalletService doesn't have any CDI attributes yet, it will still be scanned at boot time by the container because our bean discovery mode in the beans.xml file is set to all. We can explicitly add CDI features to the WalletService bean by giving it some attributes using some CDI annotations. Listing 4-3 shows the WalletService with some CDI attributes added through annotations.

[4] What is a JavaBean exactly? – Stack Overflow

[5] Jakarta Enterprise Beans 4.0 | The Eclipse Foundation

Listing 4-3. showing the WalletService with CDI attributes

```
@RequestScoped
@Transactional
public class WalletService {
}
```

Listing 4-3 shows the WalletService bean given some CDI attributes. The @RequestScoped annotation tells the CDI container in what context instances of this bean should be put. The @Transactional annotation is an interceptor that will automatically demarcate transactional boundaries for methods invoked on instances of the WalletService. The set of CDI attributes you can give a bean are Qualifiers, Scopes, Alternatives, and Name (we'll be discussing these in this chapter). This bean can be injected into other beans by annotating a field of type WalletService with the @Inject annotation as shown in Listing 4-4.

Listing 4-4. showing a dependency declaration on our WalletService CDI bean

```
public class WalletResourceImpl implements WalletResource {
@Inject
WalletService walletService;
}
```

Listing 4-4 shows an injection of the WalletService bean into the WalletResourceImpl component. The field type of the walletService variable is WalletService, which brings us to the question of how the container is able to resolve the type to use in resolving an injection point.

CDI Bean Types

An injection point is any field or parameter that is expected to be instantiated by the CDI container. So, for instance, the walletService field annotated with @Inject as shown in Listing 4-4 is an injection point. The CDI container will inject a contextual instance of type WalletService into the variable walletService. But how will the CDI container be able to know the type to resolve a variable to for any given injection point? Obviously, we will need a way to tell the runtime the types of our CDI beans so it can correctly resolve each injectable field to its type.

Technically, a CDI bean is any Java class that implements the jakarta.enterprise.inject.spi.Bean<T>[6] interface. This interface represents a bean and defines everything the CDI container needs to manage instances of the bean. The Bean interface itself extends the jakarta.enterprise.inject.spi.BeanAttributes<T>[7] interface. This interface contains the following methods:

- getName() - Get the EL name of a bean if @Named annotation has been used on the bean
- getQualifiers() - Get the set of qualifiers of the bean
- getTypes() - Get a set of bean types of the bean
- getScope() - Get the scope of the bean
- getStereotypes() - Get the set of stereotypes of the bean
- isAlternative() - Boolean method that determines if the bean is an alternative or not

These methods return relevant information that helps the CDI container resolve injection points to the right bean types. In addition, the Bean interface also contains the create() and destroy() methods which are called by the container to respectively create and destroy instances of a bean. In practice, you will not need to explicitly implement the Bean interface. CDI implementations can generate Bean<T> interface implementations from your beans on your behalf. Through implementation of the Bean<T> interface for your beans, the CDI container can resolve a bean type through its type, a combination of type and qualifiers, and by name (in expression language).

Resolution by Type

The type of any CDI bean is all superclasses of that bean up to java.lang.Object, all implemented interfaces, either directly or indirectly, and the class itself. Our WalletService bean, as an example, will have its types be java.lang.Object and WalletService because it doesn't have any superclasses other than Object nor implements any interfaces. The WalletResourceImpl however (Listing 4-4) has three types: it is an Object, a WalletResource, and WalletResourceImpl.

[6] Bean (Jakarta Context Dependency Injection API)

[7] BeanAttributes (Jakarta Context Dependency Injection API)

Resolution by Name and Qualifier

Qualifiers in CDI are a way to label or qualify CDI components to further identify them to the CDI container. The WalletResourceImpl.java class as shown in Listing 4-4 implements the WalletResource interface. This means that we can have an injection point of type WalletResource as shown in Listing 4-5.

Listing 4-5. showing injecting into a field by interface type

```
public class HelloResourceImpl implements HelloResource {

@Inject
WalletResource walletResource;
}
```

Listing 4-5 shows HelloResourceImpl declaring a dependency on WalletResource in the variable walletResource. WalletResource is an interface that is implemented by WalletResourceImpl. As interfaces can be implemented by more than one class, the injection point walletResource as declared in Listing 4-5 would need to be qualified, because the CDI container will not know at runtime which WalletResource implementation to inject into any given injection point of type WalletResource. We will come back to this when we talk about CDI Qualifiers in a bit.

Resolution by Name

The two previous bean resolution mechanisms, namely, resolution by type and by type and qualifier, are typesafe. The third way of resolving beans is by name. You can access instances of a given bean in string-based environments like the Jakarta EE platform's Expression Language.[8] A bean can be resolved when accessed in EL by annotating it with the built-in qualifier @Named. Listing 4-6 shows the WalletService annotated with @Named.

[8] Jakarta Expression Language 4.0 | The Eclipse Foundation

Listing 4-6. showing the use of @Named to resolve the bean in EL

```
@Named
@RequestScoped
@Transactional
public class WalletService {
}
```

Listing 4-6 shows the WalletService annotated with the @Named qualifier. With that qualifier in place, the WalletService can be accessed through an EL expression. By default, the WalletService can be accessed through the automatically available variable walletService in an EL expression like this: #{walletService.someMethod()}. When accessed this way, the CDI container will take care of creating an instance and injecting it into the variable.

No matter what mechanism is used to resolve a bean instance, the CDI container will always create the right instance for the given field type. The technical term for the instances of beans created by the CDI container for satisfying injection points is contextual instances, which brings us to the question: What is a contextual instance?

CDI Beans and Contextual Instances

In the previous section, we saw that a bean is a Java class that optionally has CDI metadata associated with it and can be used to satisfy injection points. A bean, then, is a source of instances used to satisfy dependency requests in your application. The instances of your bean created by the CDI container to satisfy injection points are technically called contextual instances.

The Bean<T> interface that we saw in the previous section also extends the Contextual<T> interface. The Contextual<T>[9] interface is where the Bean<T> interface inherits the create and destroy methods from. Instances created from any bean implementing the Bean<T> interface are called contextual types. Since CDI runtimes generally create implementations of the Bean<T> interface on your behalf, you end up with contextual instances injected into your injection points.

---

[9] Contextual (Jakarta Context Dependency Injection API)

When you make a request for bean instances from the CDI container via the use of the @Inject annotation on an injection point, the container must ensure that the contextual instance returned to you is associated with the right scope. Bean instances are always associated with a scope. You can explicitly define which scope a bean should be associated with. If you do not explicitly define one for a given bean, the container will associate contextual instances of that bean with a default scope.

Scopes and Contexts

CDI created instances of your beans are associated with scopes. You can think of a CDI scope as a well-defined lifetime within which a bean instance can exist. When a given scope is destroyed, so are all the bean instances associated with that scope. Different beans with different scopes can be injected into each other. The CDI container takes care of ensuring the right bean is injected into each dependent injection point.

As an example, we have a SecurityManager that we want to have only a single instance for the entire lifetime of the application – from boot to shutdown. This SecurityManager controller has a dependency on another controller, UserService, that is scoped to each HTTP request. Listing 4-7 shows the UserService controller.

Listing 4-7. showing the UserService controller

```
@RequestScoped
@Transactional
public class UserService {

    @Inject
    UserRepository userRepository;
}
```

Listing 4-7 shows the UserService class. It is annotated with @RequestScoped. This is one of the built-in scopes (more about the various scopes in a bit). This bean declares a dependency on the UserRepository, which is also another RequestScoped bean. Listing 4-8 shows the SecurityManager controller.

Listing 4-8. showing the SecurityManager controller

```
@ApplicationScoped
public class SecurityManager {

  @Inject
  UserService userService;

}
```

Listing 4-8 shows the SecurityManager controller and its dependency declaration on the UserService controller. Note that the SecurityManager is annotated with @ApplicationScoped. This is also one of the built-in scopes. Even though the UserService and SecurityManager are associated with different scopes, the CDI container will ensure that all clients of the SecurityManager see different instances of the userService context object. It achieves this through the use of the concept bean proxying.

Bean Proxying

The userService reference in the SecurityManager controller as shown in Listing 4-8 is not a direct reference to the contextual instance returned by the call to the Contextual#create(), but a client proxy object. This client proxy object implements some or all bean types of the bean and delegates method invocations on it to the target contextual object. Why this seeming indirection?

Back to our SecurityManager controller, this class will have a single instance through the entire life of the application. However, it declares a dependency on a bean that is scoped to each HTTP request. What this means is that each client of the SecurityManager should have a different instance of the UserService bean injected. This situation requires the container to create an indirect reference to the UserService contextual instance. The container needs to guarantee that when any valid injected reference to a bean belonging to any given scope is invoked, the invocation is always processed by the current instance of the injected bean.

The container needs to manage possible circular dependencies as well. The cleanest and most transparent way to be able to achieve all of that is through the use of the client proxy object. This way, you are guaranteed the right contextual instance in the right scope no matter the dependency relationship between your beans.

Built-In Scopes

CDI comes with a number of built-in scopes that cater to the common needs of most applications. You can create your own scope if you want. But in order to create a cohesive platform and provide a uniform base for other APIs to build on, the CDI spec comes with a total of five built-in scopes. They are @ApplicationScoped, @RequestScoped, @SessionScoped, @ConversationScoped, and the @Dependent pseudo-scope.

@ApplicationScoped

The @ApplicationScoped annotation on a bean makes the bean an application-scoped singleton. What this means is that for the entire lifetime of any given application running instance, only a single contextual instance of this @ApplicationScoped bean will be created. The SecurityManager controller shown in Listing 4-8 is an application-scoped bean. The application scope itself is created at container boot time. However, the first and only contextual instance of this bean will be created when a method is first invoked on a proxy. After creation, no matter how many SecurityManager bean proxies the container creates, all method invocations will be delegated to the same bean instance across the application.

It does not matter what other scope the SecurityManager gets injected into. All method invocations will eventually be serviced by the same bean instance. That instance will be destroyed by the container when the application scope is destroyed during application shutdown.

@RequestScoped

The @RequestScoped annotation on a bean associates the bean with an external user request originating from a servlet request, a web service request, and a remote EJB request. The container will also create a request scope during a CDI event (we will talk about CDI events in a later section) dispatch to an async observer method.

For a servlet request, the CDI container will create a request scope when service() or doFilter() methods are invoked on a servlet or servlet filter, respectively. For a web service, the container will create a request scope for each web service invocation, whether through JAX-RS or JAX-WS. A request is also created for each remote EJB invocation during the handling of the invocation by the EJB. A request scope will also be created when the CDI container dispatches an event to an async method observer of that particular event. For all these invocations, the request scope will be created and destroyed once the invocation ends.

The UserService controller shown in Listing 4-7 is scoped to the request context through the @RequestScoped annotation. For each web service call on the UserResourceImpl resource, a new request scope will be created and a new contextual instance of the UserService will be created and associated with that scope, because the UserResourceImpl declares a dependency on the UserService controller as shown in Listing 4-9.

Listing 4-9. showing the UserResourceImpl and its dependent declaration on the UserService controller

```
@Consumes(MediaType.APPLICATION_JSON)
@Produces(MediaType.APPLICATION_JSON)
@Path("users")
public class UserResourceImpl implements UserResource {

    @Inject
    UserService userService;
}
```

Listing 4-9 shows the @RequestScoped UserService controller injected into the UserResourceImpl REST web service class. For each REST method invoked on the UserServiceResourceImpl class, a new request scope will be created and both the UserServiceResourceImpl and the UserService contextual instances associated with that scope. After the method invocation returns, both the scope and associated contextual instances will be destroyed.

@SessionScoped

The session-scoped context can be associated with a bean through the @SessionScoped annotation. This scope is tied to a single user session and is shared between all servlet requests that occur in the same HTTP request. The session scope is active during the service method of any servlet, during the doFilter() method of any servlet filter, and when the container calls any ServletRequestListener, AsyncListener, or HttpSessionListener. This scope is destroyed when the session times out. But before the session gets destroyed, the container will make sure there are no uncalled HttpSessionListeners for that session. This ensures that the session is not destroyed while there are still listeners attached to it. Listing 4-10 shows the use of the @SessionScoped annotation on the UserSession controller in jwallet.

Listing 4-10. showing the use of the @SessionScoped

```
@SessionScoped
public class UserSession implements Serializable {

    @Inject
    SecurityManager securityManager;

}
```

Listing 4-10 shows the UserSession controller. It declares a dependency on the SecurityManager. Remember from Listing 4-8 that the SecurityManager is an @ApplicationScoped bean. The UserSession is the first bean we are seeing that implements the Serializable interface. Why? Because the @SessionScoped annotation on a bean makes the bean passivation capable. What this means is that during runtime, when the CDI container determines that there are idle instances of session-scoped beans, it can temporarily transfer the state of such bean instances to secondary storage. Effectively, the container will passivate or save the state of the idle instances. The Serializable interface marks the bean as such. In addition, all fields in a session-scoped bean should be equally serializable or transient.

@ConversationScoped

The conversation scope is a special scope for holding a "conversation" between a client and the server. It is longer than a request scope but shorter than a session or application scope. You can think of a conversation with the example of a sign-up form that spans multiple pages. Each page is a conversation between your browser and the server, and once you reach the final page and hit the submit button, the conversation terminates. CDI provides the built-in Conversation[10] bean for managing the conversation state in a conversation-scoped bean. Listing 4-11 shows a conversation-scoped SignupManager.

[10] Uses of Interface jakarta.enterprise.context.Conversation

Listing 4-11. showing the SignupManager as a conversation-scoped bean

```
@ConversationScoped
public class SignupManager implements Serializable {

    @Inject
    Conversation conversation;

    public void beginSignup() {
        beginConversation();
    }

    public void submit() {
        endConversation();
    }

    private void beginConversation() {
        if (conversation.isTransient()) {
            conversation.begin();
        }
    }

    private void endConversation() {
        if (!conversation.isTransient()) {
            conversation.end();
        }
    }
}
```

Listing 4-11 shows our Signup bean. It also implements the Serializable interface because it might get passivated by the container, just like a session-scoped bean. Similarly, all fields in a conversation-scoped bean should be passivation capable or transient. By default, a @ConversationScoped bean is in transient mode. That is, a contextual instance of a conversation-scoped bean is likely to be destroyed by the container at any time because it's transient. You will have to explicitly initiate a conversation-scoped bean into a conversation. The way to achieve that is through the use of methods on the Conversation interface.

Listing 4-11 shows the SignupManager declaring a dependency on the Conversation bean through an injection point of said type. An instance of the Conversation interface will be created by the container for us. Method beginSignup() first makes a call to method beginConversation(). The beginConversation() method first makes a check by calling Conversation#isTransient() to check if the bean is in transient mode.

This method returns true if the bean is currently not in any conversation state or, technically, a long-running conversation. Why this check? Because if we call the Conversation#begin() method on a bean that is already in a long-running conversation, an IllegalStateException will be thrown by the container. Method beginConversation() only starts the long-running conversation if that check returns true by calling the Conversation#begin() method. After this invocation, the bean is put into a long-running conversation or the conversation scope. This scope will transcend a single request, but will be shorter than a session scope.

After the registration is done and ready to be submitted, method submit() first calls method endConversation(). This method does an inverse check on the bean to see if it's in a long-running conversation, then calls the Conversation#end() method. This is also because if you invoke Conversation#end() on a Conversation that is not long-running, the container throws an IllegalStateException.

The Conversation#begin method also optionally takes a String parameter as the conversation ID. This ID will be associated with the conversation that is started by the method. In the absence of an explicit ID, the container generates one for you. You can get the ID associated with the current long-running conversation by calling the Conversation#getId() method. It returns the ID or null if the conversation is transient. You can also set and get the timeout of the conversation in milliseconds through the methods Conversation#setTimeout() and Conversation#getTimeout(), respectively.

@Dependent Pseudo-Scope

@Dependent is a pseudo-scope that is dependent upon where it is used. It is the default scope that a bean is put into when no explicit scope is defined. It is dependent because the @Dependent scoped bean takes or inherits the scope of the bean into which it is injected. A dependent-scoped bean has two distinguishing qualities, namely:

- No injected instance of the bean is ever shared between multiple injection points.
- Any instance of the bean injected into an object that is being created by the container is bound to the lifecycle of the created object.

Effectively, every request for a dependent-scoped bean always results in a new bean. And the actual scope of this dependent bean instance will be the scope of whatever bean it's being injected into. We will touch a little more on dependent scope in later sections of this book when we cover other CDI constructs.

So far, we have talked about beans and their possible scopes. At the heart of CDI is managing dependencies between these beans in their different scopes. The "entry point" to using the dependency management magic wand in CDI is through the use of the @Inject annotation at injection points.

Injection Points

An injection point in CDI is a place where you can request for contextual instances. That is, you annotate a type at a specific place with the @Inject annotation, and then the CDI container will instantiate that particular variable for you. There are three broad injection points in CDI as follows.

Field Injection Point

Field injection point is what we have seen so far. It is simply annotating a field of a given bean type in a class with @Inject. In Listing 4-11, the field conversation of type Conversation is annotated with @Inject. As we have discussed already, the container will take care of providing the right contextual instance of the annotated field type into the variable conversation. The container effectively guarantees that we will not have a NullPointerException when we invoke methods on the conversation variable at runtime. Field injection is arguably the most popular and our preferred way of using CDI for requesting contextual instances.

Constructor Injection

The second injection point available to you in CDI is the constructor injection point. Remember when we defined a CDI bean as any Java class with a no-arg constructor or a bean with at least one CDI injectable constructor? Constructor injection is when you annotate a constructor of a bean with @Inject, passing in beans that CDI can instantiate as arguments. Listing 4-12 shows the SignupManager conversation-scoped bean refactored to use a constructor injection to instantiate the conversation field.

Listing 4-12. showing the SignupManager using a constructor injection point

```
@ConversationScoped
public class SignupManager implements Serializable {

    Conversation conversation;
    @Inject
    public SignupManager(final Conversation conversation) {
        this.conversation = conversation;
    }
}
```

Listing 4-12 shows the SignupManager bean using a constructor injection to instantiate the conversation field. This constructor injection will be called automatically by the container. Even though our SignupManager doesn't have a no-arg constructor, it's still a perfectly valid CDI bean because of our constructor injection.

It is important to note that when using constructor injection, all the arguments passed to the constructor must be CDI beans or at least beans that the container knows how to instantiate (through, e.g., producer methods, which we will look at in a section later). The application will fail CDI boot validation if any of the constructor parameters is not a valid CDI bean. Also, each bean is allowed only one constructor injection. You can still have a no-arg constructor and other constructors. But having more than one constructor injection will result in errors at application boot time.

One good use of the constructor injection is for testing. When you need to create unit tests for your controllers (for instance, using Mockito[11]), you can use constructor injection to initialize your bean fields at runtime. And in your tests, you can still manually call the same constructor, manually passing in the various parameters as you would any POJO constructor.

[11] Mockito

Method Injection

A method injection point is when a method is annotated with @Inject. Similar to constructor injection, all the parameters of the method must be CDI beans, or at least the container must know how to initialize them. Method injections are called initializer methods. The container will automatically call these methods, similar to constructor injections.

These are the three main injection points in CDI. In addition to these, however, there are two other points where the parameters passed are CDI instantiated without the need for an explicit @Inject annotation. These are producer and observer methods. We cover both constructs in later sections.

Jakarta Enterprise Beans

The Jakarta Enterprise Bean, previously Enterprise JavaBeans or EJB, is a specification that precedes the CDI specification. It is a component-oriented specification for creating beans that implement business logic. It had its own dependency resolution mechanism. Annotating a Java class with any of @Stateless, @Stateful, and @Singleton made that class a component that was transactional, pooled, and secured by default.

The advent of CDI and the need to have a core inversion of control implementation on the Jakarta EE platform meant CDI had to reimplement a number of the features in EJB. However, these two specifications have been harmonized such that CDI is the single core entry point for creating business layer components. Even though CDI is the preferred way to create business services, Jakarta Enterprise Beans still remains widely in use and will be for the foreseeable future.

All Jakarta Enterprise Beans are automatically CDI beans. Annotating a bean with a Jakarta Enterprise Bean defining annotation makes that bean both a CDI and Jakarta Enterprise Bean with the features of both specifications available to the bean. From the perspective of CDI, Jakarta Enterprise Beans are called session beans. Listing 4-13 shows our SecurityManager, now with two additional annotations.

Listing 4-13. showing the SecurityManager with EJB annotations

```
@ApplicationScoped
@Singleton
@Startup
```

```
public class SecurityManager {
    @Inject
    UserService userService;
    public void saveUser(final CreateUserRequest request) {
        userService.createUser(request);
    }

}
```

Listing 4-13 shows the SecurityManager bean annotated with two Jakarta Enterprise Beans annotations - @Singleton and @Startup. The @Singleton annotation makes this bean a singleton Jakarta Enterprise Bean. The @Singleton annotation is not much different from the @ApplicationScoped annotation in the sense that both result in having just a single instance of the bean throughout the life of the application runtime.

The @Startup annotation marks the SecurityManager for eager instantiation. What this implies is that an instance of our bean will be created as part of the application startup sequence. The @Singleton annotation also makes each method invoked on the SecurityManager contextual instance transactional by default. The container will join or create transactions if none exists for each method invocation.

You can use eagerly instantiated Jakarta Enterprise Beans singletons to do some form of ahead-of-time housekeeping before all other components of your application are ready. For instance, you need to have some form of data ready when the application starts, but you need to load this application from an external service. In such a case, you can eagerly instantiate a singleton and make that call.

As you can see, metadata from both API specifications are perfectly compatible with each other. In greenfield applications however, you will most likely use CDI almost exclusively. But there is still a significant body of code out there that still uses Jakarta Enterprise Beans metadata. Maintaining or migrating such code to CDI should be quite straightforward since both specs play nicely with each other. We will get back to Jakarta Enterprise Beans in the chapter on Jakarta Persistence when we talk extensively about transactions and transactional boundaries. For now, let's continue our CDI discussion by taking a look at qualifiers.

Qualifiers

Qualifiers are a way to give the CDI container hints on the exact bean type to use to satisfy a given dependency injection point. In Listing 4-5, we injected the WalletResource into the HelloResourceImpl. Listing 4-14 shows the WalletResource interface.

Listing 4-14. showing the WalletResource interface

```
@RegisterRestClient(baseUri = BASE_URI)
@Consumes(MediaType.APPLICATION_JSON)
@Produces(MediaType.APPLICATION_JSON)
@Path("wallets")
public interface WalletResource {

 String BASE_URI = "http://wallet:3001/wallet/api";

}
```

Listing 4-14 shows the WalletResource interface. It is a REST endpoint declaration that uses the @RegisterRestClient() from the Eclipse MicroProfile REST Client API (there's a full chapter on this later in the book) to automatically create a REST client for this Jakarta REST resource.

As shown in Listing 4-5, we injected this bean by its interface into HelloResourceImpl. Trying to start the application will fail with the error "Ambiguous dependencies for type WalletResource with qualifiers @Default." This is because the WalletResource interface has two implementations in the application. One is the WalletResourceImpl that is part of our application code. The other is the REST Client that is automatically generated by the Eclipse MicroProfile REST Client.

Because there is more than one possible implementation of the interface, the CDI container will need to know exactly which concrete implementation to use at runtime to satisfy the injection point declared in HelloResourceImpl. And since we didn't specify any qualifiers, the default qualifier @Default isn't enough to tell the container which implementation to use, so during application boot validation, the runtime throws an error and truncates application boot.

To fix this, let us declare a qualifier for our WalletResource interface. Listing 4-15 shows a qualifier declaration for the WalletResource.

Listing 4-15. showing @Wallet qualifier declaration

```
@Qualifier
@Retention(RUNTIME)
@Target({FIELD, TYPE, METHOD, PARAMETER})
public @interface Wallet {

}
```

Listing 4-15 shows the @Wallet qualifier declaration. A qualifier in CDI is a normal Java annotation with the annotation @Qualifier from the CDI API. The @Wallet qualifier sets the @Target values to field, type, method, and parameter. This means it can be used on a field, class, method, or parameter. With the annotation declared, we now need to associate the qualifier with a concrete type. In this example, we want to associate the @Wallet qualifier with our WalletResource implementation. Listing 4-16 shows the use of the @Wallet qualifier on the WalletResourceImpl.

Listing 4-16. showing the use of @Wallet on the WalletResourceImpl

```
@Consumes(MediaType.APPLICATION_JSON)
@Produces(MediaType.APPLICATION_JSON)
@Path("wallets")
@Wallet
public class WalletResourceImpl implements WalletResource {

@Inject
WalletService walletService;

}
```

Listing 4-16 shows the @Wallet qualifier associated with the WalletResourceImpl. With this in place, we now have a mechanism to tell the CDI container the exact implementation of WalletResource to inject into an injection point that is declared by the WalletResource interface type. Listing 4-17 shows the WalletResource injection point in the HelloResourceImpl qualified with the @Wallet qualifier.

Listing 4-17. showing the @Wallet qualifier used to qualify the walletResource field in HelloResourceImpl

```
@Path("he
llo")
public class HelloResourceImpl implements HelloResource {

 @Inject
 @Wallet
  WalletResource walletResource;

}
```

Listing 4-17 shows us qualifying the walletResource field with the @Wallet qualifier. With these in place, we are telling the container to inject a contextual instance of the concrete type WalletResourceImpl into field walletResource in HelloResourceImpl. After this construct, the application should boot up, and no validation errors should be thrown.

@Default Qualifier

Earlier in this section, we saw the error message thrown by the container when there was an ambiguous dependency resolution with the walletResource field. The message read "Ambiguous dependencies for type WalletResource with qualifiers @Default." The @Default qualifier mentioned in that message is a built-in qualifier that every bean has in the absence of any explicit qualifier. It is implicitly annotated on each bean type by the runtime as long as that bean does not have any qualifier declared or associated with it. @Default is effectively the default qualifier.

Other Built-In Qualifiers

The Jakarta EE platform, along with the Eclipse MicroProfile project, comes with a number of built-in qualifiers. In the section "Resolution by Name", we saw the @Named qualifier. This qualifier takes an optional String value that becomes the name of the bean in an ExpressionLanguage. The @Named is a built-in qualifier.

Another built-in qualifier is the @RestClient qualifier. In Listing 4-14, we saw the WalletResource declaration as having the annotation @RegisterRestClient(baseUri

= BASE_URI). This annotation tells the Eclipse MicroProfile REST client to create an implementation of this bean for us at runtime. How do you get a hold of this created bean? Listing 4-18 shows the HelloResourceImpl again, but this time, with an additional injection of the same WalletResource type, but with a different qualifier.

Listing 4-18. showing the use of a built-in qualifier from the Eclipse MicroProfile project to qualify the WalletResource

```
@Path("hello")
public class HelloResourceImpl implements HelloResource {

    @Inject
    @Wallet
    WalletResource walletResource;

    @Inject
    @RestClient
    WalletResource restClient;
}
```

Listing 4-18 shows an additional field declaration of the same WalletResource type qualified with the @RestClient qualifier from the Eclipse MicroProfile project. The restClient variable will have a MicroProfile-generated implementation of the WalletResource injected into it at runtime. The @RestClient annotation will give us a contextual instance that implements all the methods of the interface and is ready to use. Of note is that both the walletResource and restClient fields are of the same type – WalletResource. Both fields have been defined by their interface. In the absence of qualifiers, the container would not know how to handle such ambiguous dependency declarations.

The qualifier construct in CDI is a deceptively simple yet powerful mechanism that helps you write very clean, readable, and testable code with little effort. We will continue to discuss and use qualifiers through the rest of this chapter and book. Next up, let us take a look at the CDI concept of producers. All the beans we have seen so far are beans that we have declared from scratch in one way or another – either as interfaces or concrete Java classes. However, you will sometimes find yourself needing to transform beans that are not part of your code into CDI beans in your applications.

CDI Producers

Producers in CDI are a way to transform beans or Java types that are not part of application code into CDI beans to be used in the application. We defined a CDI bean as any Java class with a no-arg constructor or one that has at least one constructor annotated with @Inject. However, there will be some Java types that are needed in an application but aren't necessarily valid CDI beans. For example, Listing 4-19 shows a field injection point of type EntityManager in the BaseRepository bean.

Listing 4-19. showing an attempt to inject a platform class into BaseRepository, an application-defined bean

```
public abstract class BaseRepository<E, K> {

@Inject
EntityManager em;

}
```

Listing 4-19 shows a field injection point declaration of type EntityManager in the BaseRepository bean. An attempt to deploy the application will fail with the error message "Unsatisfied dependencies for type EntityManager with qualifiers @Default at injection point @Inject com.example.jwallet.core.control.BaseRepository.em". The CDI container is complaining that the field type has unsatisfied dependencies. What this means is that the CDI runtime doesn't know how to instantiate a contextual instance of the EntityManager class.

EntityManager is a Jakarta EE platform class. It's an interface that Jakarta Persistence runtimes provide implementations for. Using it as an injection point type as we have done won't work because CDI doesn't have a way to instantiate it. To get around this problem, we can use producers. With CDI producers, you tell the container where a given bean type is "produced" so any time there is a request for a contextual instance of that bean, the container will go to your producer for the instance. There are two kinds of CDI producers - producer fields and methods.

Producer Fields

Producer fields refer to "producing" CDI beans from the field of another bean. Listing 4-20 shows a producer field that "produces" EntityManager instances using the @Produces annotation from CDI.

Listing 4-20. showing the EntityManager producer field

```
public class ProducerFactory {

    @Produces
    @PersistenceContext
    EntityManager entityManager;
}
```

Listing 4-20 shows a producer field for the EntityManager type. The ProducerFactory bean has a field of type EntityManager annotated with @PersistenceContext and @Produces. @PersistenceContext is an annotation from the Jakarta Persistence API used to inject instances of EntityManager. However, since this annotation is not a CDI annotation, the returned instances aren't CDI beans.

Annotating the field yet again with @Produces makes the returned instance of the EntityManager from the @PersistenceContext annotation a CDI bean. Effectively, we are using the @Produces annotation to transform the Jakarta Persistence–created EntityManager instance into a CDI bean, complete with all CDI services. When the CDI container encounters the field injection point of type EntityManager found in the BaseRepository bean (Listing 4-19), it knows to come to this field for the contextual instance.

Producers are not limited to producing bland contextual instances. You can explicitly set a scope to be associated with the produced contextual instance. In the absence of any explicit scope, the default @Dependent scope applies. In the example in Listing 4-20, the produced EntityManager contextual instances will be in @Dependent scope. There is a caveat with setting an explicit scope for the producer field, however. If the producer field contains a null value when accessed at runtime and it has any other scope other than @Dependent, then the container throws an IllegalProductException. Producer fields can be static or nonstatic default-access, protected, public, or private fields of a CDI-managed bean class.

Qualifying Producer Fields

You can also qualify producer fields using qualifiers. Let's say jwallet uses two databases – Apache Derby and Postgres. You can have two producer fields, each qualified with a specific qualifier so you can inject and qualify injection points. In the section on qualifiers, we created the @Wallet qualifier as a simple no-arg annotation. Qualifiers, however, can take arguments. Instead of creating two qualifiers to qualify the EntityManagers produced for each database, we can create a single qualifier that takes an argument. In Listing 4-21, we create the @Database qualifier that takes an argument of type DB.

Listing 4-21. showing the @Database qualifier definition

```
@Qualifier
@Retention(RUNTIME)
@Target({FIELD, TYPE, METHOD, PARAMETER})
public @interface Database {

    DB value();

    enum DB {
        DERBY,
        POSTGRES
    }
}
```

Listing 4-21 shows the @Database qualifier with a value() field of type DB for passing parameters to the qualifier. DB is an enum defined in the qualifier class consisting of two fields – DERBY and POSTGRES. Listing 4-22 shows the use of the @Database qualifier to qualify two EntityManager producer fields.

Listing 4-22. showing the use of the @Database qualifier to qualifier producer fields

```
public class ProducerFactory {
    @Produces
    @Database(DB.DERBY)
    @PersistenceContext(unitName = "jwallet-derby")
```

```
    EntityManager derby;

    @Produces
    @Database(DB.POSTGRES)
    @PersistenceContext(unitName = "jwallet-postgres")
    EntityManager postgres;
}
```

Listing 4-22 shows the ProducerFactory bean with two producer fields, both of type EntityManager. However, both fields are qualified with the @Database qualifier. The derby field producer is qualified by the @Database(DERBY) qualifier, and the postgres field by @Database(POSTGRES).

These two EntityManager fields are linked to two different persistence contexts as shown by the values passed to the unitName parameter of the @PersistenceContext annotation (Jakarta Persistence is discussed in a separate chapter). We now have two fields of the same type producing the same type but differently qualified. Listing 4-23 shows the use of the derby EntityManager producer field in BaseRepository.

Listing 4-23. showing the use of the derby producer field

```
public abstract class BaseRepository<E, K> {

    @Inject
    @Database(DB.DERBY)
    EntityManager em;
}
```

Listing 4-23 shows an injection point of type EntityManager qualified with the @Database(DERBY) qualifier. At runtime, the container is going to use the contextual instance produced from the derby field in the ProducerFactory bean to populate the em field in the BaseRepository bean. By so doing, even though the EntityManager bean is not part of the application code, through the CDI producer field construct, we have still been able to transform it into a CDI bean.

Producer Methods

Producer methods are similar to producer fields in the sense that they both produce contextual instances. Producer methods, however, produce their contextual instances based on their return types. A method annotated @Produces will produce the return type of whatever it returns. A producer method can also take parameters. However, all parameters passed to a producer method are injection points and will be taken care of by the container, because producer methods are called automatically by the container. Listing 4-24 shows a producer method that produces java.util.logging.Logger objects.

Listing 4-24. showing producer method produce Logger objects

```
public class ProducerFactory {

    @Produces
    @Database(DB.DERBY)
    @PersistenceContext(unitName = "jwallet-derby")
    EntityManager derby;

    @Produces
    @Database(DB.POSTGRES)
    @PersistenceContext(unitName = "jwallet-postgres")
    EntityManager postgres;

    @Produces
    public Logger getLog(final InjectionPoint injectionPoint) {
    return      Logger.getLogger(injectionPoint.getMember().
    getDeclaringClass().getName());
    }
}
```

Listing 4-24 shows the ProducerFactory bean, this time with the producer method getLog(). This method returns a java.util.logging.Logger object. It also takes a parameter of type InjectionPoint. This parameter will be injected by the CDI container (an example of method injection). An InjectionPoint is a CDI component that contains metadata about an injection point. The getLog method implementation sets the name of the produced Logger to the class into which it's being injected by calling the InjectionPo int#getMember#getDeclaringClass#getName(). With the producer method in place, injecting a Logger instance is as simple as using @Inject on a field of type Logger as shown in Listing 4-25.

Listing 4-25. shows the injection of the Logger into the BaseRepository bean

```
public abstract class BaseRepository<E, K> {

    @Inject
    @Database(DERBY)
    EntityManager em;

    @Inject
    Logger logger;

}
```

Listing 4-25 shows the BaseRepository with an additional field injection of type Logger. At runtime, the CDI container will consult the getLog producer method for contextual instances to satisfy this injection point. Because we have not set an explicit scope on the producer method and fields in the ProducerFactory bean, the produced contextual instances for both the EntityManager and Logger will be assigned to the @Dependent pseudo-scope.

You generally will use producer methods to instantiate beans that require some form of custom initialization that you might not be able to do in the constructor of the bean. For instance, you might have to make an external call to a web service to initialize some bean. In such a case, you can use producer methods to transform the instance of the bean that you manually instantiate into a CDI-managed object. This is because beans that you manually instantiate are not managed by the CDI runtime. The access modifier of the producer method does not matter. It could also be static or nonstatic. Through the use of CDI producer construct, we have transformed another class that is not part of application code to a CDI bean.

CDI Producers – Caveats

There are a few things you need to be aware of when using CDI producers. The following will result in CDI definition errors at application boot time:

- You cannot annotate a producer method or field with @Inject.

- A producer method parameter cannot be annotated with @Disposes, @Observes, or @ObservesAsync.
- An interceptor may not define a producer method or field.

Stereotypes

Often in application development, especially using CDI, you will find yourself having different beans created for different purposes needing the same common set of metadata. For any nontrivial application, you could end up repeating the same set of metadata on beans a significant number of times. This could get quite tedious when you need to add functionality across all those beans.

For instance, Listings 4-26 and 4-27 show the WalletService and UserService beans with their CDI metadata.

Listing 4-26. showing the WalletService bean with its metadata

```
@RequestScoped
@Transactional
public class WalletService {

}
```

Listing 4-27. shows the UserService bean with its metadata.

```
@RequestScoped
@Transactional
public class UserService {

}
```

Listings 4-26 and 4-27 both show two different CDI beans having the exact same CDI metadata. Both are request scoped and transactional. Even though both beans will carry out different functionalities, they do require the exact same set of CDI services. If we want to associate an interceptor (more on interceptors in the next section) with both beans, we would have to repeat the interceptor annotation on both beans. Clearly, repeating the same metadata over and over isn't an ideal way to write code.

The CDI specification provides the stereotype construct for grouping together commonly occurring architectural patterns into a single, common annotation. So for the beans showing in Listings 4-26 and 4-27, instead of repeating the same CDI annotations, stereotypes allow us to centralize them under one common annotation. In Listing 4-28, we create an Action stereotype that is @RequestScoped and @Transactional.

Listing 4-28. showing the Action stereotype

```
@Stereotype
@RequestScoped
@Transactional
@Retention(RetentionPolicy.RUNTIME)
@Target(ElementType.TYPE)
public @interface Action {

}
```

Listing 4-28 shows the @Action stereotype declaration. A CDI stereotype is a Java annotation annotated with @Stereotype. For the @Action stereotype, we declare that it's @RequestScoped and @Transactional. The @Target of the stereotype is also set to TYPE because we want to only associate this stereotype with beans and not methods, fields, or parameters. All beans that are annotated with this stereotype will automatically be request scoped and transactional, just as if the beans have been explicitly annotated with those annotations. With the @Action stereotype declared, we can now refactor the UserService and WalletService beans to use it. Listing 4-29 shows the WalletService refactored to use the @Action stereotype.

Listing 4-29. showing the WalletService using the @Action stereotype

```
@Action
public class WalletService {

}
```

Listing 4-30. showing the UserService using the @Action stereotype

```
@Action
public class UserService {

}
```

Listings 4-29 and 4-30 show the two CDI beans refactored to use the @Action stereotype. What this implies is that both beans are still request scoped and transactional. However, that boilerplate declarative metadata has been abstracted into a stereotype. If we need to associate all our controller beans with an interceptor, we will only have to associate the interceptor with the stereotype and our beans will automatically be intercepted.

A bean can override the scope associated with a stereotype by declaring its own scope. A bean declared scope overrides the scope associated with its stereotype. For instance, if the WalletService explicitly declares another scope in addition to the stereotype, then the scope declared by the WalletService takes precedence over the scope declared by the stereotype. You cannot associate qualifiers with a stereotype apart from the built-in @Named qualifier. Associating a stereotype with a qualifier other than @Named results in a CDI definition error. You can also associate stereotypes with other stereotypes. In doing so, the second stereotype inherits all the metadata of the first stereotype.

Lifecycle Callbacks

Contextual instances of CDI beans are fully managed by the container – from creation to destruction. However, there are times when you would want to carry out some prep work right after a bean is instantiated, or just before it is destroyed. In both cases, there are lifecycle callbacks you hook into for accomplishing such tasks. These lifecycle callbacks are automatically called by the container on your behalf at the appropriate time.

@PostConstruct

To perform some custom prep work immediately after a bean is instantiated, you can annotate a method with @PostConstruct. The method must return void and not take any parameters (except for interceptors). It can be a public, private, or package private method. It must not be static. The annotated method will be called by the container immediately after the bean is instantiated and all dependencies of the bean have been duly instantiated. Listing 4-31 shows a postconstruct lifecycle callback method in the SecurityManager.

Listing 4-31. showing the @PostConstruct method in SecurityManager

```
@ApplicationScoped
@Singleton
@Startup
public class SecurityManager {

    @Inject
    UserService userService;
    @Inject
    UserSession userSession;

    @PostConstruct
    private void init() {
        //Do prep work.
    }
}
```

Listing 4-31 shows the SecurityManager with a lifecycle callback method annotated @PostConstruct. This method will be called by the container before the contextual instance of the bean is put into service but after the bean dependencies have been initialized. In this example, the method will be called only after userService and userSession beans have been fully initialized by the container. Because this bean is application scoped, the init lifecycle callback method will only be called once – first time the bean is created and just before it's put into service. Or more technically, before the first proxy method is delegated to the (only) instance of the SecurityManager.

@PreDestroy

@PreDestroy is the opposite of @PostConstruct. A method annotated with @PreDestroy will be called by the container when the instance of the bean in which the method is declared is about to be destroyed by the container. @PreDestroy is typically used to release resources like files that the bean instance might be holding on to. The restrictions of @PostConstruct callback methods equally apply to @PreDestroy callback methods.

CDI Interceptors

Often in application development, you find that there are certain orthogonal services that some beans require that are not core to their functionality. For instance, an application could require some form of custom logging for calls to certain methods. Logging is a cross-cutting concern in the sense that more than one bean might require it.

Adding copious log messages to methods in our beans could get very unpleasant and repetitive quite fast, because almost all the logging will have the same format and message, without perhaps just a change in the method name. It would be much more elegant if we could abstract such cross-cutting concerns into some other construct – something that allows adding functionality to beans without modifying bean code.

Aspect-oriented programming (AOP)[12] is a paradigm that seeks to solve the issue of abstracting cross-cutting functionalities into a simple and customizable construct (or aspects) that can be turned on or off as and when needed. The CDI specification provides you with the concept of interceptors to implement AOP in your applications. CDI extends the Jakarta Interceptors specification.

You have already seen your first interceptor when we looked at stereotypes. The @Action stereotype, shown in Listing 4-28, has the @Transactional annotation. @Transactional is a built-in interceptor provided by the JTA[13] specification for intercepting calls to annotated beans or methods and controlling transactions for such methods.

There are two parts to implementing CDI interceptors. The first is an interceptor binding annotation. This annotation is what clients of the interceptor will use. For instance, the @Transactional annotation is one part of the transactional interceptor. The other part is linking that annotation to a bean that implements the interceptor method.

The Interceptor Annotation

For jwallet, we have a requirement to log the name of the currently logged in user, date, and time when certain methods are invoked. The interceptor binding annotation is what you will need to annotate selected methods that should be logged. The interceptor binding class is what implements the actual process of logging the stipulated information. For our logging interceptor requirement, Listing 4-32 shows the interceptor binding annotation.

[12] Chapter 1. What Is Aspect-Oriented Programming?

[13] Java Transaction API (JTA)

Listing 4-32. showing the logging interceptor binding annotation

```
@Inherited
@Target({TYPE, METHOD})
@Retention(RUNTIME)
@InterceptorBinding
public @interface Logged {

}
```

Listing 4-32 shows the @Logged interceptor binding annotation. This is a plain Java annotation with the @InterceptorBinding annotation from the Jakarta Interceptors specification. With the annotation in place, we now need to associate it with a bean that will do the actual work of the annotation. Listing 4-33 shows the interceptor binding bean LoggingBean implement the interceptor.

The Interceptor Bean

Listing 4-33. showing the LoggingBean interceptor class

```
@Interceptor
@Logged
@Priority(Interceptor.Priority.APPLICATION)
public class LoggingBean {

    @Inject
    Logger logger;

    @AroundInvoke
    //@AroundConstruct
    public Object logMethod(final InvocationContext invocationContext)
    throws Exception {
        logger.log(Level.FINE,
        () -> String.format("Method %s invoked at %s",   invocationContext.
        getMethod().getName(),
                LocalDateTime.now(ZoneOffset.UTC)));
```

```
        return invocationContext.proceed();
    }
}
```

Listing 4-33 shows the LoggingBean interceptor class. It is annotated @Interceptor and @Logged. These two annotations make this class an interceptor bean and link the @Logged annotation with it, respectively. This means whenever the @Logged annotation is used anywhere, the actual work to be done during interception will be done by a method in the LoggingBean class. It is also annotated with @Priority(Interceptor.Priority.APPLICATION). This is how interceptors are activated and ordered in Jakarta EE. The @Priority takes an int value; the lower the int value, the higher priority the annotation has.

The Interceptor.Priority.APPLICATION is a constant for the int value of 2000. If another interceptor sets its @Priority value to a lower int, that interceptor will take precedence in terms of invocation sequence over the @Logged interceptor. In the past, interceptors needed to be registered in an XML config file. But that changed in Java EE 7. Now you use the @Priority annotation to activate and order interceptors.

The LoggingBean then injects the Logger class being produced from our producer method and declares a method, logMethod, that takes a single parameter – InvocationContext. This parameter will be injected by the CDI container when it invokes the method to carry out an interception. At runtime, the container will provide an implementation of the InvocationContext interface to the method. The interface provides contextual information about the intercepted invocation and also has methods to control the behavior of the invocation chain. For the log, the InvocationContext#getM ethod#getName method is called to get the name of the method being intercepted.

The logMethod is annotated with @AroundInvoke. This annotation tells the container at what point we would want our interceptor to be put into action. @AroundInvoke, as the name implies, means that the interceptor should be dispatched just before an annotated method is invoked. So just before any method annotated with @Logged is invoked by the container, the logMethod will be automatically invoked to carry out the function of the interception. The method can invoke any service that the target method it is interposing on can invoke.

Another annotation that can be used to intercept beans is @AroundConstruct. This annotation will cause the container to invoke the annotated method just before the construct of a target bean is invoked. Generally, you would want to be careful with

@AroundConstruct because the InvocationContext bean passed to the interceptor method has access to all the parameters of the constructor. So you should exercise caution when using it.

A method annotated @AroundInvoke must return an Object. As shown in Listing 4-33, method logMethod returns Object from calling the InvocationContext#proceed() method. This call signals to the container that this method is done and execution should proceed to the next interceptor in the chain, if any or else proceed to call the actual method. An @AroundConstruct annotated method returning an Object will cause execution to move to the next interceptor in the chain or else proceed to instantiate the interposed bean.

With our interceptor fully declared, we can use it by annotating classes or methods with it. Listing 4-34 shows the @Logged interceptor applied to the WalletService.

Listing 4-34. showing the @Logged annotation applied to WalletService

```
@Action
@Logged
public class WalletService {

}
```

Listing 4-34 shows @Logged interceptor applied to WalletService. Similarly, Listing 4-35 shows the @Logged annotation applied to the UserService.

Listing 4-35. showing the @Logged interceptor applied to the UserService

```
@Action
@Logged
public class UserService {

}
```

Listing 4-35 shows the @Logged interceptor applied to the UserService. Because the interceptor is applied to the beans at the class level, all methods invoked on either class contextual instance will be intercepted by our interceptor. We could also have selectively annotated only certain methods in the beans since the @Target of the @Logged interceptor is both TYPE and METHOD.

Using Stereotypes with Interceptors

You will immediately notice that both intercepted beans have the exact same set of annotations: one a stereotype and the other an interceptor. In the section on stereotypes, we discussed the whole point of them is to abstract away common architectural patterns. Therefore, instead of separately annotating each bean with @Logged, we can add the interceptor to the @Action stereotype. This way, the interceptor automatically gets applied to all beans that are annotated with the stereotype. The interceptor can still be used separately to interceptor methods or the whole class. Listing 4-36 shows the @Logged interceptor annotation added to the @Action stereotype.

Listing 4-36. showing the @Action annotation being associated with @Logged

```
@Stereotype
@RequestScoped
@Transactional
@Logged
@Retention(RetentionPolicy.RUNTIME)
@Target(ElementType.TYPE)
public @interface Action {

}
```

Listing 4-36 shows the @Action stereotype annotated with the @Logged interceptor. This now associates the interceptor with the stereotype such that any bean that is annotated with the stereotype is also automatically intercepted. Consequently, we can remove the @Logged annotation from WalletService and UserService beans. Interceptors are a straightforward way of implementing cross-cutting concerns in an application. However, to extend or to override a bean method, CDI has another construct that can be used for that.

CDI Decorators

CDI decorators allow the wrapping of a bean inside another bean such that the wrapping bean can alter the behavior of the enclosed bean. Unlike interceptors that allow you to implement cross-cutting concerns common to a given set of beans, decorators allow the altering of the implementation of a given bean method. Thus, whereas interceptors are common to more than a single bean, decorators are tied to individual beans because they implement business methods relating to the beans they decorate. You can use decorators to change the functionality of beans you do not own, for example. CDI decorators allow you to implement the decorator design pattern in your application.

To understand them better, let us take a look at an example. The GDPR[14] legislation of the EU requires all applications used by EU residents to have their data stored on servers in the Union. To comply with this requirement, we can decorate the UserService bean so as to implement this custom requirement. First, let us refactor the UserService by introducing an interface as shown in Listing 4-37.

Listing 4-37. shows the UserFacade interface

```
public interface UserFacade {
    UserResponse createUser(final CreateUserRequest createUserRequest);

    UserResponse getUser(final Long id);

}
```

Listing 4-37 shows the UserFacade interface with two methods – createUser and getUser. This interface is a business interface that the UserService implements as shown in Listing 4-38.

Listing 4-38. shows the UserService implementing the UserFacade interface

```
@Action
public class UserService implements UserFacade {

      @Inject
      UserRepository userRepository;

      @Override
      public UserResponse createUser(final CreateUserRequest
      createUserRequest) {
            User user = fromUserWrapper(createUserRequest);

            user = userRepository.save(user);
```

[14] GDPR

```
        UserResponse userResponse = getUser(user.getId());
        return userResponse;
    }
    @Override
    public UserResponse getUser(final Long userId) {
        final User user = userRepository.findById(userId);
        return toUserResponse(user);
    }
}
```

Listing 4-38 shows the UserService implementing the UserFacade interface. Up to this point, there is nothing special about the UserService. Now to add extra functionality to the UserService bean by overriding the createUser method, Listing 4-39 shows the UserServiceDecorator for the UserService class.

Listing 4-39. shows the UserServiceDecorator that "decorates" the UserService and overrides the createUser method

```
@Decorator
@Priority(Interceptor.Priority.APPLICATION)
public abstract class UserServiceDecorator implements UserFacade {
    @Inject
    @Database(DB.MS_SQL)
    private EntityManager entityManager;

    @Inject
    @Delegate
    private UserService userService;

    @Override
    public UserResponse createUser(final CreateUserRequest
    createUserRequest) {
        final User user = UserService.fromUserWrapper(createUser
        Request);
        if (createUserRequest.getUserRegion() == UserRegion.EU) {
            entityManager.persist(user);
```

```
                final UserResponse userResponse = getUser(user.getId());
                userResponseEvent.fire(userResponse);
                //userResponseEvent.fireAsync(userResponse);
                return UserService.toUserResponse(user);
            }

            return userService.createUser(createUserRequest);
        }

}
```

Listing 4-39 shows the UserServiceDecorator. It is annotated with @Decorator. This annotation specifies that this class is a decorator. It is also annotated with @Priority. Similar to the discussion on interceptors, @Priority is the new way to activate and order the decorator. The decorator implements the UserFacade interface and is declared to be abstract. The reason it is abstract is because not all the methods on the interface are implemented by the class.

There are two injection points - one for the EntityManager and the other for the UserService. The EntityManager injection point is qualified with the @Database(MS_SQL) qualifier. The reason we are implementing this decorator is to be able to override the createUser method on the UserFacade interface. The objective is to save users in the EU to an MS SQL Server database hosted in the EU. So we inject the EntityManager, qualifying it with the requisite qualifier so that the right EntityManager instance linked to the MS SQL Server database will be injected.

The UserService injection point is annotated @Delegate. This field is called the delegate injection point of the decorator. This bean is what the UserServiceDecorator is decorating. Any calls on the delegate, in this case the UserService, will be called on the decorator, which can invoke methods directly on the delegate object. This field is what tells the CDI container what bean the UserServiceDecorator is decorating. You can qualify the delegate injection point to restrict the type of bean to be decorated.

The decorator implements the createUser method. This method is one of the two methods on the UserFacade interface. The implementation checks if the user to be persisted is in the EU region. If yes, then the actual persistence is carried out by the decorator through a call to the persist method of the injected EntityManager. Remember this EntityManager instance is linked to a SQL Server that will be hosted in the EU. If the user is not in the EU, then the decorator simply calls the createdUser method on the delegate.

This way, we have added a functionality that is custom to the UserService bean. The process of persisting a user is not a cross-cutting but actual business function. To extend that functionality, the decorator pattern is used to extend the functionality of the bean without changing the implementation. Normally, you will find yourself using the decorators to extend beans that are not part of your application. Using producers, you transform those classes into CDI beans and then use decorators to extend their functionality.

A decorator such as the UserServiceDecorator is a CDI bean, and as such, its types are all types in its chain up to java.lang.Object. A decorator cannot declare a scope other than the @Dependent pseudo-scope. Giving a decorator any other scope will be treated as a definition error by the container at application boot time. So far, you have seen how decorators and interceptors help you implement cross-cutting concerns and add functionality to beans, respectively. Next up, let us take a look at events in CDI.

CDI Events

The CDI event mechanism is a way to allow application components to emit events of any type and have one or more listeners of those events notified in a typesafe, completely decoupled way. There is no compile-time dependency between the source of the event and any observers or listeners. The publisher-subscriber paradigm of the observer design pattern is at the core of CDI events, which comprises two parts – the event object and event observers.

The Event Object

The event object is the payload of the event to be fired. Think of the payload as the data that will be passed to listeners of the event. It can be any valid Java type. In jwallet, we want to send an SMS to users who successfully sign up to the application. We could hard code this requirement into our UserService bean. However, that would mean we could get tied to a single implementation of the process of sending an SMS.

A much cleaner way would be to fire an event of the type of user representation we have in the application. This way, the SMS implementation will be fully decoupled from the process of persisting users in the system. And we can add and remove message sending implementations at will without breaking the code. We could also add other messaging options like email, all as event listeners, or observers, still completely decoupled from the event source.

To do this, we need an event object. This object will be passed to observers as the payload when the event is fired. The CDI container will map event observers to fired events based on the type of payload that the observers are observing. Listing 4-40 shows the Event interface with a payload in the UserServiceDecorator.

Listing 4-40. showing an injection of the Event object in the UserServiceDecorator

```
@Decorator
@Priority(Interceptor.Priority.APPLICATION)
public abstract class UserServiceDecorator implements UserFacade {
      @Inject
      Event<UserResponse> userResponseEvent;
}
```

Listing 4-40 shows the UserServiceDecorator with a new injection point – Event<UserResponse>. The entry point to the CDI event mechanism is the Event<T> interface. This interface takes a type, which will be the event payload. It has methods to fire different types of events. As shown in Listing 4-40, you inject an instance of the Event interface, passing in a payload type. This type is called the event type and will be used in resolving which observers are interested in this event. The CDI container will provide an implementation of the Event interface to your application at runtime. Listing 4-41 shows the use of the injected Event object.

Listing 4-41. shows the actual process of firing the UserResponse event

```
@Decorator
@Priority(Interceptor.Priority.APPLICATION)
public abstract class UserServiceDecorator implements UserFacade {
      @Inject
      Event<UserResponse> userResponseEvent;
      @Inject
      @Database(DB.MS_SQL)
      private EntityManager entityManager;

      @Inject
      @Delegate
      private UserService userService;
```

```
    @Override
    public UserResponse createUser(final CreateUserRequest
    createUserRequest) {
            final User user = UserService.fromUserWrapper(create
            UserRequest);
            if (createUserRequest.getUserRegion() == UserRegion.EU) {
                    entityManager.persist(user);
                    final UserResponse userResponse = userService.
                    getUser(user.getId());

                    userResponseEvent.fire(userResponse);

                    return UserService.toUserResponse(user);
            }

            return userService.createUser(createUserRequest);
    }
}
```

Listing 4-41 shows the amended createUser method in the UserServiceDecorator bean. The method, after persisting the User object into the database, calls the fire method on the injected event object, passing in the newly persisted User through the UserResponse object. This passed UserResponse object will be the payload of the fired event. As you can see, firing an event is as simple as calling the fire method, passing in the type of the Event interface. This simple call will cause an event to be fired that any component can subscribe to or observe. The UserResponse instance passed to the fire method of the Event bean will be passed to all event observers of the UserResponse type.

The Event Observer

The second part of the CDI event mechanism is the event observer. The observer is a subscriber to a particular event. The observers are paired to events by the container based on the types they observe. An observer that wants to be notified of the UserResponse event will have to observe a User event. Listing 4-42 shows the User event observer in the MessageCenter bean.

Listing 4-42. showing the UserResponse event observer as the MessageCenter bean

```
public class MessageCenter {

      public void sendUserSms(@Observes final UserResponse userResponse) {
            //TODO --> Send SMS through gateway... Blocking task
      }

}
```

Listing 4-42 shows the MessageCenter bean with a sendUserSms method. This method takes a single parameter of type UserResponse. This parameter determines the type of events that this observer will be notified of. The parameter is annotated with the @Observes annotation, telling the CDI runtime that this method observes events of the annotated type. When the UserResponse event is fired in the UserServiceDecorator bean, this method will be automatically called by the container and passed the UserResponse instance that was passed to the fire method of the Event interface in the UserServiceDecorator bean. Even though there is absolutely no compile-time dependency between the bean that fires the event and the one that observes it, at runtime, these beans will communicate with each other through the fired event.

Asynchronous Events

The UserResponse event we have looked at so far is a synchronous blocking event. This means when fired, the observer method will block execution until it's completed. As shown in Listing 4-42, execution will be blocked until the sendUserSms returns because the event observer method will be called in the same thread in which it was fired. However, sending an SMS most likely will require communication with an external SMS provider, over the network. This could take time, depending on the latency of the network. To circumvent such potential problems, the event mechanism supports the firing of asynchronous events.

With async events, the observers will be invoked asynchronously, executing in a separate thread from the one in which the event was fired. This way, the sending of the SMS will be in a separate thread and thus execution will return immediately to the point the event was fired. Listing 4-43 shows the firing of async events in the UserServiceDecorator bean.

Listing 4-43. showing the firing of an async event

```
@Decorator
@Priority(Interceptor.Priority.APPLICATION)
public abstract class UserServiceDecorator implements UserFacade {
    @Inject
    Event<UserResponse> userResponseEvent;
    @Inject
    @Database(DB.MS_SQL)
    private EntityManager entityManager;

    @Inject
    @Delegate
    private UserService userService;

    @Override
    public UserResponse createUser(final CreateUserRequest
    createUserRequest) {
        final User user = UserService.fromUserWrapper(createUse
        rRequest);
        if (createUserRequest.getUserRegion() == UserRegion.EU) {
            entityManager.persist(user);
            final UserResponse userResponse = userService.
            getUser(user.getId());

            userResponseEvent.fireAsync(userResponse);

            return UserService.toUserResponse(user);
        }

        return userService.createUser(createUserRequest);
    }

}
```

Listing 4-43 shows the UserServiceDecorator bean with its createUser method. This time, the event object fires an async event through the call to the fireAsync method. This method will fire an async event that only async observers will be notified of. It returns a java.util.concurrent.CompletionStage object for optional further pipeline composition on the async operation. The UserResponse observer shown in Listing 4-42 will not be called for this event because that observer is synchronous. Listing 4-44 shows the MessageCenter bean with an async UserResponse observer.

Listing 4-44. showing an async UserResponse observer

```
public class MessageCenter {

        public void sendUserSmsAsync(@ObservesAsync final UserResponse user
        Response) {
                //TODO --> Send SMS through gateway... Async
        }
}
```

Listing 4-44 shows the MessageCenter bean with a new method, sendUserSmsAsync. This method has almost the same signature as the synchronous one we saw in Listing 4-42, with the only difference being the @Observes annotation replaced with @ObservesAsync. This annotation tells the container that this method observes an async event of type UserResponse. So when the UserResponse event shown in Listing 4-43 gets fired, the sendUserSmsAsync method will be called.

Transactional Observers

The UserResponse event discussed so far should work fine. However, there is a problem. The requirement is to send a message to a user that successfully gets persisted to the database. However, we haven't checked so far if the actual act of persisting the user succeeded or not. The async event fired in Listing 4-43 is fired two lines after calling persist on the EntityManager instance. The problem is that up to the point the event is fired, the transaction in which the method is being executed has still not been committed. And until the transaction commits successfully, we really can't be certain that the act of persisting the user has succeeded or not.

To get around this problem, we can use transactional observers. A transactional observer is one that specifies at which phase of a transaction it should be invoked. With our requirement, we want the observer to be invoked only after the transaction in which the event is fired completes successfully, meaning the transaction was committed successfully, and we are certain the data is in the database. Listing 4-45 shows the MessageCenter bean with a transactional observer for sending SMS.

Listing 4-45. showing a transactional observer

```
public class MessageCenter {

    public void sendUserSms(@Observes(during = TransactionPhase.AFTER_
    SUCCESS)   final UserResponse userResponse) {
          //TODO --> Send SMS through gateway... Blocking task
     }
}
```

Listing 4-45 shows the sendUserSms method of the MessageCenter bean. This time around, the @Observes method is passed a parameter - during = TransactionPhase. AFTER_SUCCESS. This signals to the container that we want this observer to be called in the after-success phase of any transaction in which the event was fired. Because the UserResponse was fired in a transactional context, the sendUserSms observer is going to be notified only after the transaction commits successfully.

You should have noted that the sendUserSms observer is observing a synchronous event because it uses the @Observes annotation. This is because transactional observers are not supported for async events. So the event that is fired will be a synchronous event as shown in Listing 4-41 in the UserServiceDecorator.

There are a number of transactional phases available for observer methods. These are defined in the TransactionPhase enum type in the jakarta.enterprise.event package. They are

- IN_PROGRESS - The observer is called when the event is fired. This is the default.
- BEFORE_COMPLETION - The observer is called during the before completion phase of the transaction.
- AFTER_COMPLETION - The observer is called during the after completion phase of the transaction.
- AFTER_FAILURE - The observer is called during the after completion phase of the transaction, only when the transaction fails.
- AFTER_SUCCESS - The observer is called during the after completion phase of the transaction, only when the transaction succeeds.

Qualifying Events

Events can be qualified to selectively determine which observers get notified. Back to our requirement, just as we need to persist EU residents of jwallet into an EU hosted database, we can only send an email to a successfully persisted EU user and not an SMS. To meet this requirement, we can qualify our events to selectively have different observer methods called based on their qualifiers. Let's start by introducing a MessageOption qualifier that takes a MessageType parameter as shown in Listing 4-46.

Listing 4-46. showing the new MessageOption parameter

```
@Qualifier
@Retention(RUNTIME)
@Target({ FIELD, TYPE, METHOD, PARAMETER })
public @interface MessageOption {

        MessageType value();

        enum MessageType {
                SMS,
                EMAIL
        }
}
```

Listing 4-46 shows the MessageOption qualifier. With this, we can selectively determine which event observers to be notified for which event. This annotation can be used in two ways. First, we could inject two Event objects into the UserServiceDecorator, qualifying each with a separate MessageOption, as shown in Listing 4-47.

Listing 4-47. showing two qualified Event objects for each MessageOption type

```
@Decorator
@Priority(Interceptor.Priority.APPLICATION)
public abstract class UserServiceDecorator implements UserFacade {

        @Inject
        @MessageOption(MessageOption.MessageType.SMS)
        Event<UserResponse> smsEvent;
```

```
    @Inject
    @MessageOption(MessageOption.MessageType.SMS)
    Event<UserResponse> emailEvent;
}
```

Listing 4-47 shows the UserServiceDecorator bean with two Event injection points, each qualified with a MessageOption. The corresponding observers interested in each event will also need to be qualified.

Listing 4-48. shows two observers in the MessageCenter bean observing these events

```
public class MessageCenter {

    public void sendUserSmsAsync(
        @ObservesAsync @MessageOption(MessageOption.MessageType.SMS)
        final UserResponse userResponse) {
         //TODO --> Send SMS through gateway... Async
    }

    public void sendEmail(
       @ObservesAsync @MessageOption(MessageOption.MessageType.EMAIL)
       final UserResponse userResponse) {
         //TODO --> send email asynchronously
    }
}
```

Listing 4-48 shows the MessageCenter bean with two event observers, each observing the same event type but differently qualified. During observer resolution, the container will match each observer to the fired event based on type and qualifiers. So the sendSmsAsync observer will be mapped to the async event fired from the smsEvent object (Listing 4-47) and the sendEmail observer mapped to the emailEvent object (Listing 4-47). This should work as expected. However, the moment we have a dozen MessageType options in the MessageOption qualifier, we would have to inject a lot more Event objects.

Fortunately, we can dynamically add qualifiers to events based on some condition in our code. Listing 4-49 shows the UserServiceDecorator bean refactored to dynamically select a MessageOption based on the location of the persisted User.

Listing 4-49. shows a refactored UserServiceDecorator with dynamically selected event qualifiers

```
@Decorator
@Priority(Interceptor.Priority.APPLICATION)
public abstract class UserServiceDecorator implements UserFacade {

      @Inject
      Event<UserResponse> userResponseEvent;
      @Inject
      @Database(DB.MS_SQL)
      private EntityManager entityManager;

      @Inject
      @Delegate
      private UserService userService;

      @Override
      public UserResponse createUser(final CreateUserRequest
      createUserRequest) {
            final User user = UserService.fromUserWrapper(createUse
            rRequest);
            if (createUserRequest.getUserRegion() == UserRegion.EU) {
                  entityManager.persist(user);
                  final UserResponse userResponse = userService.
                  getUser(user.getId());

            userResponseEvent.select(getAnnotation(UserRegion.EU)).
            fireAsync(userResponse);

                  return UserService.toUserResponse(user);
            }else{
            final UserResponse userResponse = userService.
            createUser(createUserRequest);
userResponseEvent.select(getAnnotation(UserRegion.OTHERS)).
fireAsync(userResponse);
```

```
        return userResponse;
}
    }

    private MessageOption getAnnotation(final UserRegion userRegion) {
        if (userRegion == UserRegion.EU) {
            return new MessageOption() {
                @Override
                public MessageType value() {
                    return MessageType.EMAIL;
                }

                @Override
                public Class<? extends Annotation>
                annotationType() {
                    return MessageOption.class;
                }
            };
        }
        return new MessageOption() {
            @Override
            public MessageType value() {
                return MessageType.SMS;
            }

            @Override
            public Class<? extends Annotation> annotationType() {
                return MessageOption.class;
            }
        };
    }
}
```

Listing 4-49 shows the full UserServiceDecorator bean. In the createUser method, if a user is in the EU, we invoke the select method on the UserResponseEvent object, passing it the return type of the getAnnotation(UserRegions.EU) method. The get annotation method takes a UserRegion type parameter and returns the requisite annotation for that region. In this case, the returned qualifier will be MessageOption(MessageType.EMAIL). The Event#select method we've called takes a variable argument list of annotations.

If the user is not in the EU region, we pass UserRegion.OTHERS to the getAnnotation method, which will return the MessageOption(MessageType.SMS) that is passed to the select method of the same userResponseEvent object. This way, our observer methods as shown in Listing 4-48 stay the same. But we have made the qualifier selection process in the event firing bean much more flexible. The container will still map whichever event gets fired to the right observer method as if we had explicitly injected and qualified different event types, as shown in Listing 4-47.

It is important to note that the event observers as shown in Listing 4-48 will be conditionally called based on their types and qualifiers matching those of a fired event. However, Listing 4-50 shows a third UserResponse observer that will always be called irrespective of the qualifiers of the userResponseEvent.

Listing 4-50. shows a catch-all event observer in MessageCenter

```
public class MessageCenter {

      public void sendUserSms(
                  @Observes(during = TransactionPhase.AFTER_SUCCESS)
                  @MessageOption(MessageOption.MessageType.SMS)
                  final UserResponse userResponse) {
            //TODO --> Send SMS through gateway... Blocking task
      }

      public void sendUserSmsAsync(
                  @ObservesAsync @MessageOption(MessageOption.MessageType.
                  SMS) final UserResponse userResponse) {
            //TODO --> Send SMS through gateway... Async
      }

      public void sendEmail(
                  @ObservesAsync @MessageOption(MessageOption.MessageType.
                  EMAIL) final UserResponse userResponse) {
            //TODO --> send email asynchronously
      }
```

```
    public void sendMessage(@ObservesAsync final UserResponse
    userResponse) {
            }
}
```

In Listing 4-50, the sendMessage observer will be called for all events fired by any Event<UserResponse> object, irrespective of the qualifiers of the event object. The reason is that the sendMessage observer, in the absence of any explicit qualifiers, is implicitly qualified with the built-in @Any qualifier. The @Any qualifier is a catch-all qualifier that applies to any CDI artifact, irrespective of the qualifiers of that artifact. In this example, the sendMessage observer will be called no matter which event object fires the UserResponse event. This is something to keep in mind when working with qualifiers in CDI. If you need to restrict things exclusively to your explicitly chosen qualifiers, then you should make sure to annotate all corresponding constructs with your qualifiers to avoid subtle bugs.

Event Metadata

There may be times when you need to have some metadata regarding a fired event. In such cases, you can use the EventMetadata bean for that. Observer methods can take more than one parameter. Those we have seen so far have all taken single parameters in the form of the event payload. However, you can pass more than one parameter to the observer method, with each parameter being an injection point that will be automatically resolved by the container. Let us pass an EventMetadata bean to the sendUserSms observer method in the MessageCenter bean in Listing 4-51.

Listing 4-51. shows the passing of a second parameter to an observer method

```
public class MessageCenter {

    public void sendUserSms(@Observes(during = TransactionPhase.AFTER_
    SUCCESS) @MessageOption(MessageOption.MessageType.SMS) UserResponse
    userResponse, EventMetadata eventMetadata) {

        //TODO --> Send SMS through gateway... Blocking task
    }
}
```

Listing 4-51 shows the injection of the EventMetadata bean as the second parameter to the sendUserSms synchronous observer method. EventMetadata is an interface that will be given an implementation by the CDI runtime. It contains methods to get the qualifiers for the fired event, the InjectionPoint bean for the injection point, and the Type for the class of the event object. Injecting this metadata gives you information you can further use to make decisions dynamically in your observer methods.

Conditional Observer Methods

CDI event observer methods can be conditional. You can decide if an observer method should always be called when the event it is observing gets fired, or if it should be called only if an instance of the bean declaring the observer method already exists. By default, a new instance of the bean containing an observer method will be created if none exists. However, you can turn this off and only have observers called if an instance of the bean declaring them is already available in the current scope. To conditionally have observer methods, you will first need to give an explicit scope to the bean declaring the observer methods. The MessageCenter bean (last shown in Listing 4-51) that contains our messaging observers is @Dependent scope, because we have not explicitly associated it with a scope.

To conditionally ask that the sendUserSms synchronous observer be called only if an instance of the MessageCenter bean exists, we can pass in a second parameter to the @Observes annotation as shown in Listing 4-52.

Listing 4-52. shows the sendUserSms set to conditional

```
@RequestScoped
public class MessageCenter {

      public void sendUserSms(@Observes(during = TransactionPhase.AFTER_
      SUCCESS, notifyObserver = Reception.IF_EXISTS)
      @MessageOption(MessageOption.MessageType.SMS)
                final UserResponse userResponse, final EventMetadata
                eventMetadata) {

            //TODO --> Send SMS through gateway... Blocking task
      }
}
```

Listing 4-52 shows the MessageCenter bean, this time around with its scope set to @RequestScope. The sendUserSms observer passes the notifyObserver parameter value of Reception.IF_EXISTS to the @Observes annotation. With this construct, this observer will only be called for any fired synchronous UserResponse event if an instance of the MessageCenter bean exists within the current request scope. In the absence of an instance of the bean, the observer will not be called.

The notifyObserver takes either of the two options – Reception.IF_EXISTS or Reception.ALWAYS. The default is Reception.ALWAYS. So by default, an observer method will always be called for the event it is observing unless explicitly turned off.

Summary

In this chapter, we covered the core of the Jakarta Contexts and Dependency Injection specification. We saw the features of the specification, how to activate it, and then took a whirlwind tour of the various constructs it makes available to you for application development. There is a lot more available in the specification[15] on the Jakarta specs page. In the next chapter, we continue our discussion of Jakarta EE by looking at the Jakarta Persistence API.

[15] Jakarta Context Dependency Injection 4.0 | The Eclipse Foundation

CHAPTER 5

Persistence with Jakarta EE Persistence

Every application needs to store data at some point during its execution to a durable data store. The data store could be as simple as a flat file and as complex as a full-fledged database management system. The data store acts as the single source of truth for the application. For instance, the bank balance of your account with your bank is stored in some form of data store. This single data is the only source of truth for the bank in identifying how much money they are keeping for you.

Irrespective of the language and platform an application is written in, the process of storing application data into a durable data store generally spans three broad categories, namely, data modelling, data persistence, and data retrieval. In Enterprise Java, the Jakarta Persistence API is a fully featured specification that allows you to realize these three broad application data persistence categories through the use of annotations and intuitive interfaces.

This chapter is about persisting data to a relational database using the Jakarta Persistence API or JPA. The goal isn't to teach you everything about JPA, but rather the essentials of what you need to get very common application data persistence requirements fulfilled. For a much more comprehensive overview and reference for JPA, please take a look at the specification[1] document. The chapter is split into the three main categories of data modelling, data persistence, and data retrieval.

All the examples in this chapter use the Postgres database as the underlying database. However, the same principles should apply to all database engines out there as long as you use the JPA constructs. By the end of this chapter, you should be comfortable in using the JPA specification to persist your application data to a relational database.

[1] Jakarta Persistence 3.1 Specification

L. Saeed and G. Abdallah, *Pro Cloud Native Java EE Apps*, https://doi.org/10.1007/978-1-4842-8900-6_5

JPA at a Glance

The Jakarta Persistence API, popularly known as JPA, is the Jakarta EE specification that defines how applications can model, store into, and retrieve data from relational databases. JPA makes heavy use of annotations to prevent your Java artifacts from having to extend or implement interfaces from the API. JPA helps you solve the object-relational impedance mismatch by giving you the constructs to map plain Java classes to relational database tables.

As a Java developer, you are very familiar with object-oriented programming and design. However, this paradigm does not translate very well when it comes to database management. The JPA API allows you to model and query your data in a familiar Java context without having to dive deep into the technical aspect of relational database management systems. It also abstracts from the underlying database, leaving the handling of the different databases to the runtime. Except in very advanced cases, you as a developer will not have to know much about the database that the application uses.

It is important to note that JPA does not replace SQL or database systems knowledge. What JPA does is to make it easy for Java developers to be able to model, persist, and query data in a much more "Java way" than otherwise. That notwithstanding, some knowledge of SQL is required to be able to make full use of the JPA API.

The JPA Runtime

Throughout this chapter, there will be references to the JPA runtime. The runtime is the actual implementation of the Jakarta Persistence specification that carries out your JPA "instructions" issued through the various API constructs. It translates the high-level JPA constructs to low-level, database-specific schemas and queries. As discussed in the early chapters, Jakarta EE is made up of individual specifications, with each specification having different implementations. The JPA specification also has implementations that ship with the different Jakarta EE containers. Some of the popular implementations are Hibernate and EclipseLink.

Data Modelling

The modelling aspect of JPA is handled almost entirely by annotations found in the jakarta.persistence package. These annotations transform POJOs into JPA entities that can be modelled based on their interrelationships and hierarchies and subsequently mapped to relational database tables. For instance, one entity might extend another, contain a list of another type, and itself be contained in a collection in yet another class. All these can be mapped to relational database entity relations using the annotations found in the jakarta.persistence package.

Data Persistence

The central artifact for persisting, updating, and querying data in JPA is the EntityManager interface. This interface has all the methods needed to get data into the database, update, and query the data. As is the norm on the Jakarta EE platform, the underlying JPA specification implementation provides an implementation for the EntityManager interface at runtime.

Querying

Querying data is equally as important as persisting the data. JPA has two APIs for querying data, namely, the Java Persistence Query Language and the Criteria API. These two constructs allow you to write queries that are known ahead of time and much more dynamic, search-type queries that come up at runtime. The EntityManager interface has methods for creating queries using these two API constructs.

With the Jakarta Persistence API, you can create applications with complex data hierarchies and relationships, mapped to relational databases all through the much familiar Java language. This makes using the JPA API a critical toolset in the toolbox of every Jakarta EE developer. The rest of this chapter discusses the trio itemized earlier.

Data Modelling with JPA

The Simplest Unit

The simplest unit of a JPA artifact is a Plain Old Java Object, or POJO. Listing 5-1 shows a User POJO that will be transformed into an entity.

Listing 5-1. shows the User POJO

```
public class User {

    private String firstName;
    private String lastName;
    private String username;

}
```

Listing 5-1 shows a very basic User Java class. To map this class to a relational database table, such that each field is mapped to a table column, we need to transform it into a JPA entity. The primary annotation for transforming a Java class to a JPA entity is the @Entity annotation. Listing 5-2 shows the User class now transformed into a JPA entity.

Listing 5-2. showing the User entity

```
@Entity
public class User {
    private String firstName;
    private String lastName;
    private String username;
}
```

Listing 5-2 shows the User entity. With this, the User class is now a JPA entity that will be mapped to a database table. The name of the database table to which this class will be mapped is by default the name of the entity class, in this case User. To customize the table name, the @Table annotation can be used as shown in Listing 5-3.

Listing 5-3. shows the User entity with a customized table name

```
@Entity
@Table(name = "WALLET_USER")
public class User {

    private String firstName;
    private String lastName;
    private String username;

}
```

Listing 5-3 shows the use of the @Table annotation to customize the relational database table name to which this entity will be mapped. With these annotations, the User class is now a JPA entity that will be mapped to the relational database table wallet_user, with its instances mapped to rows in the table.

Primary Key Generation

Even though the User entity shown in Listing 5-3 will be mapped to the relational database table wallet_user, it does not have a primary key. In relational databases, the primary key is the technical unique identifier of each row in the table. The User entity, however, has not declared a primary key. To fix this, Listing 5-4 shows an updated version of the User class with a primary key field.

Listing 5-4. shows the updated User entity

```
@Entity
@Table(name = "WALLET_USER")
public class User {

    @Id
    @GeneratedValue(strategy = GenerationType.AUTO)
    protected Long id;

    private String firstName;
    private String lastName;
    private String username;

}
```

Listing 5-4 shows the User entity, now with a field of type Long named id. This field is annotated with @Id and @GeneratedValue(strategy=GenerationType.AUTO). The @Id annotation tells the runtime that the primary key of the User table should be mapped to this field. The allowed field types for the @Id annotation are Java primitive types or their corresponding wrappers, String, java.util.Date, java.sql.Date, java.math.BigDecimal, and java.math.BigInteger. The runtime takes care of mapping the annotated field to the requisite, corresponding type of the underlying database used.

Id Generation

The second annotation on the id field is the @GeneratedValue annotation. This annotation is used to tell the runtime how the primary key values should be generated through the strategy parameter. The strategy parameter is of type GenerationType and defaults to AUTO. The possible values for the GenerationType are TABLE, SEQUENCE, IDENTITY, and AUTO. With a default of AUTO, the User entity shown in Listing 5-4 can be simplified to what is shown in Listing 5-5.

Listing 5-5. shows a simplified id generation for the User entity

```
@Entity
@Table(name = "WALLET_USER")
public class User {

    @Id
    @GeneratedValue
    protected Long id;

    private String firstName;
    private String lastName;
    private String username;

}
```

Listing 5-5 shows the primary key generation set to AUTO, the default for the @GeneratedValue annotation. Listing 5-6 shows the resulting database schema diagram for the User entity declared in Figure 5-1.

Figure 5-1. *Wallet entity schema*

Listing 5-6. shows the corresponding data definition language (DDL) for the entity

```
create table wallet_user
(
    id        bigint not null primary key,
    firstname varchar(255),
    lastname  varchar(255),
    username  varchar(255)
);
```

AUTO

The AUTO primary key generation strategy delegates the decision of how primary keys should be generated to the underlying runtime. What this implies is that the application is asking the JPA runtime to select the best primary key generation strategy based on the field type and underlying database engine used.

In cases where the primary key is only used as a technical database unique row identifier, then the AUTO strategy should suffice. It also is an ideal choice for development and quick prototyping. AUTO also works best when schema generation is done by the runtime (we talk about schema generation later in the chapter). AUTO will work only for integral field types.

TABLE

The TABLE generation strategy is the most flexible and extensible generation strategy. Listing 5-7 shows the User entity using the TABLE generation strategy for the primary key generation.

Listing 5-7. shows the User entity using TABLE primary key generation

```
@Entity
@Table(name = "WALLET_USER")
public class User {

    @Id
    @GeneratedValue(strategy=GenerationType.TABLE)
    protected Long id;
```

```
    private String firstName;
    private String lastName;
    private String username;

}
```

Listing 5-7 shows the User entity with the TABLE primary key generation strategy. As is, the runtime will take care of creating the ID table (if schema generation is used). In the absence of schema generation by the runtime, the declared ID table should exist before the application starts.

The ID table is a table with two fields - a string and an integral type. The first column is the primary identifier for all generators in the table. The second integral column stores the actual ID sequence being generated. A much more elaborate example of TABLE generation is shown in Listing 5-8 where we explicitly define the ID generation table through the @TableGenerator annotation.

Listing 5-8. shows the User entity with explicit table generation

```
@Entity
@Table(name = "WALLET_USER")
public class User {
      @Id
      @TableGenerator(name = "ID_Gen",
                  table = "ID_GEN_TABLE",
                  pkColumnName = "GENERATOR_NAME",
                  pkColumnValue = "GENERATED_VALUE",
                  valueColumnName = "GEN_VAL")
      @GeneratedValue(strategy = GenerationType.TABLE,
                  generator = "ID_Gen")
      protected Long id;
      private String firstName;
      private String lastName;
      private String username;

}
```

Listing 5-8 shows the use of the @TableGenerator annotation to explicitly specify the ID table generation. The first parameter of the annotation specifies the name of the generator. This name is then passed to the generator parameter of the @GeneratedValue annotation. The other parameters of the @TableGenerator annotation are as follows:

- table – This specifies the name of the database table for this generator.
- pkColumnName – This specifies the column name for the unique identifier for this table.
- pkColumnValue – This specifies the actual value of the pkColumnName in the table.
- valueColumnName – This specifies the column name of the column for storing the ID sequence.

This TABLE ID generation will result in the DB schema shown in Listing 5-9.

Listing 5-9. shows the resulting ID generation table for the User entity

```
create table id_gen_table
(
    generator_name varchar(50) not null primary key,
    gen_val        numeric(38)
);
```

Figure 5-2 shows the resulting schema diagram for the ID generation table.

Figure 5-2. *ID generation table schema*

At application runtime, the JPA provider (runtime, implementation) will allocate a block of identifiers for this table. The default allocation block is 50. The runtime will then allocate IDs from this block from memory until it hits the size of the allocation, a request for an ID causes another round of preallocation, which will then be used in memory for assigning IDs, and so on. The allocation size can be customized through the @TableGenerator. You can also set the initial value of the gen_val column, which defaults to zero for integral types.

SEQUENCE

The SEQUENCE identity generation strategy is similar to the TABLE strategy and is used where the underlying database supports the sequence ID generation mechanism. Setting the strategy of the @GeneratedValue to SEQUENCE will cause the underlying runtime to create the requisite sequence generator on your behalf. The @SequenceGenerator can be used to explicitly create sequence generation tables, much similar to what we discussed in the TABLE strategy using @TableGenerator.

IDENTITY

The IDENTITY sequence generating strategy is used when the underlying database supports the autonumber feature. When a row is inserted into the database, the engine automatically assigns a value to the primary key column. IDENTITY is very much database dependent and thus isn't used commonly in JPA applications.

Customizing Columns

The User entity shown in Listing 5-5 will default to using the field names as database columns. However, you can customize these columns using the @Column annotation. This is very important when the application you are working on will be used with an existing schema, mostly from legacy applications. The @Column annotation can also be used to set some constraints and properties on the column in the database. Listing 5-10 shows the User entity, with @Column used to customize some fields.

Listing 5-10. shows the use of @Column annotation to customize entity fields

```
@Entity
@Table(name = "WALLET_USER")
public class User {

    @Id
    @GeneratedValue(strategy = GenerationType.AUTO)
    protected Long id;
```

```
    @Column(nullable = false)
    private String firstName;

    @Column(nullable = false)
    private String lastName;

    @Column(unique = true, length = 30, nullable = false)
    private String username;

    @Column(precision = 19, scale = 2)
    private BigDecimal totalConversions;

}
```

Listing 5-10 shows an updated User entity, with @Column customizations and constraints on some fields. The first and last names are constrained to not be null. This means the database will enforce non-null checks for every insertion into the wallet_user table. The username column is set to not be nullable and to be unique. Its length is also set to 30 variable characters. The totalConversions field, which is a numeric field, is set to a precision of 19 and a scale of 2. The updated schema diagram of the User entity is shown in Figure 5-3.

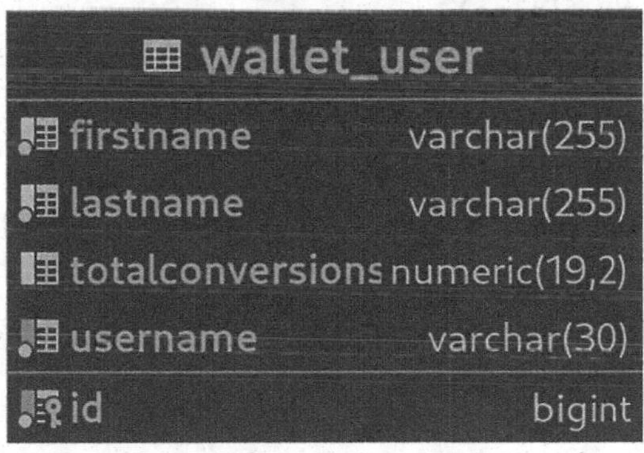

Figure 5-3. *Updated User schema*

The corresponding DDL from the new User entity is also shown in Listing 5-11.

Listing 5-11. showing the updated User entity DDL

```
create table if not exists wallet_user
(
    id                  bigint       not null primary key,
```

```
    firstname         varchar(255) not null,
    lastname          varchar(255) not null,
    totalconversions numeric(19, 2),
    username          varchar(30)  not null unique
);
```

Mapping Temporal Types

Mapping date types to database columns is a straightforward task using the Java 8 java.time packages. Listing 5-12 shows the User entity with three new java.time types.

Listing 5-12. shows temporal mapping using java.time types in the User entity

```
@Entity
@Table(name = "WALLET_USER")
public class User {

      @Id
      @GeneratedValue(strategy = GenerationType.AUTO)
      protected Long id;
      @Column(nullable = false)
      private String firstName;
      @Column(nullable = false)
      private String lastName;
      @Column(unique = true, length = 30, nullable = false)
      private String username;
      @Column(precision = 19, scale = 2)
      private BigDecimal totalConversions;

      private LocalDate birthDay;

      private LocalDateTime created;

      private LocalDateTime updated;

}
```

Listing 5-12 shows three new fields in the User entity. The birthDay field is typed to java.time.LocalDate and the created and updated fields to java.time.LocalDateTime types. The LocalDate type will be mapped to the SQL date type and the LocalDateTime type to the timestamp type in the database. The updated schema diagram of the User entity is shown in Figure 5-4.

wallet_user	
birthday	date
created	timestamp
firstname	varchar(255)
lastname	varchar(255)
totalconversions	numeric(19,2)
updated	timestamp
username	varchar(30)
id	bigint

***Figure 5-4.** Updated User entity schema*

The much older java.util.Date and java.util.Calendar types can also be used for temporal type fields. However, for these, the @Temporal type annotation will need to be used to pick which JDBC java.sql types to map the field to. The java.sql.Date, java.sql.Time, and java.sql.Timestamp can also be used. These map directly to the respective underlying database type without any hint to the runtime.

Mapping Large Objects

Oftentimes, applications need to map byte-based objects to the database. These objects can be large, depending on their type. Large objects, otherwise known as LOBs, require separate JDBC calls to the database for loading them in Java. As such, when used as field types, we need to signal the runtime to use these special calls. The way to signal the runtime about LOBs is through the use of the @Lob annotation on a large object field.

There are two types of large objects that can be mapped to the database. These are large character objects or CLOBs, represented in Java as char[] or Character[], and long String objects are mapped to the CLOB column type in the database.

Binary large objects, or BLOBs, represented in Java by byte[], Byte[], and Serializable types are mapped to BLOB database columns. Listing 5-13 shows the User entity with a BLOB field for the picture of the account holder.

Listing 5-13. shows the User entity with a BLOB field

```
@Entity
@Table(name = "WALLET_USER")
public class User {

      @Id
      @GeneratedValue(strategy = GenerationType.AUTO)
      protected Long id;
      @Column(nullable = false)
      private String firstName;
      @Column(nullable = false)
      private String lastName;
      @Column(unique = true, length = 30, nullable = false)
      private String username;
      @Column(precision = 19, scale = 2)
      private BigDecimal totalConversions;
      private LocalDate birthDay;
      private LocalDateTime created;
      private LocalDateTime updated;

      @Lob
      @Basic(fetch = FetchType.LAZY)
      private byte[] picture;

}
```

Listing 5-13 shows the picture field of type byte[] annotated with @Lob. This will be mapped to the underlying database's binary large object type.

Simple Field Types

The @Basic annotation on the picture explicitly marks the field as a basic or simple type. All the fields in the User entity are called simple types in JPA parlance. Simple fields are fields that can be mapped directly to a single database column. The @Basic annotation is used to denote simple field types. However, they can be fully omitted as has been the case with all the fields in the User entity except for the picture field.

Lazy Fetching

When a row is loaded from the table to which the User entity is mapped, all the columns mapped to simple types are loaded. By default, simple types in an entity are loaded or fetched when an instance is loaded from the database. However, there are times when fetching a simple type is not very efficient.

In the case of the User entity, we really do not want to fetch a user's picture every time an instance is loaded. To signal the runtime to not fetch the binary field by default, the FetchType.LAZY type is passed to the fetch parameter of the @Basic field.

Mapping Enums

Adding an enum field type in an entity is enough to map it to a database column. By default, the enum type will be mapped to a column of an integral type in the database. This is because by default, JPA uses the ordinal of the enum to map to the database. Listing 5-14 shows the User entity with a UserType field.

Listing 5-14. User entity with an enum field

```
@Entity
@Table(name = "WALLET_USER")
public class User {

    @Id
    @GeneratedValue(strategy = GenerationType.AUTO)
    protected Long id;
    @Column(nullable = false)
    private String firstName;
    @Column(nullable = false)
```

```
    private String lastName;
    @Column(unique = true, length = 30, nullable = false)
    private String username;
    @Column(precision = 19, scale = 2)
    private BigDecimal totalConversions;
    private LocalDate birthDay;
    private LocalDateTime created;
    private LocalDateTime updated;

    @Lob
    @Basic(fetch = FetchType.LAZY)
    private byte[] picture;
    private UserType userType;

}
```

Figure 5-5 shows the schema diagram of the User entity with the enum field type.

***Figure 5-5.** Enum ordinal schema*

The userType is mapped to an integer for this particular underlying database. This means the ordinal position of the UserType value passed to the userType field at runtime is what will persist. The problem with this approach is that the existing originals could easily change with the addition of new entries in the enum. To prevent already persisted enum fields being mapped to the wrong enum value because of changes in the ordinals, the @EnumeratedType annotation can be used to change the mapped field type to a string. Listing 5-15 shows the userType field mapped to String.

Listing 5-15. shows the mapping of enum to String

```
@Entity
@Table(name = "WALLET_USER")
@Getter
@Setter
public class User {

    @Id
    @GeneratedValue(strategy = GenerationType.AUTO)
    protected Long id;
    @Column(nullable = false)
    private String firstName;
    @Column(nullable = false)
    private String lastName;
    @Column(unique = true, length = 30, nullable = false)
    private String username;
    @Column(precision = 19, scale = 2)
    private BigDecimal totalConversions;
    private LocalDate birthDay;
    private LocalDateTime created;
    private LocalDateTime updated;

    @Lob
    @Basic(fetch = FetchType.LAZY)
    private byte[] picture;

    @Enumerated(EnumType.STRING)
    private UserType userType;

}
```

The @Enumerated annotation takes either EnumType.STRING or EnumType.ORDINAL. The ORDINAL value is the default, and as such when omitted as was done in Listing 5-14, the field is mapped to the ordinal. Figure 5-6 shows the updated schema diagram.

wallet_user	
birthday	date
created	timestamp
firstname	varchar(255)
lastname	varchar(255)
picture	bytea
totalconversions	numeric(19,2)
updated	timestamp
usertype	varchar(255)
username	varchar(30)
id	bigint

Figure 5-6. *Enum string mapping*

The userType enum field is now mapped to varchar, which represents the String type that we aim to map it to.

Transient Fields

Transient fields in an entity are fields that are not mapped to a database column. To signal the runtime that a given field should not be persistent, the transient modifier or @Transient annotation can be used on a field type. The modified or annotated field will not be mapped to a database column nor can it be queried during data retrieval. For example, the User entity shown in Listing 5-16 has an age field with the transient modifier that is computed at runtime. This field should not be persistent.

Listing 5-16. shows the use of the transient modifier

```
@Entity
@Table(name = "WALLET_USER")
@Getter
```

```
@Setter
public class User {

    @Id
    @GeneratedValue(strategy = GenerationType.AUTO)
    protected Long id;
    @Column(nullable = false)
    private String firstName;
    @Column(nullable = false)
    private String lastName;
    @Column(unique = true, length = 30, nullable = false)
    private String username;
    @Column(precision = 19, scale = 2)
    private BigDecimal totalConversions;
    private LocalDate birthDay;
    private LocalDateTime created;
    private LocalDateTime updated;

    @Lob
    @Basic(fetch = FetchType.LAZY)
    private byte[] picture;

    @Enumerated(EnumType.STRING)
    private UserType userType;

    private transient int age;

}
```

The age field could equally be annotated @Transient, and the effect would be the same.

Field and Property Access

The mappings discussed so far in the User entity have all had their respective JPA annotations on the field. What this means is that the JPA runtime will directly access these fields at runtime. This is called field access. The other access type is property access, where the getter methods of the fields are annotated with the JPA annotations. You will not see much property access in the wild as much as field access. As such, all the examples in this chapter, and the rest of the book, use field access.

Organizing with Inheritance

The User entity discussed so far is the only entity we have looked at. However, an application will seldom consist of a single entity. No matter the number of entities, a lot of the time there will be fields that are common to a set of the entities. It is very tedious to repeat these fields for each entity. In any case, the whole point of the use of an abstraction like JPA is to use the full object-oriented feature of the Java language in a database context.

As such, common entity fields can be abstracted into a common superclass that all other types that need such fields can inherit from. The id, created, and updated fields of the User entity are good candidates for abstraction into a superclass. These fields naturally would be found in other entities. To simplify the domain models, let us abstract these and more other common fields into a superclass. Listing 5-17 shows an AbstractEntity class with some common fields.

Listing 5-17. shows the AbstractEntity class

```
@MappedSuperclass
public abstract class AbstractEntity implements Serializable {

    @Id
    @GeneratedValue(strategy = GenerationType.AUTO)
    protected Long id;

    protected LocalDateTime created;
    protected LocalDateTime updated;

    protected String createdBy;
    protected String editedBy;

}
```

Listing 5-17 shows the AbstractEntity. This class is an abstract class annotation @MappedSuperclass. It's abstract because its sole purpose is to be extended by other classes. We do not want to have any concrete initialization of this class. It has five fields that all bear the protected modifier, making them available to its subclasses. The @ MappedSuperclass annotation designates this class as one whose mapping information is applied to entities that extend it. It will not have a separate table of its own.

The User entity can now extend the Abstract entity, and in the database, all the fields of the AbstractEntity class will be mapped to the wallet_user table. Listing 5-18 shows the updated User entity.

Listing 5-18. shows the User entity extending AbstractEntity

```
@Entity
@Table(name = "WALLET_USER")
public class User extends AbstractEntity {

      @Column(nullable = false)
      private String firstName;
      @Column(nullable = false)
      private String lastName;
      @Column(unique = true, length = 30, nullable = false)
      private String username;
      @Column(precision = 19, scale = 2)
      private BigDecimal totalConversions;
      private LocalDate birthDay;

      @Lob
      @Basic(fetch = FetchType.LAZY)
      private byte[] picture;

      @Enumerated(EnumType.STRING)
      private UserType userType;
      private transient int age;

}
```

The User entity now takes the common fields from the AbstractEntity it extends. The updated database diagram of the wallet_user table is shown in Figure 5-7.

wallet_user	
birthday	date
created	timestamp
createdby	varchar(255)
editedby	varchar(255)
firstname	varchar(255)
lastname	varchar(255)
picture	bytea
totalconversions	numeric(19,2)
updated	timestamp
usertype	varchar(255)
username	varchar(30)
id	bigint

Figure 5-7. *Updated entity diagram*

The structure of the wallet_user table only changed because of the addition of the two new createdBy and editedBy fields. It still looks exactly like it was in Figure 5-6. Though from the database perspective the structure remains the same, from the Java perspective, the code is better organized and easy to read and maintain.

Embeddables

An embeddable is an object that derives its identity from an enclosing object. In JPA, an embeddable is a Java class whose fields are mapped to its enclosing entity's table. Listing 5-19 shows an Address embeddable that can be used by other entities.

Listing 5-19. shows an Address embeddable

```
@Embeddable
public class Address {

     protected String apartment;
     protected String street;
     protected String city;
     protected String state;
     protected String zip;
```

```
    private PhoneType phoneType;
    protected String phone;

    public enum PhoneType {
        MOBILE,
        FIXED,
        VOIP
    }
}
```

The Address embeddable is a POJO with no special annotation or mapping other than the @Embeddable annotation. This annotation signals the runtime that this class will not have an identity of its own, but rather derive such from its embedding entity. Any entity that embeds this Address object will have all its fields mapped to the table of the embedding class. Listing 5-20 shows the User entity embedding the Address class.

Listing 5-20. shows the User embedding Address

```
@Entity
@Table(name = "WALLET_USER")
public class User extends AbstractEntity {

    @Column(nullable = false)
    private String firstName;
    @Column(nullable = false)
    private String lastName;
    @Column(unique = true, length = 30, nullable = false)
    private String username;
    @Column(precision = 19, scale = 2)
    private BigDecimal totalConversions;
    private LocalDate birthDay;
    @Lob
    @Basic(fetch = FetchType.LAZY)
    private byte[] picture;
    @Enumerated(EnumType.STRING)
    private UserType userType;
        private transient int age;
```

```
    @Embedded
    private Address address;

}
```

The User entity embeds the Address through the use of the @Embedded annotation. The wallet_user table will have all the fields of the Address class mapped to it. Figure 5-8 shows the updated wallet_user table.

wallet_user	
birthday	date
created	timestamp
createdby	varchar(255)
editedby	varchar(255)
firstname	varchar(255)
lastname	varchar(255)
picture	bytea
totalconversions	numeric(19,2)
updated	timestamp
usertype	varchar(255)
username	varchar(30)
apartment	varchar(255)
city	varchar(255)
phone	varchar(255)
phonetype	integer
state	varchar(255)
street	varchar(255)
zip	varchar(255)
id	bigint

Figure 5-8. *Updated wallet_user table*

All the Address fields are mapped to the User entity table. Embeddables are another way of organizing code to make it much clearer and easy to read and maintain while taking advantage of SQL's ability to have a lot of columns in a database.

Relationships

JPA is an object-relational mapper. The relation in that name refers to the ability of entities to have some form of relationship with each other. The kinds of relationships or associations that entities can have with each other are generally grouped into four types, namely:

- Many-to-one
- One-to-one
- One-to-many
- Many-to-many

There are two broad types of entity relationships in JPA, namely, single-valued relationships and collection-valued relationships.

Single-Valued Relationships

A single-valued relationship or association is one in which an entity has an association to another entity instance where the cardinality[2] of the target is one. In Java, this association means that one entity has a field of the target entity as one of its properties. In the database, the primary key of the target entity will become a foreign key column in the originating entity table.

Many-to-One

The many-to-one relationship is an association where N number of entities are associated with one of a given target entity. There is always a single target entity from the perspective of the originating entities. Listing 5-21 shows a new entity, TransactionHistory, that saves the transaction history of a User.

[2] Cardinality in Data Modeling | Vertabelo

Listing 5-21. shows the TransactionHistory entity

```
@Entity
public class TransactionHistory extends AbstractEntity {

    private String sourceCurrency;
    private String targetCurrency;
    private String amount;
    private LocalDateTime transactionDate;

    @ManyToOne
    private User accountOwner;

}
```

The TransactionHistory entity has an association with the User entity. This association is a many-to-one, in that many transactions can belong to the same user. The @ManyToOne annotation is used to denote this kind of association. From the perspective of every TransactionHistory instance, there is always a single user. In the database, a foreign key column will be created in the TransactionHistory table that points to the wallet_user table. Listing 5-22 shows the generated DDL for the TransactionHistory entity when mapped to the database.

Listing 5-22. showing the TransactionHistory schema

```
create table if not exists transactionhistory
(
    id              bigint not null primary key,
    amount          varchar(255),
    created         timestamp,
    createdby       varchar(255),
    editedby        varchar(255),
    sourcecurrency  varchar(255),
    targetcurrency  varchar(255),
    transactiondate timestamp,
    updated         timestamp,
```

```
    accountowner_id bigint
        constraint fk_transactionhistory_accountowner_id
            references wallet_user
);
```

The accountOwner_id field is the foreign key column in the TransactionHistory table that references the User entity table. In JPA, the foreign key column is referred to as a join column. Because we did not explicitly specify any name for the join column, the default is the field name followed by an underscore and the name of the primary key column, in this case id. This column can be customized through the use of the @JoinColumn annotation.

In the association shown in Listing 5-21, the TransactionHistory is said to be the owning side of the relationship because the foreign key column is found in its table. Thus, the owning side of an association is one that has the primary key of the target entity as a foreign key column. The @JoinColumn annotation is used on the owning side of the association to customize the foreign key column.

By default, a single-valued relationship is loaded when the originating entity is loaded. This means when an instance of TransactionHistory is fetched from the database, its accountOwner field will be fetched as part of it. This behavior can be customized by passing a FetchType value to the fetch parameter of the @ManyToOne annotation.

The directionality of this example association is unidirectional, meaning only one side knows about the association. The TransactionHistory knows it has a relationship with the User entity. But the User entity is oblivious of any such association. From the perspective of the User entity, it is "single." The other kind of directionality is bidirectional, where both entities know about each other through associations.

One-to-One

A one-to-one association is one in which one entity has an association with another entity. In this case, there is only a single entity from the perspective of either side of the relationship. Listing 5-23 shows a new entity, UserCredentials, with an association to the User entity.

Listing 5-23. shows UserCredentials

```
@Entity
public class UserCredentials extends AbstractEntity {

    @Column(unique = true, length = 30, nullable = false)
    private String email;
    @Column(nullable = false)
    private String password;
    private String salt;

    @OneToOne
    @JoinColumn(name = "wallet_user_id")
    private User user;

}
```

UserCredentials is an entity that contains login credentials for a User. It has a one-to-one association with the User, denoted by the @OnetoOne annotation. It also bears the @JoinColumn annotation to set a custom name for the foreign key column. This implies the UserCredentials is the owning side of the relationship. Listing 5-24 shows the updated User entity (showing only new parts for brevity).

Listing 5-24. shows the updated User entity

```
@Entity
@Table(name = "WALLET_USER")
public class User extends AbstractEntity {

    @OneToOne(mappedBy = "user")
    private UserCredentials userCredentials;

}
```

The User entity also declares an association with the UserCredentials entity, denoted by the @OnetoOne annotation. This annotation here is passed the mappedBy parameter, set to the name of the field of the User type in the target entity, in this case UserCredentials. This denotes that UserCredentials is the owning side of the association. The kind of association between User and UserCredentials is a bidirectional one-to-one mapping or association. Figure 5-9 shows the updated schema diagram for the User and UserCredentials classes.

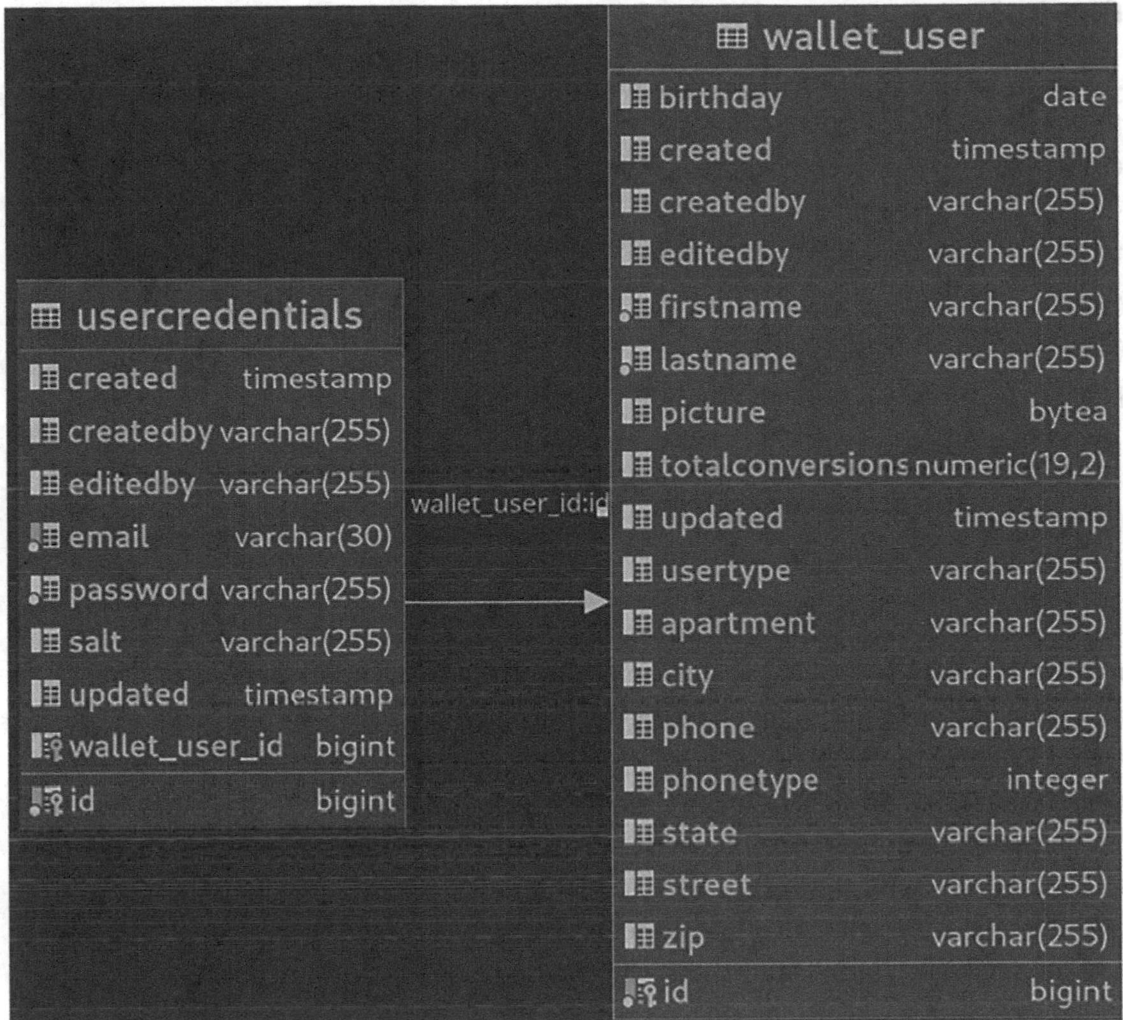

***Figure 5-9.** User and UserCredentials*

Collection-Valued Relationships

Collection-valued relationships or association is where a source entity references one or more instances of the target entity. Unlike the association shown in Listings 5-23 and 5-24 where the source entity targets a single instance of the target entity, collection-valued relationships are modelled with the collection type to represent the N number of target entity instances. The one-to-many and many-to-many are the association types that use collection-valued fields.

One-to-Many

An entity has a one-to-many association with a target entity when it has a collection of the target entity as a field. Listing 5-25 shows the User entity declaring a one-to-many association to transaction history.

Listing 5-25. User entity with one-to-many relationship

```
@Entity
@Table(name = "WALLET_USER")
public class User extends AbstractEntity {

    @OneToMany
    private List<TransactionHistory> transactionHistory;

}
```

A User can have one or more transaction histories. This is denoted by the one-to-many relationship between the User and TransactionHistory entities. This association, as shown in Listing 5-25, is declared by the use of the @OneToMany annotation. The current state of the relationship is bidirectional, because the TransactionHistory also declares an association back to the User entity.

In every one-to-many relationship, the owning side of the association is always the many side. In the case of the User and TransactionHistory, the latter will be the owning side of the relationship because the primary key of the User entity will be placed as a foreign key column in the TransactionHistory table. To declare the many side of the association as the owning side, the mappedBy parameter of the @OneToMany annotation should be set to the name of the field in the TransactionHistory entity, as shown in Listing 5-26.

Listing 5-26. shows the updated User entity

```
@Entity
@Table(name = "WALLET_USER")
public class User extends AbstractEntity {

    @OneToMany(mappedBy = "accountOwner")
    private List<TransactionHistory> transactionHistory;

}
```

In the TransactionHistory table, a foreign key column will contain the primary key of the target entity to which the TransactionHistory history has an association with. The TransactionHistory table will remain unchanged from what it was as shown in Figure 5-9.

A one-to-many association can also be unidirectional from the perspective of the one side of the association. In this case, the target entity type in the collection field of the one side of the association is oblivious to the relationship. In a unidirectional one-to-many relationship, there is only one side, which is also automatically the owning side of the association. Since the association field is a collection type, a join table is used to map the relationship. A join table is a simple table that contains two primary key fields - one to the primary key of the owning or source entity of the association and the other to the target entity.

Many-to-Many

Many-to-many association is one in which both the source and target of the relationship have a collection of each other. The @ManyToMany annotation can be used to express such an association. Many-to-many relationships can also be bi- or unidirectional. Getting this type of relationship right can be tricky, and so except in very complex cases, a one/many-to-one relationship should suffice.

Lazy Fetching

Collection-valued associations are lazily loaded or fetched by default. What this means is that when an instance of the User entity is loaded, its collection field of type TransactionHistory will not be loaded unless it is traversed to in the same transaction. You can change the default loading strategy by setting the fetch parameter of the @OneToMany or @ManyToMany to FetchType.EAGER.

Collections of Simple Types

The collection-valued associations discussed so far have all been between entities. JPA also has support for mapping a collection of simple types. Remember simple types refer to the basic Java types that are not entities, for example, String, Integer, and embeddables. Listing 5-27 shows the UserCredentials entity with a collection of Strings to represent the email history of a user.

Listing 5-27. shows UserCredentials with a collection of simple type

```
@Entity
public class UserCredentials extends AbstractEntity {

    @ElementCollection
    private Set<String> emailHistory;

}
```

The emailHistory field is a set of Strings annotated @ElementCollection. This is a simple type that has no existence of its own. As such, in the database, a table will be created with two fields. One field will be a foreign key column that points to the primary key column of the UserCredentials table and another field that contains the value of each element in the set.

The name of this table, by default, is the name of the declaring entity class underscore the name of the field. So for the field shown in Listing 5-27, the resulting table will be userCredentials_emailHistory. Element collections can also be eagerly fetched. By default, they are lazily fetched. You can set them to be eagerly fetched by passing FetchType.EAGER to the fetch parameter.

Maps

JPA supports declaring entity associations through the use of the java.util.Map construct. A map is a collection that associates a key to any arbitrary object type. There can be any number of combination types of declaring associations using maps based on the key-value type permutation. The value type of a map determines the type of association that is being created. If the value type of the map is an entity, then either a @OneToMany or @ManyToMany association annotation should be used. However, if the value is a simple or embeddable type, then @ElementCollection must be declared.

If the key of the map is a simple or embeddable type, the @MapKeyColumn can be used to customize the key column in the database. If the value of the map is an entity and the key is to be mapped to an attribute of that entity, then the @MapKey annotation can be used to tell the runtime which field in the target value entity the key should be mapped to.

Given the very flexible nature of modelling associations using maps, it can be very hard to get right. A lot of the time, the use of java.util.Collection types should suffice. Unless in very rare and extreme cases where you need the flexibility offered by maps, we do not recommend its use.

Data Persistence

The second of the trio of using JPA involves persisting the data. This is where instances of the entities you modelled get persisted to their respective database tables. The central artifact responsible for taking your entity instances and persisting them to the database is the EntityManager. There are four components to data persistence with JPA that you should understand. These are the persistence unit, persistence context, transactions, and the EntityManager interface.

Persistence Unit

A persistence unit is a logical grouping of a set of entities that share the same configuration. This configuration includes the datasource and other persistence properties such as schema creation. A datasource is simply a connection to a database that can be used by JPA. The persistence unit declares the datasource and the transaction type, along with a set of entities that belong to that persistence unit.

The datasource in Jakarta EE is a managed resource that is mostly defined as part of the server and passed to the persistence unit as a JNDI resource. If schema generation is enabled, then the database user used to create the datasource should have the requisite permissions to create tables in the database. Listing 5-28 shows the persistence unit declaration for the account module of the jwallet application.

Listing 5-28. shows a sample persistence unit

```
<?xml version="1.0" encoding="UTF-8" standalone="yes"?>
<persistence xmlns="https://jakarta.ee/xml/ns/persistence"
             xmlns:xsi="http://www.w3.org/2001/XMLSchema-instance"
             xsi:schemaLocation="https://jakarta.ee/xml/ns/persistence
             https://jakarta.ee/xml/ns/persistence/persistence_3_0.xsd"
             version="3.0">

    <persistence-unit name="jwallet" transaction-type="JTA">
        <jta-data-source>jdbc/jwallet</jta-data-source>
```

```
        <properties>
            <property name="jakarta.persistence.schema-generation.
            database.action" value="create"/>
        </properties>
    </persistence-unit>
</persistence>
```

The persistence unit is named jwallet and declares the transaction type as JTA. The declared datasource is created in the application server. This is one of the flexibilities of JPA. The underlying database could be anywhere in the world; as long as there is a valid datasource that JPA can connect to, it will work. The declared property tells the runtime to create the database tables when the application starts.

This property can be configured to do nothing, drop and create the tables, create or drop the tables. There are properties that can be used to load SQL scripts to populate the database when an application starts. As is, the persistence unit does not explicitly add any entities. This means all entities found in the module will be bound to this persistence unit. This file is put in the resource/META-INF folder of the application.

Persistence Context

A persistence context is akin to an instance of a persistence unit. It is a managed set of entity instances belonging to a given persistence unit. The persistence context is similar to a giant cache of all the entities that are bound to the persistence unit from which the persistence context is created. The persistence context is critical to understanding how JPA works with regard to persisting and loading data. We will look at this shortly when we talk about the entity manager.

Transactions

Methods called on the EntityManager that alter the state of an entity, or the set of entities in the database, require a transaction. In Jakarta EE, transactions are managed on your behalf by the application server. You generally would not worry about transactional boundaries. The container will automatically spawn or join a transaction and commit it when the operation ends.

EntityManager

The EntityManager is an interface that has methods for carrying out create, read, update, and delete operations on JPA entities. It is a managed object in Jakarta EE, meaning you do not explicitly create it. Rather, you request an instance from the JPA runtime which should inject one for you. You can leverage the CDI runtime to inject the EntityManager object as long as you have a producer for it. This construct is discussed in the preceding chapter on Jakarta Contexts and Dependency Injection.

Requesting for an EntityManager instance entails you telling the JPA runtime which persistence unit to associate the given EntityManager with. The returned instance is then bound to that persistence unit, from which a persistence context is created. This persistence context is what the EntityManager will use to manage the CRUD of the entities bound to the persistence unit.

Persisting Entities

Injecting the EntityManager

To persist an entity, we need to first get an instance of the EntityManager. Listing 5-29 shows the BaseRepository class injecting a database-qualified EntityManager (for details of this construct, please refer to Chapter 4).

Listing 5-29. showing injected EntityManager

```
public abstract class BaseRepository<E, K> {

    @Inject
    @Database(POSTGRES)
    EntityManager em;
}
```

The @Inject annotation is a CDI annotation for requesting contextual instances. There is a place where the EntityManager instances are "produced" as shown in Listing 5-30.

Listing 5-30. shows EntityManager production

```
public class ProducerFactory {

    @Produces
    @Database(DB.POSTGRES)
    @PersistenceContext(unitName = "jwallet")
    EntityManager postgres;
}
```

The @PersistenceContext annotation is a JPA construct for requesting EntityManagers. The postgres field will be populated by the JPA runtime with an instance of the EntityManager scoped to the persistence unit. Injection is the recommended way of getting an instance of the EntityManager on the Jakarta EE platform.

Persisting Data

Once you have an entity manager instance, you can invoke methods on it to persist data. The EntityManager#persist method is the primary means of persisting entity instances. It takes an entity instance and persists it in the database. Listing 5-31 shows the save method in BaseRepository for persisting entities.

Listing 5-31. shows BaseRepository

```
public abstract class BaseRepository<E, K> {

    @Inject
    @Database(POSTGRES)
    EntityManager em;

    public E save(E entity) {
        em.persist(entity);
        return entity;
    }
}
```

The BaseRepository is a generic class that takes an entity type and its corresponding primary key type. It contains common CRUD methods to avoid repeating the same for all entities. The em.persist call will cause the entity manager to put the passed entity instance into the persistence context. For simplicity, the persistence context is created when a transactional method starts. Remember the persistence context is sort of an instance of the persistence unit. The BaseRepository is extended by the UserRepository, as shown in Listing 5-32.

Listing 5-32. shows the UserRepository

```
public class UserRepository extends BaseRepository<User, Long> {
    public UserRepository() {
        super(User.class);
    }

}
```

The UserRepository is then injected into the UserService to be used for persisting users. The createUser method of this class takes a CreateUserRequest and delegates to the userRepository as shown in Listing 5-33.

Listing 5-33. shows the UserService persisting users

```
@Action
public class UserService implements UserFacade {

      @Inject
      UserRepository userRepository;

      @Override
      public UserResponse createUser(final
      CreateUserRequest                     createUserRequest) {
            User user = fromUserWrapper(createUserRequest);

            user = userRepository.save(user);
            UserResponse userResponse = getUser(user.getId());
            return userResponse;
      }

}
```

The UserService uses the @Action stereotype to declare a request-scoped transactional bean. Please refer to Chapter 4 for detailed CDI discussion. The @Transactional annotation is a CDI interceptor that will cause a transaction to be created for every method invoked on the UserService. When the save method is called on the userRepository contextual object, the entity manager will persist the passed entity to the persistence context created when the method execution started.

At this point, the entity instance would have its primary key field set, but the instance would still not be in the database. The persistence context contains the instance and all other instances that have any kind of operation performed on them through a method invocation on the entity manager. When the method returns successfully, the container will automatically commit the transaction, and it is at this point that the persistence context will get flushed to the database.

Transaction Rollback

During entity manager operations, errors can occur. A typical example is constraint violation. The User entity we have seen so far has no validation. However, every entity in any application will have some form of validation constraints on its fields based on the business context. On the Jakarta EE platform, the Jakarta Bean Validation specification[3] is the default means of declaring constraints on artifacts. Listing 5-34 shows the updated User entity with validation constraints on its fields.

Listing 5-34. shows constrained User entity

```
@Entity
@Table(name = "WALLET_USER")
public class User extends AbstractEntity {

      @Column(nullable = false)
      @NotEmpty
      private String firstName;

      @Column(nullable = false)
      @NotEmpty
      private String lastName;

      @Column(precision = 19, scale = 2)
      private BigDecimal totalConversions;
```

[3] Jakarta Bean Validation 3.0 Specification

```
    @NotNull
    @Past
    private LocalDate birthDay;

    @Lob
    @Basic(fetch = FetchType.LAZY)
    private byte[] picture;

    @Enumerated(EnumType.STRING)
    private UserType userType;

    @Embedded
    @Valid
    private Address address;

    @OneToOne(mappedBy = "user", cascade = CascadeType.ALL)
    @Valid
    private UserCredentials userCredentials;

    @OneToMany(mappedBy = "accountOwner", cascade = CascadeType.ALL)
    private List<TransactionHistory> transactionHistory =
                                                new ArrayList<>();

    private transient int age;

}
```

A number of the validation constraints are self-explanatory, for instance, @NotNull means the field should not be null. The @Past annotation on the dateOfBirth field requires the set value to be in the past. The @Valid annotation on the Address and UserCredentials tells the runtime to cascade validation to the annotated field type. So when the User entity is being validated, the validation will be cascaded to the two @Valid annotated fields, and their respective fields will also be validated if they have constraint annotations. The constrained UserCredentials entity is shown in Listing 5-35.

Listing 5-35. shows the constrained UserCredentials entity

```
@Entity
public class UserCredentials extends AbstractEntity {

    @Column(unique = true, length = 30, nullable = false)
    @NotEmpty
    @Email
    private String email;

    @Column(nullable = false)
    @NotEmpty
    @Size(min = 8, max = 30)
    private String password;
    private String salt;

    @OneToOne
    @JoinColumn(name = "wallet_user_id")
    private User user;

    @ElementCollection
    private Set<String> emailHistory;

}
```

The @Email annotation on the email field will enforce a valid email constraint for any passed email. The @Size annotation sets the minimum character length of the password to 8 and maximum to 30. The Address entity has similar constraints for the address fields.

When the persist method is called on an EntityManager instance, in this case the save method on the userRepository contextual instance, just before the entity is persisted, the runtime will automatically validate the constraints. This validation is enabled automatically when a bean validation provider is found on the classpath.

If any validation constraint fails, a ConstraintViolationException will be thrown by the bean validation runtime, which will result in a rollback of the transaction. In this case, the transaction will not be committed and will be rolled back. All of this is done by default without you needing to set anything. If there is no exception thrown, the entity gets merged into the persistent context, and when the method exits successfully, the transaction gets committed with it being flushed to the database.

Updating and Removing Data

Persisting entities is done with the persist method on the EntityManager. Updating is equally done with the merge method. Listing 5-36 shows the merge method of the BaseRepository class.

Listing 5-36. shows the merge method in UserRepository

```
public abstract class BaseRepository<E, K> {

    @Inject
    @Database(POSTGRES)
    EntityManager em;
    public E merge(E entity) {
        return em.merge(entity);
    }
}
```

The merge method similarly takes an entity and merges the state of the entity into the currently active persistence context. Similar to persisting, validations will be performed, and if everything works correctly, the persistence context gets flushed when the transaction is committed.

Deleting an entity is done with the remove method of the EntityManager. This method takes an entity instance and removes the entity first from the persistence context. And when the persistence context is merged, the row gets removed.

Cascading Operations

The various association annotations, @OneToOne, @ManyToOne, @OneToMany, and @ManyToMany, have the cascade parameter that can be set to any of the CascadeType enum types. The User entity shown in Listing 5-34 shows the CascadeType.ALL value passed to the @OneToMany association for the TransactionHistory. This means that the persistence runtime should cascade operations on the parent entity, in this case the User entity, to the child entity, in this case TransactionHistory.

So when persisting a user instance, if there are any TransactionHistory instances in the list, these will also get persisted. Effectively, all operations on the parent entity will be cascaded to the child. A lot of the time, the decision to cascade will depend on the business domain.

For instance, a rule of thumb is the direction an association can be traversed. In the User entity, it is natural to traverse from a user to its transaction history. It really would be weird to traverse a history back to its user. For such, it makes sense to cascade operations from the User to its TransactionHistory.

Callback Methods

JPA has callback methods that entities can implement to carry out operations just before a checkpoint operation is executed. The @PrePersist, @PreUpdate, @PostLoad, and @PostRemove are annotations that can be placed on a method either in the entity or in an entity listener to mark as a callback. As the names of the annotations imply, annotating a method with any of them results in the method being called just before the event for which it's listening occurs. Listing 5-37 shows the user entity with a @PostLoad callback method to compute the age of the user.

Listing 5-37. shows the @PostLoad callback

```
@Entity
@Table(name = "WALLET_USER")
public class User extends AbstractEntity {
      private transient int age;

      @PostLoad
      private void computeAge() {
      age = (int) ChronoUnit.YEARS
                        .between(birthDay, LocalDate.now(ZoneOffset.UTC));
      }
}
```

The computeAge method is annotated with @PostLoad, the implementation of which simply calculates the years between today's date and the birthday of the user, setting the transient age field to the result. This method will be called right after the entity is loaded from the database. When a callback method is created within the entity as we have it, the method has access to the fields of the entity. The signature of the callback method within the entity is that it returns void and takes no parameter. The caveat with a callback method within the entity is that you cannot inject any dependency into it.

Entity Listeners

Another way to attach callbacks to entities in JPA is through the use of entity listeners. An entity listener is a class that declares one or more callback methods. This class can then be registered with an entity, and every callback method in the listening class will be called when the listening event occurs for the entity. Listing 5-38 shows an entity listener with two callback methods.

Listing 5-38. shows an entity listener

```
@ApplicationScoped
public class AbstractEntityEntityListener {
      @PrePersist
      void init(final Object entity) {
          final AbstractEntity abstractEntity = (AbstractEntity) entity;
          abstractEntity.setCreated(LocalDateTime.now(ZoneOffset.UTC));
          abstractEntity.setCreatedBy("Dummy User");
      }

      @PreUpdate
      void update(final Object entity) {
          final AbstractEntity abstractEntity = (AbstractEntity) entity;
          abstractEntity.setUpdated(LocalDateTime.now(ZoneOffset.UTC));
          abstractEntity.setEditedBy("Dummy User");
      }

}
```

The AbstractEntityListener is an application-scoped CDI bean that declares two methods annotated @PrePersist and @PreUpdate, respectively. A callback method in an entity listener takes a single parameter of type java.lang.Object. This is because within the entity, the instance is known to be the instance of the declaring entity. But a listener is a separate class, and as such, there needs to be a way to pass the instance on which the event occurred to the method. This is why the method takes an Object.

Within the method implementations, the passed Object type is cast to the AbstractEntity type, and some fields are set on it. An entity listener is also a CDI bean as shown by the @ApplicationScoped annotation. This means we can inject dependencies into it and then carry operations on the entity.

Once an entity listener is declared as done in Listing 5-38, it has to be registered with an entity. Listing 5-39 shows the AbstractEntityEntityListener registered with the Abstract entity.

Listing 5-39. shows registering an entity listener

```
@MappedSuperclass
@EntityListeners({AbstractEntityEntityListener.class})
public abstract class AbstractEntity implements Serializable {

    @Id
    @GeneratedValue(strategy = GenerationType.AUTO)
    protected Long id;

    protected LocalDateTime created;
    protected LocalDateTime updated;

    protected String createdBy;
    protected String editedBy;

}
```

Registering an entity listener on an entity is done through the @EntityListeners annotation. As shown in Listing 5-39, this annotation takes an array of entity listeners and calls them for each registered event. Since the AbstractEntity is just a mapped superclass, this declaration is equivalent to registering the entity listener with each child of the AbstractEntity.

Querying Data

There are two primary ways of querying for data in JPA, namely, the Jakarta Persistence Query Language (JPQL) and the Criteria API. In between these two are a number of overridden find methods on the EntityManager that can be used to directly find an entity based on its primary key.

Finding by Primary Key

The EntityManager has the find method for finding an entity by primary key. This is the simplest way of loading an entity instance if the primary key is known. Listing 5-40 shows the BaseRepository's implementation of finding an entity by its ID in the find method.

Listing 5-40. BaseRepository's find method

```
public abstract class BaseRepository<E, K> {

    @Inject
    @Database(POSTGRES)
    EntityManager em;
    public E findById(K id) {
          return em.find(clazz, id);
    }

}
```

The find method returns the entity instance if found or null. You should keep this in mind when using the find method to load an entity. You should null-check the returned value.

Jakarta Persistence Query Language (JPQL)

The Jakarta Persistence Query Language, otherwise known as JPQL, is a string-based, SQL lookalike language for querying entities. JPQL is very similar to SQL, except instead of querying across database tables and rows, you query across your persistent entities and objects. The JPA runtime takes care of translating the JPQL to the requisite SQL dialect of the underlying database.

JPQL is not a SQL alternative. It is a query language you can use in addition to SQL. It's important to not get bogged down by dogma about which is better. JPQL is well suited to Java developers. Knowing JPQL does not negate the need to know SQL. Both languages complement each other and help you write very sophisticated applications.

The Structure of JPQL

A typical JPQL query is made up of at least a select and from clause, with an optional where and order by clauses. Listing 5-41 shows the simplest JPQL for querying a User entity.

Listing 5-41. Simplest JPQL

```
select u from User  u
```

The first difference between this query and its SQL counterpart is that the JPQL is querying an entity, and not a database table. The User in the query refers to the User entity. This name is the unqualified class name of the User entity. This name can be customized by passing a name parameter to the @Entity annotation, though this is rare in practice. The entity is then aliased to the u variable. The variable u is arbitrary. It could equally have been foo or bazz. In JPQL, an alias variable is mandatory, while it's optional in SQL. The u alias variable can then be used in the rest of the query to reference each entity instance in the database row.

The query also makes a select clause for the User entity. This means the full user entity instance will be returned for each row of the User table. In SQL, you would enumerate the columns of the table you want to query. The runtime takes care of translating this query to the most optimal SQL dialect of the underlying database.

Selecting with Select

The JPQL select clause can take more than an entity. It can take path expressions as well. The final returned type is dependent upon the type passed to the select clause. In the query shown in Listing 5-41, the returned type of the query will be a list of User instances. It is possible to also traverse an entity to one of its properties or even to a different entity. Listing 5-42 shows traversing the User entity to its UserCredentials entity.

Listing 5-42. shows path property traversal

```
select u.userCredentials from User  u
```

The path traversal to the UserCredentials field of the User entity will cause the result list returned from the query to be of type UserCredentials, even though the query started from the User table. It is possible to also traverse simple fields of the entity. Listing 5-43 shows traversing simple properties.

Listing 5-43. shows traversing simple properties

```
select u.lastName, u.lastName, u.userCredentials.email from User  u
```

This query traverses to simple types in the User and UserCredentials entities. The returned type of this query will be zero, or more instances of object arrays will be returned. This is because for such expressions, the final property could be any type, and as such, the runtime returns everything as an array of objects.

At its core, this is very much how the JPQL select clause works. You can select an entity or traverse to a property in that entity or even the property of an entity in the primary entity. The return type of the result will depend on what the type or types passed to the select clause resolve to. If it resolves to a single type, the returned result will be of that type. If it resolves to more than one type, then you get an array of objects.

The From Clause

The FROM clause defines the entity or entities across which the query should span. The queries shown in Listings 5-41 to 5-43 all had the FROM clause declaring the query domain entity and aliasing it to a variable. The FROM clause, however, can also declare more than one entity to query across through JOINS.

The query shown in Listing 5-42 will create an implicit inner join from the User to the UserCredentials table. The query can be rewritten as shown in Listing 5-44.

Listing 5-44. showing explicit join

```
select u.userCredentials from User  u join u.userCredentials c
```

The query now joins the User to the UserCredentials table and aliases the latter to the c variable. These aliased variables can then be used in the where clause. As used, the type of JOIN created is the inner JOIN. The JOIN type can be explicitly declared, but in its absence, it defaults to inner join. You can declare multiple JOINs and alias them all to variables that will be available in the rest of the query context. An outer JOIN can also be created using the LEFT JOIN syntax instead of just JOIN.

Fetch joins can also be used to create joins, but unlike traditional joins, a fetch join does not return the joined entity. A fetch join signals the runtime to eagerly load the fetched entity so when it is accessed from the primary entity, there is no extra database call. Listing 5-45 shows the User entity with a fetch joined query for its transaction history.

Listing 5-45. User entity with fetch join

```
select u from User  u join fetch  u.transactionHistory
```

The fetch join of the transaction history of the user tells the runtime to prefetch the transaction history of each user row. The transactionHistory is declared to be lazily fetched. Within the transaction, with the join fetch in place, when this query is executed, the runtime will not make a second call to the database. The fetch join effectively eagerly fetches the joined entity.

The WHERE Clause

The where clause of a JPQL query is where the results are filtered to only those matching the where criteria. The where clause in JPQL is very similar to the SQL where clause. Listing 5-46 shows the User query restricting the result set to only users with a certain total conversion threshold.

Listing 5-46. shows where for a User query

```
select u.userCredentials from User u
where u.totalConversions >= :totalConversions
```

The where clause uses the aliased variable in the from clause to set a condition. The aliased variable, being an instance of the User entity, can be traversed with the . operator. The where clause traverses the totalConversions field and uses the >= operator to restrict the result. The variable on the right-hand side of the operator is called a named parameter. This is the recommended way to pass variables to JPQL queries. The value will be escaped by the runtime on your behalf for security reasons.

The where clause supports a number of the Java operators like >, <, <=, >=, and the keywords LIKE, IN, IS, EMPTY, BETWEEN, and the NOT for inverting any of the keywords. It also has support for the logical AND that you can use to create logically related conditions. The JPA specification has much more details about using the where[4] clause in your queries.

[4] Jakarta Persistence 3.1 Specification | WHERE Clause

Aggregate Queries

JPQL also has support for aggregate queries. There are five aggregate queries that can be used to create summaries of data. These are AVG, COUNT, MAX, MIN, and SUM. Listing 5-47 shows the count of all Users with total conversions exceeding a passed amount.

Listing 5-47. shows the use of the COUNT aggregate query

```
select COUNT(u) from User u
where u.totalConversions >= :totalConversions
```

The count aggregate function is used in the select clause to count the number of users with total conversions exceeding a passed value. This query will return an integral type denoting the total count.

Executing Queries

After creating queries, they need to be executed. The way to execute JPQL queries is through the EntityManager interface. There are two kinds of JPQL, namely, dynamic and named queries.

Dynamic Queries

Dynamic queries are JPQL queries created directly in a method. These are said to be created on the fly or dynamically because they will be constructed for each call of the method. Listing 5-48 shows the query for loading all Users executed dynamically.

Listing 5-48. shows dynamic query execution

```
public List<User> loadAllUsers() {
        return em.createQuery("select u from User  u", User.class)
                .getResultList();

}
```

The createQuery method is an overloaded method on the entity manager that takes a query, and optionally a type, to which the results should be cast, and then returns a TypedQuery<T> where T is the type passed to the method. If no type is specified in the createQuery method, then a Query is returned. In this case, the result will be untyped.

Generally, we do not recommend the use of the raw Query type. You should pass in a type as long as you know it beforehand.

The returned TypedQuery interface has a number of methods that you can call to get the result of the query. The getResultList, getResultStream, and getSingleResult methods return a typed list of the query result, a typed java.util.stream.Stream interface, or a single result. We recommend avoiding the use of the getSingleResult because it is a little quirky.

Named Queries

The example shown in Listing 5-48 can be transformed into a named query by moving the JPQL to an element on the entity class as shown in Listing 5-49.

Listing 5-49. shows a named query

```
@Entity
@Table(name = "WALLET_USER")
@NamedQuery(name = User.LOAD_ALL_USERS, query = "select u from User  u")
public class User extends AbstractEntity {
public static final String LOAD_ALL_USERS = "User.loadAllUsers";

}
```

Creating a named query entails annotating an entity class with the @NameQuery annotation. This annotation takes the name of the query and the actual JPQL. The example shown in Listing 5-49 shows the User.loadAllUsers query that selects all users from the user entity. Using a named query is just a matter of passing the name of the query to the EntityManager as shown in Listing 5-50.

Listing 5-50. shows using the LOAD_ALL_USERS named query

```
public List<User> loadAllUsers() {
        return em.createNamedQuery(User.LOAD_ALL_USERS, User.class).
        getResultList();
}
```

The createNamedQuery method of the EntityManager interface takes the name of the query and optionally the type. This is practically the only difference between executing a named and dynamic query. The jury is still out on which is much more efficient. Our general recommendation is to use named queries as much as possible because they are easier to read and can be found at one central place, mostly on the entity being queried.

Passing Parameters

The TypedQuery interface has methods to set the parameters of JPQL queries. Listing 5-51 shows the execution of the query that was shown in Listing 5-46.

Listing 5-51. shows passing parameters to queries

```
public List<User> loadUsersByTotalConversion(final BigDecimal
totalConversion) {
    return em.createNamedQuery(LOAD_USERS_BY_CONVERSIONS, User.class)
            .setParameter("totalConversions", totalConversion)
            .getResultList();
}
```

The setParameter method on the returned TypedQuery takes a String representing the named parameter and the value. The passed value will be automatically escaped by the JPA runtime.

JPQL is a powerful but simple query language that complements the use of SQL for application development. The question of when to use JPQL is something we do not have any strong opinions about. In the end, a lot of things come down to technical decisions of the particular domain. A general rule of thumb is to use what is available on the platform as much as possible because doing so makes your application portable across different providers.

Criteria API

The Criteria API is another API for querying entities in JPA. Unlike JPQL, the Criteria API is typesafe but much more verbose. It lends itself better to creating search type queries in applications. JPQL, on the other hand, is much more suited to creating queries that are known beforehand. Listing 5-52 shows the Criteria API equivalent of the JPQL shown in Listing 5-52.

Listing 5-52. shows the Criteria API for getting users

```
public List<User> loadAllUsersCriteria() {

    CriteriaBuilder criteriaBuilder = em.getCriteriaBuilder();
    CriteriaQuery<User> query = criteriaBuilder.createQuery(User.class);
    Root<User> from = query.from(User.class);
    return em.createQuery(query.select(from)).getResultList();

}
```

The Criteria API starts with a call to the getCriteriaBuilder method on the EntityManager. This returns a CriteriaBuilder that is used to build the query. The CriteriaBuilder creates a typed CriteriaQuery with a call to the createQuery method that takes a class. The query then uses the from method to create a typed Root<T> object that acts as the root entity of the query. The query is finally executed by passing the query. select(from) to the createQuery method of the EntityManager. The CriteriaQuery.select method returns yet another CriteriaQuery that is passed to the EntityManager.

As you can see, the Criteria API can be very verbose. A one-line JPQL translated to the Criteria API takes about three. There is also support for passing parameters to the query. The query shown in Listing 5-46 is rewritten using the Criteria API in Listing 5-53.

Listing 5-53. Passing parameters with the Criteria API

```
public List<User> loadUsersByConversionCriteria(final BigDecimal
totalConversion) {

    CriteriaBuilder criteriaBuilder = em.getCriteriaBuilder();
    CriteriaQuery<User> query = criteriaBuilder.createQuery(User.class);
    Root<User> from = query.from(User.class);

    CriteriaQuery<User> where =
        query.select(from).where(
           criteriaBuilder.greaterThanOrEqualTo(
              from.get("totalConversions"),totalConversion));
    return em.createQuery(where).getResultList();

}
```

The Criteria API has methods for all the keywords we saw with JPQL such as the where clause. The query.select method returns a CriteriaQuery on which the where method is called to set the predicate for the query. The CriteriaBuilder has methods representing the various operators available in JPQL such as greaterThanOrEqualTo as used earlier. To access a field of the entity, the get() is called on the Root object and passed the name of the field.

The Criteria API lends itself much better to creating search type queries. Listing 5-54 shows a simple search for a user based on the passed search object.

Listing 5-54. shows Criteria API search

```
public List<User> searchUsers(final UserSearchRequest searchRequest) {

   CriteriaBuilder criteriaBuilder = em.getCriteriaBuilder();
   CriteriaQuery<User> query = criteriaBuilder.createQuery(User.class);
   Root<User> from = query.from(User.class);
   final Set<Predicate> predicateSet = new HashSet<>();
   if (searchRequest.getFirstName() != null) {
     Predicate firstName = criteriaBuilder
       .like(from.get("firstName"),
                         "%" + searchRequest.getFirstName() + "%");
     predicateSet.add(firstName);
   }
   if (searchRequest.getLastName() != null) {
     Predicate lastName = criteriaBuilder
       .like(from.get("lastName"),
                         "%" + searchRequest.getLastName() + "%");
     predicateSet.add(lastName);
   }

   if (searchRequest.getTotalConversions() != null) {
     Predicate totalConversions = criteriaBuilder
       .greaterThanOrEqualTo(from.get("totalConversions"),
                              searchRequest.getTotalConversions());
     predicateSet.add(totalConversions);
   }
```

```
    if (searchRequest.getUserType() != null) {
      Predicate userType = criteriaBuilder
        .equal(from.get("userType"), searchRequest.getUserType());
      predicateSet.add(userType);
    }

   CriteriaQuery<User> where = query
       .select(from).where(predicateSet.toArray(new Predicate[] {}));
   return em.createQuery(where).getResultList();

}
```

The method takes a UserSearchRequest object that contains some fields of the User entity. It then traverses each field, checking if it's not null and then creating a jakarta.persistence.criteria.Predicate object from it. These predicates are added to a set that is then converted to an array and passed to the where method on the CriteriaQuery. This is a very simple search implementation using the Criteria API. Because of its dynamic nature, it is well suited to this kind of use. The Jakarta Persistence specification has much details on the Criteria API in the relevant section.[5]

Summary

In this chapter, we discussed the Jakarta Persistence API,[6] the standards-based object-relational mapping API for bridging the object-relational divide. We looked at the three broad components of data handling, namely, modelling which entailed creating entities and organizing their interrelationships; data persistence, where we actually put the data into the database; and querying data, which entailed getting the data out of the database.

The Jakarta Persistence API is a very complex and extensive specification. The goal of this chapter has been to introduce you to the API in the hopes that you can better continue your study of the specification on your own. With what you have learned in this chapter, pursuing the specification should be easy and straightforward.

---

[5] Jakarta Persistence 3.1 Specification | Criteria API

[6] Jakarta Persistence 3.1 Specification (Spec document)

CHAPTER 6

REST with Jakarta EE REST API

The REpresentational State Transfer or REST architecture is a stateless, HTTP-based communication standard for modern applications. Originally proposed by Dr. Roy Fielding in his PhD thesis,[1] it is the de facto means of enabling simple, stateless, predictable, fast, and representation-based communication between applications written in different languages and frameworks. An application written in the Django framework in Python can have REST resources that are consumed by another application written in Java with Jakarta EE. Similarly, a Jakarta EE application can create resources that can be consumed by a C# application.

REST resource consuming clients do not always have to be external applications. A single application written as a collection of microservices will use the REST architecture as a way for the different services to communicate with each other. As a platform-agnostic communication means, the HTTP protocol allows the implementation of REST resources to be completely abstracted from the client.

The Jakarta RESTful Web Services specification[2] is the Jakarta EE standard for creating REST web services on the platform. The specification defines a number of interfaces and annotations for creating sophisticated web services in combination with other Jakarta EE specifications like the Jakarta Contexts and Dependency Injection.

This chapter introduces you to the Jakarta RESTful Web Services specification. You will learn how to create different types of web resources using the very simple set of API constructs from the specification, along with how it integrates with other Jakarta EE specifications to create a cohesive platform for developing modern applications.

[1] Architectural Styles and the Design of Network-based Software Architectures | Roy Thomas Fielding

[2] Jakarta RESTful Web Services 3.1 | Specification

L. Saeed and G. Abdallah, *Pro Cloud Native Java EE Apps*, https://doi.org/10.1007/978-1-4842-8900-6_6

The chapter will also take a look at the Eclipse MicroProfile REST client for consuming REST resources in a typesafe way. By the end of this chapter, you will have a solid foundation in creating web services on Jakarta EE and using the Eclipse MicroProfile Client.

Modelling REST Services

REST web services are called resources because they represent application resources. The actual resource being represented is domain specific. Designing REST web services to expose resources to consuming clients entails crafting the web resources along the lines of what operations can be carried out on a given resource. As the REST architecture is based on HTTP, resources are exposed as HTTP paths. Identifying what operations can be carried out on a resource can clarify what HTTP paths those operations can be exposed on.

Once the set of operations and their corresponding HTTP paths are identified, then the application data format would also need to be considered. As HTTP is language agnostic, it can be used to expose resources in any number of formats including JSON, XML, and plain text. This is important because different clients will want the same resource in different formats. The issue of resource format, however, is becoming less of a major consideration because the JSON format has emerged as the lingua franca of the Web. Thus, it is mostly the default format for exposing resources over HTTP. That notwithstanding, the issue of resource formats merits consideration especially when the resources are being exposed to different clients.

With the application paths and data format considered, the next step is to map HTTP methods[3] to the identified paths. This step entails mapping the right HTTP method to each corresponding action that can be performed on the resource in question.

The User Resource

Let us model a REST resource for the User entity looked at extensively in the previous chapter on Jakarta Persistence. For our User resource, we want to allow a client to create, update, find a user by an ID, get all users, search a user, find all users with a certain total conversion threshold, and finally remove a user. Table 6-1 shows the various actions mapped to HTTP paths and their corresponding HTTP methods.

[3] HTTP Methods | Mozilla

***Table 6-1.** shows the possible mappings for UserResource*

Action	HTTP Path	Return Type	HTTP Method
Create a user	/users	Created user	POST
Update a user	/users	Updated user	PUT
Find a user by id	/users/<userId>	The user or an exception	GET
Get all users	/users	List of users	GET
Search users	/users/search	List of users	GET
Find users by conversion	/users/<threshold>	List of users	GET
Delete a user	/users	Void	DELETE

The table shows the mapping between the actions that can be carried out on a user resource and the corresponding HTTP paths and methods. Naming resource methods requires adhering to general good REST practices.[4] Because resources are consumed through the HTTP standard which is itself language or platform agnostic, it is important to name resources in a way that is intuitive, simple, and consistent. Table 6-1 will serve as the discussion context for the rest of the chapter.

Jakarta REST Resources

For ease of application maintenance, REST resources should be organized in a hierarchical manner. Oftentimes, an application will have a base path where all other resource paths are accessed relative to. For instance, the currency conversion API from `https://api.apilayer.com/currency_data` has all the currency conversion resource methods hosted relative to the currency_data path. This can be said to be the root application path or root resource for the currency conversion API from apilayer.com.

[4] RESTful web API design | Microsoft

The Root Resource

In Jakarta REST, the root resource is defined as a subclass of the jakarta.ws.rs.core.Application class. Listing 6-1 shows the root resource declaration for the jwallet application.

Listing 6-1. shows the root resource declaration

```
@ApplicationPath("api")
public class RootResourceConfiguration extends Application {
}
```

The root resource class is declared as a subclass of the Application class. This class contains three methods that can be overridden to explicitly register resource classes, extensions, and properties. Most of the time, you would not need to override these methods as done in Listing 6-1.

The class is annotated @ApplicationPath and passed the value "api." This annotation defines the root resource for the application. All resources in the application will be accessed through the base or root path /api.

A Jakarta REST Resource

A REST resource in Jakarta REST is defined as a Java class. This class will have a path that matches an HTTP path. The class then is said to be hosted at that path. Listing 6-2 introduces the UserResource to implement the various resources identified in Table 6-1.

Listing 6-2. shows the first UserResource class

```
@Consumes(MediaType.APPLICATION_JSON)
@Produces(MediaType.APPLICATION_JSON)
@Path("users")
public class UserResource {

    @Inject
    UserService userService;
}
```

The UserResource class is a POJO with a number of Jakarta REST annotations. These annotations transform this POJO into a REST HTTP resource even though we are yet to add to any resource methods. The @Consumes and @Produces annotations both determine the Multipurpose Internet Mail Extensions (MIME[5]) media type that the methods in the resource class can consume and produce. As JSON is the most popular data exchange format across the Web and within microservices applications, the constant MediaType.APPLICATION_JSON is passed to both annotations. This constant is a String with the value application/json.

The @Path annotation is passed the value "users," designating this class as hosted at the path /api/users. This annotation takes a value that denotes the HTTP resource path at which the annotated object will be hosted. Remember the root or base path is set as "api" through the @ApplicationPath on the RootResourceConfiguration class as shown in Listing 6-1. The declaration shown in Listing 6-2 creates a resource at the path /api/users that when accessed by a client will cause the Jakarta REST runtime to instantiate an instance of the UserResource to serve the request.

The runtime is able to map the /users to be hosted at the base path /api because in the RootResourceConfiguration, the getClasses method is not overridden. This means, by default, all resource classes will be scanned and added as child resources of this root resource.

HTTP Methods

With the resource class in place, we can start implementing the HTTP methods shown in Table 6-1. A resource method in Jakarta REST is a Java method annotated with any of the requisite annotations denoting the HTTP method the Java method responds to. There are seven annotations that map to the corresponding HTTP methods for creating resource methods. These are @POST, @GET, @PUT, @DELETE, @PATCH, @HEAD, and @OPTIONS.

@POST

The @POST annotation on a resource class method denotes the method as responding to HTTP POST requests. Listing 6-3 shows the createUser method in the UserResource class annotated @POST.

[5] MIME types | Mozilla

Listing 6-3. shows the @POST method

```
@Consumes(MediaType.APPLICATION_JSON)
@Produces(MediaType.APPLICATION_JSON)
@Path("users")
public class UserResource {

    @Inject
    UserService userService;

    @POST
    public UserResponse createUser(CreateUserRequest createUserRequest) {
        return userService.createUser(createUserRequest);
    }

}
```

The createUser method is annotated @POST, meaning it responds to HTTP POST requests. In the absence of any explicit @Path annotation, this method will be hosted at /api/users path. A POST request to that path will cause the runtime to invoke the createUser method on an instance of the UserResource class. So far, everything is pure Java with a few annotations. The method consumes a strongly typed Java class, the CreateUserRequest.

The @Consumes annotation at the class level means that the createUser method consumes JSON. By consuming JSON, we mean the client will post a JSON representation of the Java type that the method consumes, in this case the CreateUserRequest. When the runtime matches the client request to this method, the request body, in this case JSON string, will be passed to an artifact called a message body reader.

Message Body Readers

A message body reader is an instance of the parameterized jakarta.ws.rs.ext. MessageBodyReader<T> interface that takes the InputStream of a MediaType and converts it to T, where T is some Java type. Each message body reader is associated with a single MediaType whose InputStream it can transform into a Java type. The runtime ships with a number of message body readers for the popular MediaTypes. You do not need to provide an instance of the MessageBodyReader unless you want to customize the conversion process.

Message Body Writers

A message body writer is the opposite of a message body reader in that it takes a Java type and converts it to the type represented by the MediaType it is associated with. The message body writer takes the Java type instance and writes it to the output stream that is returned to the client. Similar to the body reader, you generally will only provide your own custom writer implementation when you need to do some customization of the process. The UserResponse object returned by the createUser method will equally be transformed into JSON and written to the output stream of the response sent to the client.

The HTTP request shown in Listing 6-4 will be mapped to the CreateUserRequest Java type automatically by the automatically provisioned message body reader.

Listing 6-4. shows a sample POST request

```
POST http://localhost:3003/account/api/users
Content-Type: application/json

{
        "firstName":"John",
        "lastName":"Jakes",
        "email":"a@b.com",
        "userRegion":"AFRICA",
        "birthDay":"08-02-1975",
        "password":"_myStrong_pswd&^_I"
}
```

The JSON in the request body will be mapped to the CreateUserRequest shown in Listing 6-5.

Listing 6-5. shows the CreateUserRequest

```
public class CreateUserRequest {

    private String firstName;
    private String lastName;
    private String email;
```

```
    private LocalDate birthDay;
    private UserRegion userRegion;
    private String password;

}
```

The actual implementation of the resource method is completely business specific. The REST runtime will transform the request body to the method parameter and hand it over to you. As declared in Listing 6-3, if the client passes no method body or an empty string, the method parameter will be null. This means you will have to do null-check on the passed value. To prevent this, the REST spec integrates with the Jakarta Bean Validation specification to allow declarative validation.

Validating Resources

As discussed in the previous chapter on persisting data with Jakarta Persistence, the Bean Validation API is a set of annotations and interfaces that you can use to constrain values to only what an application requires. To prevent the client from passing null or invalid values for user creation, Listing 6-6 shows the createUser method with some validation constraints.

Listing 6-6. shows bean validation

```
@Consumes(MediaType.APPLICATION_JSON)
@Produces(MediaType.APPLICATION_JSON)
@Path("users")
public class UserResource {

    @Inject
    UserService userService;

    @POST
    public UserResponse createUser(@NotNull @Valid  CreateUserRequest
    createUserRequest) {

        return userService.createUser(createUserRequest);
    }

}
```

The two constraint annotations, @NotNull and @Valid, will cause the method parameter to be validated. It first will validate that the converted POST body is not null. Then it will cause a recursive validation of the converted object. In this case, all constraint validations on the CreateUserRequest will be validated. The method body will only be executed when there is no validation exception. If there is a validation exception resulting from a constraint violation, the REST runtime will send HTTP 400 (Bad Request) to the client. The CreateUserRequest is shown in Listing 6-7 with validation constraints.

Listing 6-7. shows updated CreateUserRequest

```
public class CreateUserRequest {

    @NotEmpty
    private String firstName;

    @NotEmpty
    private String lastName;

    @NotEmpty
    @Email
    private String email;

    @NotNull
    @Past
    private LocalDate birthDay;

    private UserRegion userRegion;
    @NotEmpty
    @Size(min = 8, max = 30)
    private String password;

}
```

Because the createUser method did not explicitly declare any resource paths with the @Path annotation as done on its class, the runtime will know to call it when a POST request is made to the parent /users path as declared by the @Path annotation on the class. Only one each of the HTTP methods is allowed to be hosted in a class without an explicit @Path annotation. If we declare another @POST method without a @Path annotation in the same UserResource class, this will be an error.

A sample POST request to the /users path with valid data as shown in Listing 6-4 returns the JSON data shown in Listing 6-8.

Listing 6-8. shows a successful call to the /users resource

```
http://localhost:3003/account/api/users
HTTP/1.1 200 OK
Content-Type: application/json
Content-Language: en-US
Content-Length: 114
Date: Fri, 26 Aug 2022 17:08:13 GMT

{
      "data": {
            "firstName": "John",
            "lastName": "Jakes",
            "userId": 5
      },
      "response": {
            "responseCode": "0",
            "responseMessage": "OK"
      }
}
```

The response header generated by the Jakarta REST runtime contains some metadata about the response. It tells us the HTTP version used, the response code, which in this successful invocation is 200. The returned JSON in the response body is a representation of the UserResponse object returned by the createUser method. Listing 6-9 shows the UserResponse object.

Listing 6-9. shows the UserResponse class

```
public class UserResponse extends Response<UserResponse.UserResponseData> {
  public static UserResponse of(UserResponseData data) {
    UserResponse userResponse = new UserResponse();
    userResponse.setData(data);
```

```
    return userResponse;
  }

  @Getter
  @Setter
  public static class UserResponseData {

    private Long userId;
    private String firstName;
    private String lastName;
    private String username;

  }
}
```

The call to the /users resource method with the request shown in Listing 6-10 will result in an HTTP response code 400 because the data is not correct. As the request object is being validated with the @Valid and @NotNull annotations, the runtime will automatically validate the request and return the appropriate response.

Listing 6-10. Calling /users with bad data

```
POST http://localhost:3003/account/api/users
Content-Type: application/json

{
     "firstName":"John",
     "lastName":"Jakes",
     "userRegion":"AFRICA",
     "birthDay":"08-02-1975",
     "password":"_myStrong_pswd&^_I"
}
```

The request data misses the email field, which is annotated @NotEmpty in the CreateUserRequest. The preceding call results in the response shown in Listing 6-11.

Listing 6-11. Response data

```
http://localhost:3003/account/api/users

HTTP/1.1 400 Bad Request
Content-Type: text/plain;charset=UTF-8
validation-exception: true
Content-Language: en-US
Content-Length: 60
Connection: Close
Date: Fri, 26 Aug 2022 17:35:41 GMT
```

This is automatic and only requires you to annotate your fields with the relevant Jakarta Bean Validation annotations. A POST method does not necessarily need to return data. The createUser method could as well return void. What a resource method returns is a business domain decision that will be made on a case-by-case basis.

@GET

Creating a method that responds to the HTTP GET request entails annotating a Java method with the @GET annotation. There are four GET requests in the list of resource methods shown in Table 6-1. Three of those return collections of users. When you have such similar return types for different resource methods, it is an indicator to refactor the endpoints to simplify them.

Looking again at Table 6-1, the endpoint to search for users and to filter users by total conversions can be combined into one. So the search endpoint supports filtering or searching for users by total currency conversions. This way, the search endpoint can be expanded such that you can filter by conversions based on a predicate like greater than or equal to, less than or equal to, and such. With this new approach, we end up with three GET requests: one for getting a user by ID, one for getting all users, and another for searching. Listing 6-12 shows the first attempt at crafting the GET requests for the UserResource.

Listing 6-12. GET requests for users

```
@Consumes(MediaType.APPLICATION_JSON)
@Produces(MediaType.APPLICATION_JSON)
@Path("users")
```

```
public class UserResource{

  @Inject
  UserService userService;

  @GET
  @Path("{userId}")
  public UserResponse getUser(@PathParam("userId") Long userId) {
    return userService.getUser(userId);
  }

  @GET
  @Path("search")
  public List<UserResponse> searchUsers(@NotNull @BeanParam
  UserSearchRequest userSearchRequest) {
    return userService.searchUsers(userSearchRequest);
  }

  @GET
  public List<UserResponse> getAllUsers() {
    return userService.getAllUsers();
  }

}
```

@PathParam

The getUser method takes the java.lang.Long type. This parameter is annotated @PathParam. The value passed to the @PathParam annotation is the same value passed to the @Path annotation of the method. The @Path annotation value, however, is surrounded by curly braces. This is one way a variable in a resource path or path segment is captured in Jakarta REST. The {userId} is a variable that will be substituted at runtime with the actual value passed. The @PathParam grabs the value and injects it into the userId method parameter. The path /api/users/1 will be matched to this method.

The path parameter doesn't have to be one. A resource path can have /{param1}/{param2}/{param3} or any such combination. Just keep in mind that if you use the same variable twice, the last match wins. So if you have /{same}/{same}, and you inject the variable with @PathParam("same"), the path /foo/bazz will have the value bazz injected for all instances of @PathParam("same"). Keep this in mind when creating resource paths. The @Path annotation also supports the use of regular expressions to limit the set of characters that can be passed as the path. The method parameter can also be further constrained with @NotNull.

Similar to the POST method, the returned type will be automatically marshalled to the JSON representation and returned to the client as such. Because the class is annotated @Produces("application/json"), all returned types will be automatically transformed to JSON.

@BeanParam and @QueryParam

The searchUsers resource method is hosted at the /api/users/search path. This method takes a UserSearchRequest object and returns a list of UserResponses. The method parameter is annotated @BeanParam, which is used for aggregating resource parameters into the annotated object. Listing 6-13 shows the annotated UserSearchRequest class.

Listing 6-13. UserSearchRequest

```
public class UserSearchRequest implements Serializable {

  @QueryParam("firstName")
  private String firstName;

  @QueryParam("lastName")
  private String lastName;

  @QueryParam("totalConversions")
  private BigDecimal totalConversions;

  @QueryParam("conversionFilter")
  private ConversionFilter conversionFilter = ConversionFilter.EQ;

  @QueryParam("userType")
  private UserType userType;

  public enum ConversionFilter {
    GT,
    GTE,
    LT,
    LTE,
```

```
    EQ,
    NEQ
  }

}
```

The UserSearchRequest class has its fields annotated @QueryParam. This annotation binds the value of the passed HTTP query parameter name to the annotated field. It can also be used on method parameters, similar to @PathParam. As used in Listing 6-13, with the @BeanParam annotation annotating the method parameter, the runtime will grab all query parameters for the search resources and inject them into an instance of this class, passing that instance to the method.

For example, the HTTP GET request /api/users/search?firstName=Joe&conversionFilter=GTE will cause an instance of UserSearchRequest to be created and the field firstName set to Joe and the conversionFilter field set to GTE. @BeanParam is a very powerful annotation for creating search type resources because instead of having many method parameters, you can abstract all possible query parameters into an object as we have done with the searchUsers method.

In simple cases, this search resource should be enough. But, when returning a list, you might have very large datasets that instead of returning all at a go, it would be much more efficient for both client and server to page. Pagination would require that the client be given the option to pass a limit, that is, the maximum data to return per page, and an offset. The returned information would also include some metadata about the searched dataset, for instance, the total number of elements in the set. Listing 6-14 shows the UserSearchRequest updated to give the client the option to page.

Listing 6-14. Updated UserSearchRequest

```
public class UserSearchRequest implements Serializable {

  @QueryParam("firstName")
  private String firstName;

  @QueryParam("lastName")
  private String lastName;
  @QueryParam("totalConversions")
  private BigDecimal totalConversions;
  @QueryParam("conversionFilter")
```

```
    private ConversionFilter conversionFilter = ConversionFilter.EQ;
    @QueryParam("userType")
    private UserType userType;

    @QueryParam("limit")
    @DefaultValue("150")
    @Positive
    private Integer limit;

    @QueryParam("offset")
    @DefaultValue("0")
    private Integer offset;

    public enum ConversionFilter {
        GT,
        GTE,
        LT,
        LTE,
        EQ,
        NEQ
    }
}
```

@DefaultValue

The limit and offset fields are also query parameters that we expect to be grabbed from the request and injected into the respective fields. The @DefaultValue on both fields sets a default value in the absence of any explicit value set by the client. This means that if there is no limit and offset values passed as query parameters, the instantiated class instance will have the limit field set to 150 and the offset field set to 0. The limit field is also annotated @Positive, which is a bean validation constraint that constrains the possible values of the field to a positive integer.

We have refactored the UserSearchRequest without changing anything in our resource method at all. This is why we recommend the use of the @BeanParam annotation when dealing with query parameters. With the paging option created, we can now refactor the returned type to also contain some metadata that the client uses in creating a meaningful paging request. Listing 6-15 shows a new parameterized class, SearchResult, with some metadata.

Listing 6-15. SearchResult

```
public class SearchResult<T> implements Serializable {
      private List<T> searchResult = new ArrayList<>();

      private Long totalSize;
      private Long offset;
      private Long limit;
}
```

SearchResult takes a type and binds that type to the searchResult list. This list will contain the actual search result. The totalSize field refers to the total size of the matched search request. The offset and limit simply return what the client passed, if any. With this new construct, we can refactor the searchUsers resource method to return a SearchResult object typed to UserResponse. Listing 6-16 shows the updated resource method.

Listing 6-16. Updated searchUsers resource method

```
@GET
@Path("search")
public SearchResult<UserResponse> searchUsers(@NotNull @BeanParam
UserSearchRequest userSearchRequest) {
    return userService.searchUsers(userSearchRequest);
}
```

Listing 6-17 shows the full search implementation in the UserRepository using the Criteria API of the Jakarta Persistence specification. As discussed in the previous chapter, the Criteria API is better suited to such application search cases.

Listing 6-17. Search user implementation with the Criteria API

```
public SearchResult<UserResponse> searchUsers(final UserSearchRequest
searchRequest) {
    CriteriaBuilder criteriaBuilder = em.getCriteriaBuilder();
    CriteriaQuery<User> query = criteriaBuilder.createQuery(User.class);
    Root<User> from = query.from(User.class);
```

```
final Set<Predicate> predicateSet = new HashSet<>();

if (searchRequest.getFirstName() != null) {
  Predicate firstName = criteriaBuilder.like(from.get("firstName"), "%"
  + searchRequest.getFirstName() + "%");
  predicateSet.add(firstName);

}
if (searchRequest.getLastName() != null) {
  Predicate lastName = criteriaBuilder.like(from.get("lastName"), "%" +
  searchRequest.getLastName() + "%");
  predicateSet.add(lastName);

}
if (searchRequest.getTotalConversions() != null) {
  if (searchRequest.getConversionFilter() == UserSearchRequest.
  ConversionFilter.EQ) {
    predicateSet.add(criteriaBuilder.equal(from.
    get("totalConversions"),
        searchRequest.getTotalConversions()));
  }
  if (searchRequest.getConversionFilter() == UserSearchRequest.
  ConversionFilter.GT) {
    predicateSet.add(criteriaBuilder.greaterThan(from.
    get("totalConversions"),
        searchRequest.getTotalConversions()));
  }
  if (searchRequest.getConversionFilter() == UserSearchRequest.
  ConversionFilter.GTE) {
    predicateSet.add(criteriaBuilder.greaterThanOrEqualTo(from.
    get("totalConversions"),
        searchRequest.getTotalConversions()));
  }

  if (searchRequest.getConversionFilter() == UserSearchRequest.
  ConversionFilter.LT) {
```

```
      predicateSet.add(criteriaBuilder.lessThan(from.
      get("totalConversions"),
          searchRequest.getTotalConversions()));
    }
    if (searchRequest.getConversionFilter() == UserSearchRequest.
    ConversionFilter.LTE) {
      predicateSet.add(criteriaBuilder.lessThanOrEqualTo(from.
      get("totalConversions"),
          searchRequest.getTotalConversions()));
    }

    if (searchRequest.getConversionFilter() == UserSearchRequest.
    ConversionFilter.NEQ) {
      predicateSet.add(criteriaBuilder.notEqual(from.
      get("totalConversions"),
          searchRequest.getTotalConversions()));
    }
  }

  if (searchRequest.getUserType() != null) {
    Predicate userType = criteriaBuilder.equal(from.get("userType"),
    searchRequest.getUserType());
    predicateSet.add(userType);
  }

  CriteriaQuery<User> where = query.select(from).where(predicateSet.
  toArray(new Predicate[] {}));
  TypedQuery<User> typedQuery = em.createQuery(where);
  if (searchRequest.getOffset() != null) {
    typedQuery = typedQuery.setFirstResult(searchRequest.getOffset());
  }
  if (searchRequest.getLimit() != null) {
    typedQuery = typedQuery.setMaxResults(searchRequest.getLimit());
  }
  List<UserResponse> response =
      typedQuery.getResultList().stream().map(UserService:
      :toUserResponse).collect(Collectors.toList());
```

```
    SearchResult<UserResponse> searchResult = new SearchResult<>();
    searchResult.setSearchResult(response);

    CriteriaQuery<Long> countQuery = criteriaBuilder.
    createQuery(Long.class);
    Root<User> userCountRoot = countQuery.from(User.class);
    countQuery.select(criteriaBuilder.countDistinct(userCountRoot.
    get("id")))
        .where(predicateSet.toArray(new Predicate[] {}));
    Long count = em.createQuery(countQuery).getSingleResult();

    searchResult.setTotalSize(count);
    searchResult.setLimit(Long.valueOf(searchRequest.getLimit()));
    searchResult.setOffset(searchResult.getOffset());

    return searchResult;

}
```

As discussed in the previous chapter, the Criteria API can be very verbose and unwieldy. However, it is the best tool for these kinds of database queries. You generally will break the search implementation query down into smaller methods. They are only reproduced here as one large body for ease of reference.

With the search method implemented, complete with pagination, we need to make an architectural decision about the last GET method. This method simply returns all the users in the system. But do we really need it? As the search resource method also returns a similar result, we can decide to remove the last GET method because it is almost redundant. You can search for a collection of users which will return a list. Having an endpoint that returns all users will also require paging for better performance. Since this is already implemented in the searchUsers endpoint, we can omit the final GET method from an architectural point of view.

@PUT

The @PUT method is used to create or update a resource. The general pattern is to use @POST for creating and @PUT for updating. We will stick to this convention. So @PUT is used to update a user. Listing 6-18 shows the @PUT method in the UserResource class.

Listing 6-18. @PUT method

```
@Consumes(MediaType.APPLICATION_JSON)
@Produces(MediaType.APPLICATION_JSON)
@Path("users")
public class UserResource {

     @Inject
     UserService userService;
     @PUT
     public UserResponse updateUser(@NotNull UpdateUserRequest
     updateUserRequest) {
     return       userService.updateUser(updateUserRequest);
     }
}
```

As this method does not explicitly declare any @Path param, it will be hosted at the root /users path. An HTTP PUT request to /api/users will be matched to this method. The method parameter is annotated @NotNull because we do not want the client to pass null. But the actual UpdateUserRequest does not declare any constraint validation. Listing 6-19 shows the UpdateUserRequest.

Listing 6-19. UpdateUserRequest

```
public class UpdateUserRequest implements Serializable {
  private Long userId;
  private String firstName;

  private String lastName;

  @JsonbDateFormat("dd-MM-yyyy")
  private LocalDate birthDay;

  private CreateUserRequest.UserRegion userRegion;
}
```

This class only allows the updating of select fields of a user. This is because in application development, you will often have some entity fields that impact a lot of other parts of the application. For instance, the user email might be linked to other artifacts that the user owns. Allowing ad hoc updating of such a field could cause data corruption. Such core fields are generally updated in more complex ways like through the use of business processes. This way, all other places that the field is used get updated in a single shot. This is why architecturally, and from a business perspective, the UpdateUserRequest allows updating of only select fields.

The @JsonbDateFormat annotation on the birthDay field is used to set the date format of the passed value. This annotation is from the Jakarta JSON Binding specification,[6] an API for converting JSON to and from Java. This specification is the default underlying provider for marshalling the response types to JSON. The annotation takes the same date formats as the DateTimeFormatter in the java.time package.

@DELETE

The @DELETE method is used to create a resource method that responds to the HTTP DELETE method. Similar to updating certain fields, deleting a resource is a very serious operation that must be carried out in a controlled, well-thought-out way. In enterprise applications, deleting resources requires a business process that ensures all places where the resource to be deleted is used are taken care of. However, for the sake of completeness, a @DELETE method is shown in Listing 6-20.

Listing 6-20. @DELETE method

```
@DELETE
public void deleteUser(@NotNull @Positive Long userId) {
    userService.removeUser(userId);

}
```

The Response Object

The resource methods seen so far have all directly returned Java types which are then marshalled to JSON. The jakarta.ws.rs.core.Response object can be used to provide custom metadata to the client. Listing 6-21 shows the createUser resource method refactored to return a custom Response object containing the path to the newly created entity.

[6] Jakarta JSON Binding | Specification

Listing 6-21. Returning a Response object

```
@POST
public Response createUser(@NotNull @Valid CreateUserRequest
createUserRequest, @Context UriInfo uriInfo) {
    UserResponse user = userService.createUser(createUserRequest);
    URI uri = uriInfo.getAbsolutePathBuilder()
                    .path(user.getData().getUserId().toString())
                    .build();
    return Response.created(uri).entity(user).build();
}
```

The createUser method now takes two parameters. The second one is the UriInfo that is injected into the variable uriInfo through the use of the @Context annotation. This annotation is used to inject Jakarta REST artifacts into fields and method parameters. The UriInfo interface contains methods for getting information about the current request URI. The createUser implementation first saves the passed user and then builds a path to the location of the newly created user.

Remember in Table 6-1, we set the path to getting a user by ID to /api/users/{userId}. The URI info instance calls the getAbsolutePathBuilder method which returns the full path to the current resource class, then appends the newly created user ID to it. Listing 6-22 shows the returned response when a POST request like shown in Listing 6-4 is made.

Listing 6-22. Returned custom Response object

```
http://localhost:3003/account/api/users

HTTP/1.1 201 Created
Content-Type: application/json
Location: http://localhost:3003/account/api/users/1
Content-Language: en-US
Content-Length: 114
Date: Sat, 27 Aug 2022 00:07:22 GMT

{
  "data": {
    "firstName": "John",
```

```
    "lastName": "Jakes",
    "userId": 1
  },
  "response": {
    "responseCode": "0",
    "responseMessage": "OK"
  }
}
```

The Location header field is set to the full URI to the newly created user. Clients then navigate through that path to then load the newly created user from the resource class. It is also worthy of note that in Listing 6-21 when the createUser resource method returned a UserResponse, the HTTP response code was 200. But in Listing 6-22 when returning the Response object, the HTTP response code is 201. The Response class can be used to create all forms of custom response data that is returned to the client.

Exception Mappers

Exception mapping is a Jakarta REST construct for mapping exceptions to client responses. Business exceptions are a way to signal to the client that there is a problem with the normal execution of the application. The way to convey exception messages to clients is through the use of exception mappers. When a POST request was made in Listing 6-10 to create a user, the server responded with HTTP status code 400 telling the client that the request was bad. This message is not very helpful. A much better experience would be to tell the client exactly what is wrong with the data being passed. This can be achieved through the use of exception mappers.

An exception mapper is an implementation of the jakarta.ws.rs.ext.ExceptionMapper interface. This interface takes a Throwable type and maps it to a Response object in the toResponse method. Listing 6-23 shows an exception mapper for returning validation constraint violation messages to the client.

Listing 6-23. Exception mapper

```
@Provider
public class ConstraintViolationExceptionMapper implements ExceptionMapper<
ConstraintViolationException> {
```

```
  @Override
  public Response toResponse(ConstraintViolationException exception) {
    StringBuilder builder = new StringBuilder();

    for (ConstraintViolation<?> cv : exception.getConstraintViolations()) {
      String path = cv.getPropertyPath().toString().split("\\.")[2];

      builder.append(path).append(" - ")
              .append(cv.getMessage()).append("\n");
    }
    return  Response.status(Response.Status.BAD_REQUEST)
        .entity(builder.toString())
        .build();
  }
}
```

The ConstraintViolationExceptionMapper maps the jakarta.validation.ConstraintViolationException exception to a Response object. When a constraint violation occurs, the ConstraintViolationException is thrown, with a set of the constraints that occurred. Each constraint object has the name of the field on which the violation occurred. The toResponse method maps these to a string and sets that as the entity on the Response. The @jakarta.ws.rs.ext.Provider annotation on the class registers it as a Jakarta REST artifact that will be scanned and registered automatically by the runtime. Listing 6-24 shows the response from a call with malformed data to the createUser resource method.

Listing 6-24. Mapped response

```
HTTP/1.1 400 Bad Request
Content-Type: application/json
Content-Language: en-US
Content-Length: 55
Connection: Close
Date: Sat, 27 Aug 2022 00:46:22 GMT

lastName - must not be empty
email - must not be empty
```

The request omitted the email and lastName fields of the CreateUserRequest object. This caused a validation exception to take place, and the ConstraintViolationException was mapped to the client through the exception mapper that we registered. The response body shows each violated field and the corresponding helper message.

The Jakarta REST Client

Jakarta REST comes with an HTTP client for making REST calls. This client is a very simple and straightforward construct that revolves around the jakarta.ws.rs.client.WebTarget interface. The WebTarget targets a resource by its URI. A WebTarget is obtained by calling the static target method on the jakarta.ws.rs.client.Client instance returned by the jakarta.ws.rs.client.ClientBuilder class. Listing 6-25 shows the construction of a Client and using it to target a resource to obtain a WebTarget in the test class of the account module.

Listing 6-25. Obtaining a Client

```
public class AbstractAccountIT {
  protected static final WebTarget target;
  protected static final Client client;
  static {
    client = ClientBuilder.newClient();
    target = client.target("http://localhost:3003/account/api");
  }
  @AfterAll
  protected static void cleanUp() {
    if (client != null) {
      client.close();
    }
  }
}
```

The ClientBuilder.newClient method returns a Client. Clients are heavy objects, and as such, you should not create more than necessary instances. In the preceding example, the returned instance is assigned to the static client variable. The target method is then invoked with the full base resource path being targeted to return a WebTarget instance which is assigned to the target variable. The instantiation is done in a static block because the WebTarget and Client instances are static. Just this initialization is enough to use the target for all calls.

Once everything is done, the Client should be closed to prevent resource leakage. According to the API, "Clients are heavy-weight objects that manage the client-side communication infrastructure. Initialization as well as disposal of a Client instance may be a rather expensive operation." As such, we close the Client instance after all the tests are run in the cleanUp method annotated with @AfterAll from the JUnit test suite.

With the WebTarget initialized, HTTP REST calls can be made by specifying the relative path of the resource of interest. Listing 6-26 shows making both POST and GET requests to the /users and /users/{userId} resource paths, respectively.

Listing 6-26. Making calls with the client

```
@Test
    void createUser() {
        UserResponse createdUser = target.path("users")
                .request().post(Entity.json(createUserRequest),
                UserResponse.class);

        assertEquals("0", createdUser.getResponse().getResponseCode());
        assertEquals("OK", createdUser.getResponse().getResponseMessage());
        // get created user
        UserResponse userResponse = target.path("users/{userId}")
                .resolveTemplate("userId", createdUser.getData().
                getUserId()).request()
                .get(UserResponse.class);

        assertEquals("0", userResponse.getResponse().getResponseCode());
        assertEquals("OK", userResponse.getResponse().
        getResponseMessage());

    }
```

The path method on the WebTarget returns another WebTarget instance that resolves to the original path passed to the client.target invocation in Listing 6-25 and this new path. So the target.path("users") call in Listing 6-26 resolves the returned WebTarget to `http://localhost:3003/account/api/users`. The request method is then called on the implicitly returned WebTarget instance to return a jakarta.ws.rs.client.SyncInvoker instance. This interface has all the HTTP methods that can be invoked to make the actual request.

The post method invoked in Listing 6-26 passes in an instance of the CreateUserRequest. This instance is transformed to JSON using the static json method on the jakarta.ws.rs.client.Entity class. The second parameter passed to the post method is the class type to which the returned response should be transformed. As per the resource paths shown in Table 6-1, a POST request to the /api/users resource returns the created user. The post invocation response is directly assigned to a UserResponse variable because the runtime will automatically read and convert the returned entity from JSON to the concrete Java type for us.

The second call is a GET call to the /api/users/{userId} endpoint. This endpoint takes a path parameter. The path method is passed the raw path with the variable name which is then resolved to the ID of the user with the resolveTemplate method. This method takes the name of the variable to resolve and the value to resolve to. The get method is then invoked to make the HTTP get request. The returned response is directly assigned to a Java type because the get method was passed a class type to which the body of the response should be converted.

The Jakarta REST client is a feature-rich API for making all forms of HTTP calls to web resources. You can chain paths and resolve variables to create complex resource paths. You can also get the raw jakarta.ws.rs.core.Response object returned by a call for use in your code.

The MicroProfile REST Client

The Eclipse MicroProfile REST client specification[7] provides another way to make REST calls in a much more typesafe way. Even though the Jakarta REST client looked at in the previous section gets the job done, it can get verbose and unwieldy at times. The MicroProfile REST client is another way to consume HTTP resources in Java without

[7] MicroProfile Rest Client 3.0 Release

having to do the plumbing work of creating client objects. Listing 6-27 shows a complete MicroProfile REST client declaration for making external calls to apilayer.com's currency conversion service.

Listing 6-27. MicroProfile client

```
@RegisterRestClient(baseUri = BASE_URI)
@ClientHeaderParam(name = "apikey", value = "INSERT_API_KEY_FROM_SERVICE")
@Path("exchangerates_data")
public interface ApiLayer {

    String NAME = "ApiLayer";
    String BASE_URI = "https://api.apilayer.com";

    @GET
    @Path("convert")
    ApiLayerConvertResponse convertCurrency(@BeanParam
    ApiLayerConvertRequest apiLayerConvertRequest);

    @GET
    @Path("list")
    JsonObject getCurrencySymbols();
}
```

Creating a REST client entails describing the resources that should be targeted. The ApiLayer interface declares two HTTP GET methods. The first one takes an ApiLayerConvertRequest object that is annotated @BeanParam that has the query params that the apilayer.com currency service expects. The two methods return an ApiLayerConvertResponse and JsonObject, respectively. The first return type is an application-specific object, and the second, JsonObject, is part of the Jakarta JSON Processing API.

The interface is annotated @RegisterRestClient(baseUri = BASE_URI). This annotation is a MicroProfile REST client stereotype that marks this interface as a REST client targeting the baseUri. All calls using this client will be relative to the passed value for the baseUri, in this example, `https://api.apilayer.com`. The @ClientHeaderParam(name = "apikey", value = "API_KEY") is used to add HTTP header information to the outbound request. As used on the interface level, every outbound request made through this client will have a header entry as key-value pair from this annotation. For the preceding example, each request will have an apiKey="YOUR_API_KEY_FROM_API_LAYER" in the request header.

The @Path annotation is used to specify the relative path that methods invoked on this client will be made relative to. As is, all methods invoked on an instance of this client will be made relative to `https://api.apilayer.com/exchangerates_data`. The first GET method will be made to `https://api.apilayer.com/exchangerates_data/convert` and the second one to `https://api.apilayer.com/exchangerates_data/list`. With the client declaration in place, using it is as simple as injecting it with @Inject and the MicroProfile-specific qualifier, @RestClient. Listing 6-28 shows the use of the ApiLayer REST client in the RateService bean.

Listing 6-28. REST client use

```
@ApplicationScoped
public class RateService {

  @Inject
  @RestClient
  ApiLayer apiLayer;

    private ConvertCurrencyResponse convert(final ConvertCurrencyRequest
    currencyRequest) {
    ApiLayerConvertRequest request = new ApiLayerConvertRequest();
    request.setFromCurrency(currencyRequest.getSourceCurrency());
    request.setToCurrency(currencyRequest.getTargetCurrency());
    request.setAmount(currencyRequest.getAmount().toPlainString());

    ApiLayerConvertResponse response = apiLayer.convertCurrency(request);

    ConvertCurrencyResponseData data = new ConvertCurrencyResponseData();
    data.setCurrency(currencyRequest.getTargetCurrency());
    data.setAmount(response.getResult());
    data.setSource(ApiLayer.NAME);

    return ConvertCurrencyResponse.of(data);
  }
}
```

To use the REST client, we inject it using @Inject and qualify it with the @RestClient CDI qualifier from the MicroProfile REST Client API. The implementation of the interface will be provided at runtime by the underlying REST Client implementation. The convert method calls the convertCurrency method on the inject client like any other Java instance. The implementation will take care of creating the actual HTTP request, making the invocation to the target resource, and getting and converting the response to the declared Java types. The ApiLayerConvertRequest and ApiLayerConvertResponse classes are shown in Listings 6-29 and 6-30, respectively.

Listing 6-29. ApiLayerConvertRequest

```
public class ApiLayerConvertRequest {

      @QueryParam("from")
      private String fromCurrency;
      @QueryParam("to")
      private String toCurrency;
      @QueryParam("amount")
      private String amount;

}
```

Listing 6-30. ApiLayerConvertResponse

```
public class ApiLayerConvertResponse {
      private boolean success;
      private Info info;
      private LocalDate date;
      private BigDecimal result;

      @Getter
      @Setter
      public static class Info {
            private Long timestamp;
            private BigDecimal rate;

      }
}
```

The ApiLayerConvertResponse is the Java representation of the JSON that the endpoint returns. The REST Client runtime takes care of marshalling the returned JSON to the Java representation automatically. Listing 6-31 shows a sample JSON returned by the `https://api.apilayer.com/exchangerates_data/convert` endpoint.

Listing 6-31. Sample return data


```
{
  "date": "2005-01-01",
  "historical": true,
  "info": {
    "quote": 0.51961,
    "timestamp": 1104623999
  },
  "query": {
    "amount": 10,
    "from": "USD",
    "to": "GBP"
  },
  "result": 5.1961,
  "success": true
}
```


The getCurrencySymbols endpoint in the ApiLayer interface returns a JsonObject. For this endpoint, we want to have the JSON data directly for further processing. The REST Client runtime will convert the JSON string representation of the response to a JsonObject when the method is invoked on the client instance. The MicroProfile REST Client API is a powerful, intuitive, and much more typesafe way of consuming REST resources in Jakarta EE applications.

Summary

This chapter looked at creating RESTful web services using the Jakarta REST API. We looked at modelling the domain resource to HTTP resource paths, proceeded to use the various constructs from the API to create these resources, and learned how to use the Client API to make REST calls. We also looked at the Eclipse MicroProfile REST client and saw how simple it is to consume REST resources using that API. You can find out much more advanced topics in the respective Jakarta REST and Eclipse MicroProfile REST Client specifications. They are both written in an easy-to-understand language and should serve your authoritative source of knowledge for advanced usage.

CHAPTER 7

Managing Configurations

Every application will go through different stages on its way to production. From development to testing to staging to production, all these stages will have different configurations just for those environments. For instance, an app that uses an external service like a fraud detection API will have different configurations for the service depending on the stage the application is being run in. Another application that needs to import data in a batch service, for instance, will also have different configurations for which data to import depending on which stage the application is in.

Applications need to behave differently depending on some configuration values provided. It would be tedious if these configuration values were bundled with the application, which would mean having to repackage and deploy the application for each stage. It would be ideal to have a mechanism that gives you the developer a way to define different configuration values for different application stages without having to repackage and redeploy your application.

This is what the Eclipse MicroProfile Config API is designed for. It is a specification that gives your application transparent access to different configuration sources without having to touch the application itself. So, for instance, in the fraud detection example cited earlier, you can have a dummy URL for the development stage, a test URL from the service provider for the testing and staging stages, and finally the live URL for the production stage.

The Config specification allows you to define these configuration values in a hierarchical way such that the right value is returned automatically depending on the stage. This chapter is about the Eclipse MicroProfile Config specification. By the end of this chapter, you will learn how to incorporate the Config API into your application and use it to externalize dynamic application configuration values.

L. Saeed and G. Abdallah, *Pro Cloud Native Java EE Apps*, https://doi.org/10.1007/978-1-4842-8900-6_7

What Is the Config Specification?

The Eclipse MicroProfile Config specification defines a flexible system for managing application configuration. Based on the examples in the introduction section, an application will need to have at least three different configurations for the stated stages. The Config specification provides the constructs to realize this in a flexible and intuitive way. There are three core parts to the Config specification, namely, config sources, converters, and config values.

Config Sources

A config source is simply a source for configuration. If an application makes a request for a certain configuration value, for instance, *foo*, the Config runtime will need to load the value associated with property key *foo*. The place where the key-value pair for configurations is defined is the config source. The config source could be anything or anywhere: database, system properties, environment variables, etc. All these possible sources of configuration properties are abstracted into a ConfigSource by the Config runtime.

Your application interacts with these config sources in a transparent way through the ConfigSource abstraction. This way, the application does not concern itself with the actual source of the configuration values. This results in the flexibility of having various combinations of config sources to satisfy even the most complex application requirements.

Because you can have myriad config sources, there needs to be a way to sort or prioritize the sources. For instance, if property *foo=someValue* is defined in more than one config source, which config source should take precedence?

For this, the specification provides the concept of ordinal. Each config source is assigned an ordinal value that determines its priority. Sources with higher ordinals have higher priorities over those with lower originals. So in the preceding example, if property *foo=someValue* is defined in config source A with an ordinal of 100 and *foo=thatValue* is defined in config source B with an ordinal of 300, a call to get the value of property foo will return the *thatValue* because its source has a higher ordinal. If multiple ConfigSources happen to share the same ordinal, then they will be sorted by name.

The Config specification defines three default config sources, along with their default ordinal values, as shown in Figure 7-1.

Figure 7-1 shows the default config sources.

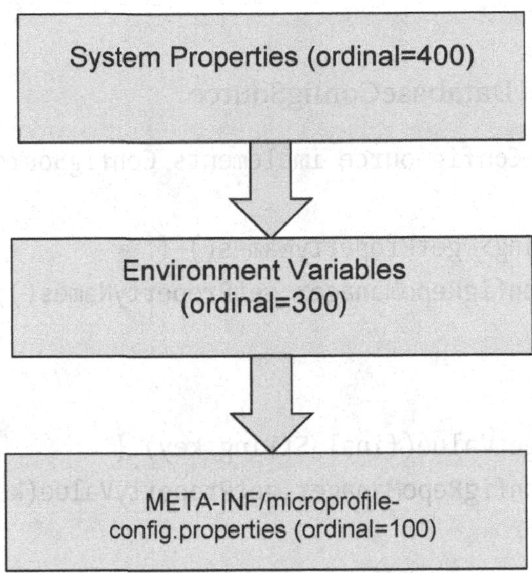

***Figure 7-1.** Config ordinals*

The first source is mapped to what you would get if you invoked System.getProperties(). The second source is what you get when you call the System.getenv() method. The third source, the microprofile-config.properties file, is normally bundled with the application. This is found in the META-INF folder under the resources folder.

The Config runtime searches for config properties starting from the config source with the highest ordinal to the lowest. The first match in that search order wins. This way, you can define different values for the same property in different config sources. For example, defining the property *foo=someValue* in the microprofile-config.properties file shipped with the application, and the same property *foo=thatValue* as a system property, a call for the foo property at runtime will return *thatValue*. This is because it is defined in a source with a higher ordinal.

Custom Config Sources

Your application is not limited to the three default config sources. For instance, you might be interacting with a legacy system that stores configuration values that your application needs in a database. You can define a database config source for your application and register it with the Config runtime. It will get scanned and picked up just like the default config sources. Listing 7-1 shows a DatabaseConfigSource custom config source for jwallet.

Listing 7-1. shows the DatabaseConfigSource

```
public class DatabaseConfigSource implements ConfigSource {
    @Override
    public Set<String> getPropertyNames() {
        return ConfigRepoManager.getPropertyNames();
    }

    @Override
    public String getValue(final String key) {
        return ConfigRepoManager.getPropertyValue(key);
    }

    @Override
    public String getName() {
        return this.getClass().getSimpleName();
    }
    @Override
    public int getOrdinal() {
        return 450;
    }
}
```

Listing 7-1 shows the custom config source declared in the DatabaseConfigSource class. The class starts by implementing the ConfigSource interface. The first three methods are the required methods to be implemented from the interface from a total of five methods. The other two are optional. The DatabaseConfigSource is a config source for fetching configuration values from a database. Those values could be put in by anyone or any system. The DatabaseConfigSource abstracts away that into the implemented ConfigSource view.

Method getPropertyNames returns the set of property names found in this config source. The getValue method returns the value associated with the passed key. For instance, passing in the key foo should return the value associated with it. The getName method returns the name of this config source, mainly for logging and debugging purposes. These are the three methods required to be overridden from the ConfigSource interface.

The getOrdinal method is an optional method that returns the ordinal of this config source. Remember an ordinal determines the priority of a config source. If this method is not overridden, the default ordinal of 100 defined in the ConfigSource interface will be used. For the DatabaseConfigSource, we want it to be the first place that is searched for configurations. Thus, the ordinal is set to 450, putting it above the three default config sources.

The ConfigRepoManager is a utility class that instantiates a dataSource and uses JDBC to query the database. For this example, we assume a database table with two fields, PROPERTY_KEY and PROPERTY_VALUE, corresponding to a config key and its value, respectively. Listing 7-2 shows the getPropertyValue in the ConfigRepoManager utility class.

Listing 7-2. shows the getPropertyValue method implementation

```
public static String getPropertyValue(final String keyName) {
 try {
      final PreparedStatement query;
      try (final Connection connection = dataSource.getConnection()) {
      query = connection.prepareStatement("SELECT PROPERTY_VALUE FROM
      CUSTOM_CONFIGURATIONS WHERE PROPERTY_KEY = ?");}
                query.setString(1, keyName);
                final ResultSet propertyValue = query.executeQuery();
                if (propertyValue.next()) {
                     return propertyValue.getString(1);
                }
                propertyValue.close();
                query.close();
           } catch (final SQLException e) {
                e.printStackTrace();
           }
           return null;
      }
```

Listing 7-2 shows the getPropertyValue method in ConfigRepoManager using JDBC to retrieve config property values from the database based on the passed key. Based on what you've learned so far in this book, you might be wondering why the use of plain JDBC instead of CDI and JPA. The answer is that a ConfigSource is not a CDI bean. It's treated by the Config runtime as a Plain Old Java Object.

This is because making a ConfigSource a CDI bean could cause a circular startup loop when a given custom config source depends on a bean that in turn also depends on the config source for configurations. To prevent the likelihood of such problems occurring, custom ConfigSource implementations are treated as POJOs.

With the ConfigSource interface implemented, we need to register the implementation with the MicroProfile Config runtime. To do so, the fully qualified class name of the DatabaseConfigSource must be added to the /META-INF/services/org.eclipse.microprofile.config.spi.ConfigSource file. With an ordinal of 450, the Config runtime will first attempt to resolve the property foo in the newly registered custom config source, because it has an ordinal of 450, before going down to the system properties, then environment variables, and finally to the microprofile-config.properties file.

Converters

The second component in the Config trio is the concept of converters. By default, the MicroProfile Config runtime treats all configurations as String/String pairs. It doesn't matter the type of the value specified in a given configuration source. It will be loaded as a String. For instance, the config property *rate.minimum=15* will be loaded as "15" when a request for the property *rate.minimum* is made to the Config runtime.

Assuming the target Java field type for the preceding property is BigDecimal, clearly there will be a problem since the runtime will be attempting to assign incompatible types. The solution is the use of converters. When the property value associated with *rate.minimum* is loaded, the Config runtime will look at the target field type into which the value is going to be set, then call an appropriate converter to convert the loaded value into the target field type.

So when *rate.minimum* is loaded, a converter that can take a String and return a BigDecimal from it will be called and pass the loaded String of 15. This converter will then return a BigDecimal with the value of 15. The Config specification provides some default converters and a mechanism to create custom converters as well. The default converters are

- boolean and java.lang.Boolean, values for true (case insensitive) "true", "1", "YES", "Y", "ON". Any other value will be interpreted as false
- byte and java.lang.Byte
- short and java.lang.Short
- int and java.lang.Integer
- long and java.lang.Long
- float and java.lang.Float, a dot "." is used to separate the fractional digits
- double and java.lang.Double, a dot "." is used to separate the fractional digits
- char and java.lang.Character
- java.lang.Class based on the result of Class.forName

These converters have a default jakarta.annotation.Priority of 1. A priority is used to determine the hierarchy of a set of converters. Two converters targeting the same type will be sorted by their @Priority values. Converters with higher @Priority values have higher precedence over converters with lower @Priority values.

Automatic Converters

When there is no default or custom converter for a given target Java type, the Config runtime will create an automatic dynamic converter if the target Java type

- Has a public static T of(String) method
- Has a public static T valueOf(String) method
- Has a public Constructor with a String parameter
- Has a public static T parse(CharSequence) method

For the *rate.minimum* property, the runtime will create an automatic converter on our behalf because the target Java type of BigDecimal has a valueOf(String) method.

Custom Converters

If you need to pass custom types through the configuration mechanism and none of the converters will get the job done, you can create your own custom converter and register it with the Config runtime. Listing 7-3 shows a custom converter for the ConvertCurrencyRequest type.

Listing 7-3. shows the ConvertCurrencyRequest custom converter

```
public class CurrencyRequestConverter implements Converter<ConvertCurrency
Request> {
      @Override
      public ConvertCurrencyRequest convert(final String value) {
            if (value == null || value.isBlank()) {
      throw new NullPointerException("Value must not be null or empty
      string");
            }
      final String[] split = value.split(",");
      if (split.length != 3) {
      throw new IllegalArgumentException("The resulting array has less than
      3 elements.");
            }
            return  ConvertCurrencyRequest
                    .builder()
                    .sourceCurrency(split[0])
                    .targetCurrency(split[1])
                    .amount(new BigDecimal(split[2])).build();
      }
}
```

Listing 7-3 shows the CurrencyRequestConverter. A custom Config converter needs to implement the parameterized org.eclipse.microprofile.config.spi.Converter<T>, passing in the type that the converter will convert. The specification expects custom converter implementations to throw a NullPointerException if a null value is passed for conversion. This is done in the first check in the CurrencyRequestConverter.

The implementation then splits the passed string using the expected comma separator into an array. Remember config values are passed as raw Strings. And so even though the target type is a custom type, the passed config value will just be a comma-separated list of field values of the target type. The custom converter then checks if the resulting array length is three, because the target class, shown in Listing 7-4, has three fields.

Listing 7-4. shows the target ConvertCurrencyRequest type

```
public class ConvertCurrencyRequest {
      private String sourceCurrency;
      private String targetCurrency;
      private BigDecimal amount;

}
```

The custom converter then constructs a ConvertCurrencyRequest using the builder pattern, passing in each field taken from the array. This way, custom ConvertCurrencyRequest can be passed as config values and read automatically to make currency conversions without having to make REST calls to the application. This is especially suited to batch jobs and interfacing with legacy applications.

As an example, the preceding converter can be used to read ConvertCurrencyRequest config values from a database that was populated by a legacy COBOL application. Because jwallet already has a custom database config source (Listing 7-2) and now a custom converter, the application can be used to interface with a legacy application without much need for refactoring. The legacy application will fill the database, and jwallet will read and convert the currencies.

Config Value

The third of the config trio is the actual config value. The whole essence of the Config specification is to abstract away all possible sources of application configuration values into a transparent, single view in the form of config sources. Using these config sources, you can then get config values based on the keys for each value needed.

For the given configuration *convert_request="USD,GHS,5"*, there are six different ways to get the config value using the Config API. This configuration should get mapped to the ConvertCurrencyRequest type. What happens in the absence of a value for a given property request depends on the retrieval method. These retrieval methods are as follows.

The Config Bean

Config values can be retrieved by injecting an org.eclipse.microprofile.config.Config bean. This bean resolves the property value by searching through all available config sources. The ordinal of the config sources determine which config value is returned when the same property is found in more than one config source. Listing 7-5 shows the use of the Config bean to retrieve the property *convert_request="USD,GHS,5"*.

Listing 7-5. shows the Config bean for retrieving config values

```
@ApplicationScoped
public class RateService {

      @Inject
      Config config;

public ConvertCurrencyResponse batchConvertWithConfig() {
ConvertCurrencyRequest request = config.getValue("convert_request",
ConvertCurrencyRequest.class);
      return convert(request);

      }

}
```

Listing 7-5 shows the use of the Config bean to get configuration values. In the batchConvertWithConfig method, the getValue method is called on the injected Config bean. This method takes the key of the configured property, in this case, convert_request and the target type. Because we have a custom converter for the ConvertCurrencyRequest, we just pass it as the second parameter type. The method returns an instance of ConvertCurrencyRequest representing the read and converted property. If the value associated with the passed property key resolves to an empty string or null, a java.util.NoSuchElementException will be thrown.

Direct Injection of Target Type

You can directly inject the target type using @Inject and a qualifier as shown in Listing 7-6.

Listing 7-6. showing the direct injection of an expected config value

```
@ApplicationScoped
public class RateService {

    @Inject
    @ConfigProperty(name = "convert_request")
    ConvertCurrencyRequest convertCurrencyRequest;

    public ConvertCurrencyResponse batchConvertWithSimpleProperty() {
        return convert(convertCurrencyRequest);
    }
}
```

Listing 7-6 shows the direct injection of the ConvertCurrencyRequest using @Inject and the @ConfigProperty qualifier. This qualifier takes two parameters: name and defaultValue. If the name parameter is omitted, then the runtime will default to using the class_name.injection_point_name, where injection_point_name is the field name or parameter name, and class_name is the fully qualified name of the class being injected to. The second parameter is the defaultValue.

The defaultValue parameter acts as the lowest config source because it becomes a fallback to when no value is set. If this is omitted like done in Listing 7-6 and there is no value set, then a deployment exception will be thrown and the application cannot be deployed.

Optional Injection

Config values can be read by injecting optional types. Rather than directly injecting the target type as done in Listing 7-6, the target value can be wrapped in a java.util. Optional<T> value as shown in Listing 7-7.

Listing 7-7. shows injecting config values as Optional type

```
@ApplicationScoped
public class RateService {

@Inject
@ConfigProperty(name = "convert_request")
Optional<ConvertCurrencyRequest> convertRequest;

public ConvertCurrencyResponse batchConvert() {
   return convertRequest.map(this::convert).orElseGet(ConvertCurrencyRespo
   nse::new);

      }

}
```

Listing 7-7 shows retrieving config values through the injection of an Optional type wrapping the target value. Similar to the direct injection, the Optional field is also annotated with the same @ConfigProperty annotation. However, as an Optional type, if the value associated with the passed key, in this case convert_request, resolves to an empty string or null, an empty Optional is returned instead of a DeploymentException being thrown. A default value can also be passed as the second parameter to the @ConfigProperty qualifier.

Provider Injection

Config values can be retrieved through injection of the jakarta.inject.Provider<T> bean. A target type is wrapped in the Provider interface and annotation @Inject and @ConfigProperty, as shown in Listing 7-8.

Listing 7-8. shows the use of Provider for retrieving config values

```
@ApplicationScoped
public class RateService {
   @Inject
   @ConfigProperty(name = "convert_request")
   Provider<ConvertCurrencyRequest> currencyRequestProvider;

    public ConvertCurrencyResponse batchConvertWithProvider() {
```

```
        return convert(currencyRequestProvider.get());
    }
}
```

Listing 7-8 shows the use of Provider to retrieve config values. As usual, the field currencyRequestProvider is annotated @Inject and @ConfigProperty. This construct is similar to using Optional<T>, except that unlike Optional, a call to Provider#get as done in the batchConvertWithProvider method will always get the latest value from the underlying config.

The three previous ways you have seen all read the config value once. So if the data changes in the underlying config source, it is not reflected in values returned through any of the first three constructs. However, the use of Provider<T> and calling the get method on it as done in Listing 7-8 will always resolve the latest value from the underlying config source.

The call to the Provider#get method will throw a RuntimeException if the value resolves to null or an empty string. Listing 7-8 did not explicitly pass in a defaultValue, which means a value is expected to be available, the absence of which will throw a RuntimeException when get is called on the currencyRequestProvider field.

Supplier Injection

The java.util.Supplier<T> interface can also be used to read config values through injection. Listing 7-9 shows the use of the Supplier interface to retrieve config values.

Listing 7-9. shows the use of the java.util.Supplier interface

```
@ApplicationScoped
public class RateService {

    @Inject
    @ConfigProperty(name = "convert_request")
    Supplier<ConvertCurrencyRequest> convertCurrencyRequestSupplier;

    public ConvertCurrencyResponse batchConvertWithSupplier() {
        return convert(convertCurrencyRequestSupplier.get());
}
```

Listing 7-9 shows the use of the Supplier functional interface. Similar to the Provider<T> interface, the Supplier interface is also injected using @Inject and the @ConfigProperty qualifier. Also similar to the Provider<T> interface, the call to get as done in the batchConvertWithSupplier method will resolve the latest value in the underlying config source. The absence of a default value means the value must exist, absence of which will cause a RuntimeException to be thrown.

The ConfigValue Metadata

The org.eclipse.microprofile.config.ConfigValue interface can also be injected and used to get config values. Unlike the other constructs discussed earlier, the ConfigValue interface has methods to get the ConfigSource name, the ordinal, the raw config value, the name of the property, and the value. Unless you need to do something at runtime with the config source, you will seldom use the ConfigValue.

Summary

The Eclipse MicroProfile Config specification is a simple set of API constructs that helps you load application properties at runtime without having to redeploy the application nor the application needing to know the actual underlying source of the configuration. This chapter looked at the three core components that make up the Config specification, namely, config source, converters, and config value. These three components together give you all that you need to abstract your application from its properties.

CHAPTER 8

Resilience with Fault Tolerance API

Modern cloud-native applications are generally crafted as a set of microservices that communicate with each other, mostly over the network. Users of such applications have come to expect applications to always be available. However, there are a number of things that can always go wrong during the runtime of an application instance.

The network may be unavailable, a database service might take too long to respond, an application might go viral overnight and have an unexpected surge in concurrent users, a web service might be offline, and a multitude of other potential problems. For an application to be able to weather such inevitable mishaps, it needs to be fault-tolerant and resilient.

The Eclipse MicroProfile Fault Tolerance specification provides a number of declarative API constructs that can be used to create fault-tolerant and resilient modern, cloud-native applications. The goal of this chapter is to show you how you can use the Eclipse MicroProfile Fault Tolerance API to add retry policies, bulkheads, circuit breakers, timeouts, and fallbacks to your microservices, transforming them into much more resilient cloud-native versions.

Fault Tolerance

The Fault Tolerance specification provides a number of interceptor bindings that can be used declaratively to achieve fault tolerance on applications. These interceptor bindings can be used individually or in combination with each other. Because the specification is built on the Jakarta Interceptors specification, it can be used directly with CDI beans. So all existing CDI services can be transformed into fault-tolerant components with the Fault Tolerance specification.

L. Saeed and G. Abdallah, *Pro Cloud Native Java EE Apps*, https://doi.org/10.1007/978-1-4842-8900-6_8

The set of fault tolerance interceptor bindings available covers the following aspects of creating resilient, fault-tolerant applications:

- Fallback
- Timeout
- Retry policy
- Circuit breaker
- Asynchronous
- Bulkhead

Fallback

The @Fallback interceptor binding is a method-level annotation that tells the runtime to fall back on a designated method if the annotated method throws an exception. The type of exception that triggers the fallback can be customized. Specific exceptions can also be set to be skipped when thrown, that is, those methods will not trigger the runtime to invoke the fallback method. Listing 8-1 shows the RateService bean with two methods: calculateAmount and calculateAmountFallback.

Listing 8-1. The RateService bean with a fallback method

```
@ApplicationScoped
public class RateService {

    @Inject
    @RestClient
    RateResource rateResource;

    @Fallback(fallbackMethod = "calculateAmountFallback")
    public BigDecimal calculateAmount(TransactionRequest
    transactionsRequest, Wallet wallet) {
        ConvertCurrencyRequest convertCurrencyRequest = new
        ConvertCurrencyRequest();
        convertCurrencyRequest.setSourceCurrency(wallet.getCurrency());
        convertCurrencyRequest.setTargetCurrency(transactionsRequest.
        getCurrency());
```

```
        convertCurrencyRequest.setAmount(transactionsRequest.getAmount());

        ConvertCurrencyResponse convertCurrencyResponse = rateResource.
        convertCurrency(convertCurrencyRequest);
        return convertCurrencyResponse.getData().getAmount();
    }

    public BigDecimal calculateAmountFallback(TransactionRequest
    transactionsRequest, Wallet wallet) {
        return transactionsRequest.getAmount();
    }
}
```

Listing 8-1 shows the RateService application-scoped bean. It has two methods. The first one, calculateAmount, has the @Fallback annotation. This annotation has the parameter fallbackMethod set to the name of the second method, calculateAmountFallback. At runtime, by default, any exception that is a subclass of java.lang.Throwable thrown will cause the runtime to invoke the fallback method. The fallback method must have the same method signature as the one it's acting as a fallback for.

The @Fallback annotation can also be passed a class instead of using the fallbackMethod parameter. The passed class must be an implementation of the org.eclipse.microprofile.faulttolerance.FallbackHandler<T> interface. This interface takes the type of the return type of the method for which it is acting as a fallback. Listing 8-2 shows a FallbackHandler implementation in the RateCalcFallback class.

Listing 8-2. showing the RateCalcFallback handler class

```
public class RateCalcFallback implements FallbackHandler<BigDecimal> {
     @Override
     public BigDecimal handle(final ExecutionContext context) {
           final TransactionRequest transactionRequest =
           (TransactionRequest) context.getParameters()[0];
           return transactionRequest.getAmount();
     }
}
```

Listing 8-2 shows the RateCalcFallback class implementing the FallbackHandler interface. This class takes a BigDecimal value, which is the return type of the method it is acting as a fallback for. The interface has a single method named handle that gets passed an org.eclipse.microprofile.faulttolerance.ExecutionContext type. This object contains metadata about the failed method for which the fallback is kicking in.

As shown in Listing 8-2, the handle method implementation calls the getParameters method on the passed ExecutionContext object to get the method's parameters, pick the first one, and return a default value. Listing 8-3 shows the RateService bean again, but this time using the RateCalcFallback handler instead of a method in the class itself.

Listing 8-3. shows the RateCalcService using the RateCalcHandler fallback handler

```
@ApplicationScoped
public class RateService {

    @Inject
    @RestClient
    RateResource rateResource;

    @Fallback(RateCalcFallback.class)
    public BigDecimal calculateAmount(TransactionRequest
    transactionsRequest, Wallet wallet) {
        ConvertCurrencyRequest convertCurrencyRequest = new
        ConvertCurrencyRequest();
        convertCurrencyRequest.setSourceCurrency(wallet.getCurrency());
        convertCurrencyRequest.setTargetCurrency(transactionsRequest.
        getCurrency());
        convertCurrencyRequest.setAmount(transactionsRequest.getAmount());

        ConvertCurrencyResponse convertCurrencyResponse = rateResource.
        convertCurrency(convertCurrencyRequest);
        return convertCurrencyResponse.getData().getAmount();
    }

}
```

Listing 8-3 shows the RateService's calculate method using the RateCalcFallback class as the fallback instead of a method. At runtime, a noncontextual instance of the RateCalcFallback will be automatically created if an exception gets thrown. The @Fallback annotation has two other parameters, namely, applyOn and skipOn.

applyOn takes an array of exceptions that should trigger the fallback mechanism. When a value is specified for this parameter, then only the passed exception types, when thrown, will cause the fallback method to be invoked. Leaving this out is equal to passing in Throwable.class.

The skipOn parameter also takes an array of exceptions, but these exceptions, when thrown, will cause the fallback method to be skipped. You can use this parameter to prevent the fallback method being called when the target method throws a business exception, for example, a custom validation exception.

Timeout

The @Timeout annotation is used to set a timeout, after which a method execution should be timed out or truncated. Microservices applications will generally talk to each other, as well as make external calls to other services. It is important to not let a single method execution take an unreasonable amount of time to execute. No timeboxing could end up costing significant amounts of money.

The @Timeout annotation takes two parameters, the value and the unit. The value refers to the length of execution after which the method should time out. The default is 1000. The unit refers to the java.time.Duration.ChronoUnit. The default is ChronoUnit. MILLIS. So by default, annotating a method with @Timeout will cause the method to time out after 1000 milliseconds of execution if it has not returned yet.

The timeout can also be used with other fault-tolerant constructs like the @Fallback. When a method is annotated both @Timeout and @Fallback, when the method times out, the fallback method will be called to return the fallback value. Listing 8-4 shows the RateService method calculateAmount annotated with the @Timeout annotation, leaving it with the default of timing out after 1000 milliseconds.

Listing 8-4. shows the RateService using the @Timeout annotation

```
@ApplicationScoped
public class RateService {

    @Inject
```

```
    @RestClient
    RateResource rateResource;

    @Fallback(RateCalcFallback.class)
    @Timeout
    public BigDecimal calculateAmount(final TransactionRequest
    transactionsRequest, final Wallet wallet) {
        ConvertCurrencyRequest convertCurrencyRequest = new
        ConvertCurrencyRequest();
        convertCurrencyRequest.setSourceCurrency(wallet.getCurrency());
        convertCurrencyRequest.setTargetCurrency(transactionsRequest.
        getCurrency());
        convertCurrencyRequest.setAmount(transactionsRequest.getAmount());

        ConvertCurrencyResponse convertCurrencyResponse = rateResource.
        convertCurrency(convertCurrencyRequest);
        return convertCurrencyResponse.getData().getAmount();
    }
}
```

Listing 8-4 shows the RateService using the @Timeout annotation on the calculateAmount method. The existence of the @Fallback and @Timeout means if no exception is thrown, but the method still does not complete execution after 1000 milliseconds, the runtime will time it out and call the RateCalcFallback handler to return a default value.

The @Timeout annotation can be used at the class and method level. When used on a class, all methods on the class will time out based on the configuration of the annotation at the class level. If a bean declares the annotation at both the class and method levels, the annotation at the method level takes precedence over that of the class level.

Retry

Almost all modern applications will need to make some form of call over the network. This call could be to another service within the same network or a completely separate call outside the network the application is deployed on. A network glitch could cause the call to fail. In such cases, it would be good to have a mechanism that will automatically retry the method invocation.

The @Retry annotation is used to invoke the same operation again if that operation terminates exceptionally. The types of exceptions that can trigger the retry can be customized. So are exceptions that should be skipped. Listing 8-5 shows the RateService bean's calculateAmount method bearing the @Retry annotation.

Listing 8-5. showing the use of the @Retry annotation in the RateService bean

```
@ApplicationScoped
public class RateService {

    @Inject
    @RestClient
    RateResource rateResource;

    @Fallback(RateCalcFallback.class)
    @Timeout
    @Retry
    public BigDecimal calculateAmount(TransactionRequest
    transactionsRequest,  Wallet wallet) {

        ConvertCurrencyRequest convertCurrencyRequest = new
        ConvertCurrencyRequest();
        convertCurrencyRequest.setSourceCurrency(wallet.getCurrency());
        convertCurrencyRequest.setTargetCurrency(transactionsRequest.
        getCurrency());
        convertCurrencyRequest.setAmount(transactionsRequest.getAmount());

        ConvertCurrencyResponse convertCurrencyResponse = rateResource.
        convertCurrency(convertCurrencyRequest);
        return convertCurrencyResponse.getData().getAmount();
    }

}
```

Listing 8-5 shows the RateService bean's calculateAmount method bearing the @Retry annotation. As is, the method will be retried if an exception is thrown during its execution. Because it is used alongside the @Timeout annotation, if the method should time out with a timeout exception, it will be retried. By default, the maximum number of retries is three. If after the three retries the method still throws an exception, then the fallback handler passed in the @Fallback annotation will be called.

The @Retry annotation has a number of parameters that you can pass to customize its behavior according to the needs of a given application. These parameters are shown in Table 8-1.

Table 8-1. *The parameters of the @Retry annotation*

Parameter	Description	Default Value
maxRetries	The maximum number of retries	3
delay	Delays between each retry	0
delayUnit	The delay unit	ChronoUnit.MILLIS
maxDuration	Maximum duration to perform the retry for	180000
durationUnit	Duration unit for maxDuration	ChronoUnit.MILLIS
jitter	The random vary of retry delays	
jitterDelayUnit	The jitter unit	ChronoUnit.MILLIS
retryOn	Specify the failures to retry on	Exception.class
abortOn	Specify the failures to abort on	–

The jitter parameter is used to add randomness to the retry delay. The default jitter value of 200 means that the effective delay between each retry will be [delay - jitter, delay + jitter]. With the default delay of 0 value is, we end up with -200, or 200 for effective delay. However, a negative effective delay is treated as 0. So in the absence of a value for the delay, the effective delay is 200 milliseconds.

The maxDuration sets the maximum duration of the whole retry process. It is critical to have a maximum duration to not end up in an infinite retry situation. The default value is 180000 milliseconds, meaning the entire retry duration will last for that period after which another of the fault tolerance annotations takes over.

The abortOn parameter is used to specify exceptions that when thrown in a method, the method will not be retried. You can use this to specify custom business exceptions like validation exceptions that should not be retried. If a method client, for instance, passes an invalid value and a method throws a validation exception, it is much more efficient to not retry the method since the cause of the exception is anticipated and a normal part of the business process.

The @Retry annotation can be used on a class or a method as done in Listing 8-5. When used on a class, all methods in the class will be retried. When used on a class and a method, the annotation on the method takes precedence over the class-level annotation for that particular method.

Circuit Breaker

A circuit breaker acts as a guard over a resource method, preventing the method from tying down computer resources by failing fast if a set criteria is met. When consistent calls to a method keep failing, the failing method could end up taking up resources and in some cases cascading the failure to other components of the application. To prevent such occurrences, the circuit breaker pattern is used to stand guard on a method and prevent invocations from reaching that method when some preset failure threshold is reached. A circuit breaker is always in one of three states – closed, open, half-open.

Closed

The circuit breaker is closed when invocations are allowed through to the guarded method. This is the normal state of being for the circuit breaker. It records whether each method invocation succeeded or not and keeps tally up to a preset count. If the preset count is reached and the proportion of failed method invocations exceeds a preset failure ratio (relative to the preset count), the circuit breaker transitions to the open state.

Open

In the open state, calls to the guarded method will fail immediately with an org.eclipse.microprofile.faulttolerance.exceptions.CircuitBreakerOpenException. This exception will keep being thrown for all method invocations until a configurable delay is reached, after which the circuit breaker then transitions to half-open state.

Half-Open

In the half-open state, the circuit breaker allows a configurable number of trial invocations through to the guarded method. By default, if one of those invocations fails, the circuit breaker transitions back to the open state. If all the trial executions succeed, the circuit breaker transitions to the closed state.

The @CircuitBreaker annotation can be used to create a circuit breaker for a method. If the annotation is used on a class, then all methods in the class will have circuit breakers. If used on a class and a method inside that class, then the @CircuitBreaker at the method level takes precedence over the class-level annotation for that method. Listing 8-6 shows the @CircuitBreaker annotation used on the convertCurrency method in the Rate service bean.

Listing 8-6. showing the @CircuitBreaker used in the RateService bean

```
@ApplicationScoped
public class RateService {

@CircuitBreaker
@Fallback(fallbackMethod = "convertCurrencyFallback")
public ConvertCurrencyResponse convertCurrency(final ConvertCurrencyRequest
convertCurrencyRequest) {
return convert(convertCurrencyRequest);
      }

}
```

Listing 8-6 shows the @CircuitBreaker method used on the convertCurrency method in the RateService bean. As is, the circuit breaker will consider all exceptions of type java.lang.Throwable thrown in the method as a failure and transition to the open state if 10 or more failures occur during 20 consecutive requests. The circuit breaker will then delay for 5000 milliseconds in the open state before transitioning to the half-open state, during which a single successful call will cause it to transition to the closed state.

The parameters of the @CircuitBreaker annotation are shown in Table 8-2.

***Table 8-2.** showing the @CircuitBreaker annotation parameters*

Parameter	Description	Default Value
failOn	The exceptions to be considered a failure	Throwable. class
skipOn	Exceptions that should not be considered failures	–
delay	How long the circuit breaker should stay in the open state	5000
delayUnit	The delay unit	ChronoUnit. MILLIS
requestVolumeThreshold	The total number of consecutive requests in a rolling window	20
failureRatio	The ratio of failures relative to the requestVolumeThreshold that should trip the circuit to open	0.50
successThreshold	The number of successful invocations that should transition the circuit from half-open to closed	1

The @CircuitBreaker annotation can be used alongside other fault-tolerant annotations. As shown in Listing 8-6, it is used in combination with the @Fallback annotation. In this case, when the circuit breaker opens, failed invocations will cause the fallback method, in this case convertCurrencyFallback, to be invoked.

Asynchronous

The @Asynchronous annotation is used to transform a method into an asynchronous one that executes on a separate thread from the calling thread. A method annotated @Asynchronous must return either of java.util.concurrent.CompletionStage or java. util.concurrent.Future. To maximize the use of this annotation with other fault-tolerant annotations, the specification recommends the use of CompletionStage as the return type.

@Asynchronous can be used at the class or method level. When used at the class level, all methods in the class will be executed asynchronously. This annotation does not take any parameters. The only requirement, as stated earlier, is that the method returns either Future<T> or CompletionStage<T>. Listing 8-7 shows an asynchronous method, convertCurrencyAsync, in the RateService that makes use of the @Asynchronous annotation.

Listing 8-7. shows the RateService method convertCurrencyAsync using @Asynchronous

```
@ApplicationScoped
public class RateService {

@Asynchronous
@Retry
public CompletionStage<ConvertCurrencyResponse> convertCurrencyAsync(
        final ConvertCurrencyRequest convertCurrencyRequest) {
        return CompletableFuture.completedFuture(convert(convertCurrency
        Request));
    }
}
```

Listing 8-7 shows the RateService method convertCurrencyAsync annotated with the @Asynchronous and @Retry annotations. The method returns a CompletionStage wrapped ConvertCurrencyResponse object. When this method is invoked, a new thread will be spawned for its execution. As the @Asynchronous is used alongside @Retry, the retrying, should the method complete exceptionally, will happen in the spawned thread. All other fault-tolerant interceptors used with @Asynchronous will take place in the spawned thread.

If @Asynchronous is used with @Fallback, the fallback method must have the same signature as the original method. That is, the fallback method must also return a Future<T> or CompletionStage<T> exactly as the method it is acting as a fallback for.

Bulkhead

The @Bulkhead annotation is a fault-tolerant annotation that is used to limit the number of concurrent requests that can hit a given method instance. By default, the annotation allows ten concurrent requests to an application. Depending on how the annotation is used, you can optionally specify how many requests can wait in a queue. The bulkhead implementation has two main styles, namely, semaphore and thread pool isolation.

Semaphore Style

The semaphore style bulkhead is when a non-@Asynchronous method is annotated @Bulkhead. Listing 8-8 shows the RateService convertCurrency method annotated @Bulkhead.

Listing 8-8. showing the use of @Bulkhead in RateService

```
@ApplicationScoped
public class RateService {

@CircuitBreaker
@Fallback(fallbackMethod = "convertCurrencyFallback")
@Bulkhead
public ConvertCurrencyResponse convertCurrency(final ConvertCurrencyRequest
convertCurrencyRequest) {
        return convert(convertCurrencyRequest);
  }
}
```

Listing 8-8 shows the RateService's convertCurrency method annotated @Bulkhead. This bulkhead use is the semaphore style because the annotated method is not asynchronous. As is, the method will allow only ten concurrent users at a time to the method. If the number of concurrent users exceeds ten, an org.eclipse.microprofile.faulttolerance.exceptions.BulkheadException will be thrown. In this case, because the annotation is used with the @Fallback, the fallback method will be called if the exception is thrown. The number of current users can be customized by setting the value parameter of the annotation.

Thread Pool Style

The thread pool style bulkhead is when an asynchronous method is annotated @Bulkhead. This style also allows the setting of the maximum number of requests that can be available in the waiting queue. Listing 8-9 shows the RateService's convertCurrencyAsync method annotated with the @Bulkhead.

Listing 8-9. showing the thread pool bulkhead in RateService

```
@ApplicationScoped
public class RateService {

@Asynchronous
@Retry
@Bulkhead
public CompletionStage<ConvertCurrencyResponse> convertCurrencyAsync(
      final ConvertCurrencyRequest convertCurrencyRequest) {
return CompletableFuture.completedFuture(convert(convertCurrencyRequest));

   }

}
```

In Listing 8-9, the convertCurrencyAsync method bears both the @Asynchronous and @Bulkhead annotations. By default, only ten concurrent requests will be allowed to the method at any point in time, with ten more in the waiting queue. The parameter waitingTaskQueue can be used to set the size of the waiting queue.

If a request cannot be added to the queue, an org.eclipse.microprofile.faulttolerance.exceptions.BulkheadException is thrown. If a bulkhead-related exception is thrown in the method shown in Listing 8-9, the method invocation will be retried because of the @Retry annotation. Since the method did not declare a fallback, if the retry cycle completes and the method still throws an exception, that exception will be directly thrown to the client.

Configuring Fault Tolerance with Config

The Eclipse MicroProfile Fault Tolerance specification integrates with other specifications from the project. As such, the six fault-tolerant annotations discussed earlier can be configured through the use of the Config specification. Fault-tolerant annotation parameters can be overridden individually or globally.

Individual Overrides

You can override individual fault tolerance annotations through config properties using the Config API. The property format is <classname>/<methodname>/<annotation>/<p arameter>, where the class name refers to the fully qualified class name, methodName being the method bearing the fault-tolerant annotation, and annotation being the interceptor whose parameter you wish to set or override.

For example, the @Retry annotation shown in Listing 8-9 can be configured using config properties in, for instance, the microprofile-config.properties as com.example. jwallet.rate.rate.control.RateService/convertCurrencyAsync/Retry/maxRetries=5. This will set the maxRetries of the @Retry annotation on the convertCurrencyAsync method in RateService to 5.

Setting fault-tolerant parameters through the Config mechanism overrides the same parameter if passed in the method. Also, because of the ordinal algorithm for setting the precedence of config sources, you can define different fault-tolerant parameters for the same method in different config sources for different environments.

Global Parameter Overrides

You can also set global fault-tolerant properties that will apply to all fault-tolerant interceptors in a given class or the entire application. For class-level overrides, the property format is <classname>/<annotation>/<parameter>, the difference with the individual level override being that the method name is omitted for the class-level override. For instance, to set the maxRetries for all @Retry annotations in RateService to 8, we can pass the property com.example.jwallet.rate.rate.control.RateService/Retry/ maxRetries=8.

Fault-tolerant parameters can also be overridden at the application level. The property format for that is <annotation>/<parameter>. Still on @Retry, to set the default application-level maxRetries to 10, we can set the property Retry/maxRetries=10. This will apply the maxRetries=10 to all @Retry annotations in the application.

Configurations closest to a component win in terms of precedence. Thus, individual fault-tolerant configurations take precedence over class-level ones, which, in turn, take precedence over application-level ones. This way, you can define sophisticated parameters for the fault-tolerant interceptors for different stages of the application.

Summary

This chapter discussed the Eclipse MicroProfile Fault Tolerance specification. Using annotations, we saw how you can make methods more resilient and fault tolerant using fallback, timeout, retry, circuit breaker, asynchronous, and bulkhead patterns. The chapter also discussed how you can configure the fault-tolerant annotations using the Eclipse MicroProfile Config API.

CHAPTER 9

Keeping Count with Metrics

Deployed, user-facing applications need to be monitored to ensure they are delivering as expected. Cloud-native applications deployed to complex cloud hosting environments need to be monitored even more because any unexpected deviation from preset expectations could mean significant extra hosting bills.

The way to monitor deployed, running applications is through the use of application metrics. Metrics such as how many times a method has been called and how many seconds a given method takes to return are all different kinds of metrics that can give insights into how an application is performing.

The Eclipse MicroProfile Metrics API provides a set of API constructs for exposing different types and kinds of application metrics. With this API, you can expose application, implementation runtime, and JVM metrics through annotations and a Java API in the OpenMetrics[1] format, consumable by monitoring applications like Prometheus.

This chapter covers the Metrics specification within a Jakarta EE context. By the end of the chapter, you will be able to use the Metrics API to expose different kinds of metrics in your cloud-native Jakarta EE application.

The Structure

The Eclipse MicroProfile Metrics specification is mostly a metadata-driven API for exposing metrics in an application. The scope and type of metrics you can expose depend on the application requirements. All the metrics exposed through the use of this API are hosted automatically under the context path /metrics.

[1] OpenMetrics

L. Saeed and G. Abdallah, *Pro Cloud Native Java EE Apps*, https://doi.org/10.1007/978-1-4842-8900-6_9

For local development, this will mostly be http://localhost:8080/metrics, and for an application deployed to foo.com, the metrics will be hosted at `https://foo.com/metrics`. The specification defines three scopes or categories of metrics. These are base-, application-, and vendor-specific metrics.

Base Metrics

The base metrics are metrics that all implementations are mandated to provide. These metrics expose information about the underlying JVM and operating system. Some of these base metrics are available processors, used, maximum, and committed heap memory, among others. There are some metrics under base metrics that could be optional as they could pertain to specific JVM or operating system release. These metrics are hosted at the path /metrics/base.

Application Metrics

Application metrics are the set of custom metrics that you would like to collect about your application. You can use either annotations or the Java API to expose these metrics. Examples of such metrics are how long it takes for a given method to execute. These metrics are accessible at /metrics/application.

Vendor Metrics

Vendor metrics are custom metrics that a compatible implementation of the Eclipse MicroProfile specification optionally provides on top of the mandatory base metrics. The vendor metrics are hosted at /metrics/vendor.

Metrics Data Format

By default, when a GET request is made to the /metrics resource, the returned metrics information is in the OpenMetrics text format. This is an open standard format for metrics supported by a number of monitoring applications like Prometheus.

However, the same metrics data can be returned in the JSON format if the Accept header of the HTTP request matches application/json. If the Accept header of the request matches both application/json and text/plain or no Accept header is specified, then the data is returned in the default OpenMetrics text format.

The Metrics Registry

The metrics registry is a registry of all metrics that can be accessed under the /metrics resource and their metadata. There is a shared singleton registry for each of the three metrics scopes of base, application, and vendor. Metrics are identified in the registry through their metrics ID comprising their names and tags (if available). Think of the metrics registry as a database of the metrics found in each scope. The registry will be transparent to you as an application developer most of the time. But you should know it's there when you have to interact with it.

Using Metrics

There are two ways you can use the Metrics API in your application. One is through annotations, and the other is through the Java API. Whichever you choose is only a matter of application requirements and developer preference. The annotations are interceptor bindings that are managed by the CDI runtime. Consequently, only proxyable managed beans can use the annotations for collecting metrics.

Annotations

There are six annotations for creating different kinds of metrics. These are

- @Counted
- @ConcurrentGauge
- @Gauge
- @Metered
- @SimplyTimed
- @Timed

All these annotations have parameters that are common to all of them. These are shown in Table 9-1.

Table 9-1. *showing common metrics annotation parameters*

Name	Type	Description	Option/Required
name	String	Sets the name of the metric	Optional. Defaults to name of annotated object
absolute	boolean	If true, name is used as the absolute name of the metric. If false, prepends the package name and class name before the given name	Optional. Defaults to false
displayName	String	Human-readable name for metadata	Optional. Defaults to null
description	String	A description of the metric	Optional. Defaults to null
unit	String	The unit of the specific metric	Optional. Different defaults
tags	String[]	An array of "key=value" tags for the metric	Optional. Empty array

@Counted

The @Counted metric annotation counts the number of times the annotated method, constructor, or type is invoked or instantiated. This annotation can be used on a method, constructor, or class. If used at the class level, all methods in that class will have their invocations counted. Listing 9-1 shows method convertCurrency in the RateResourceImpl class annotated with @Counted, passing in some parameters.

Listing 9-1. shows the use of @Counted

```
@Consumes(MediaType.APPLICATION_JSON)
@Produces(MediaType.APPLICATION_JSON)
@Path("rates")
public class RateResourceImpl {

      @Path("convert")
```

```
    @POST
    @Counted(name = "convert_currency",
            absolute = true,
            displayName = "Convert currency method",
            description = "Method to convert one currency to
            the other",
            tags = { "info=conversions", "type=meta" })
    ConvertCurrencyResponse convertCurrency(@Valid ConvertCurrency
    Request convertCurrencyRequest){
  return rateService.convertCurrency(convertCurrencyRequest)
};
}
```

Listing 9-1 shows the @Counted annotation used on the convertCurrency method. It has the name parameter set and the absolute set to true. This means the name of this metric that will be registered in the registry is convert_currency. If absolute was not set to true, the name of the metric would be package name + class name + passed value to name parameter. The tags are also set to some method-specific info.

Tags play an important role in metrics because in a cloud-native environment where orchestration of deployed containers is done by engines like kubernetes, the traditional mapping of application runtime and host is no longer the case. In the context of metrics, tags add an additional dimension for identifying metrics in addition to the name of the metrics.

The counted metric can be accessed directly from the /metrics/application/convert_currency when the application is deployed. The name of the metric is enough to access it via the REST endpoint because the absolute parameter was set to true. A sample call for this metric in the OpenMetrics format returns the result shown in Listing 9-2.

Listing 9-2. showing a sample metric for @Counted

```
# TYPE application_convert_currency_total counter
# HELP application_convert_currency_total Method to convert one currency to
the other
application_convert_currency_total{info="conversions",type="meta"} 75
```

Listing 9-2 shows the @Counted annotation when accessed directly from the /metrics/application context path. The returned data is annotated with TYPE and HELP that shows the type and description of the metric, respectively. The metric count is preceded by application_. This is how application-level metrics are differentiated from base- and vendor-level metrics. The tags passed to the @Counted annotation are also returned as part of the full metric ID. As per the count, the convertCurrency method has been called a total of 75 times.

@ConcurrentGauge

This annotation is used to gauge concurrent invocations of an annotated method or constructor or instantiations of an annotated class. This metric works by incrementing the parallel count by one when the annotated element is entered and decremented by the same number when exited. This metric gauges the number of concurrent invocations of the annotated element.

When used on a class, any parallel invocation counter for the current, the previous minute maximum, and previous minute minimum is created and registered in the metric registry for each constructor and method of the class using the name and absolute field values of the annotation.

When used on a method, the metric gauges for the current, previous minute maximum, and previous minute minimum are created and registered in the metric registry. When used on a constructor, the same gauges for that constructor are registered. Listing 9-3 shows the convertCurrency method annotated with @ConcurrentGauge.

Listing 9-3. showing @ConcurrentGauge on convertCurrencyMethod

```
@Consumes(MediaType.APPLICATION_JSON)
@Produces(MediaType.APPLICATION_JSON)
@Path("rates")
public class RateResourceImpl {

    @Path("convert")
    @POST
    @ConcurrentGauge(name = "convert_currency_concurrent_gauge",
            absolute = true,
            description = "Method to convert one currency to
            the other",
```

```
            tags = { "convert=custom" }
    )
    ConvertCurrencyResponse convertCurrency(@Valid ConvertCurrencyRequest
    convertCurrencyRequest){};
}
```

Listing 9-3 shows the convertCurrency method annotated with @ConcurrentGauge. The name, absolute, and description are set, along with some custom tags. This is accessible at /metrics/application/convert_currency_concurrent_gauge. A sample call for the default text format returns the data as shown in Listing 9-4.

Listing 9-4. showing the result for the @ConcurrentGauge metric

```
# TYPE application_convert_currency_concurrent_gauge_current gauge
# HELP application_convert_currency_concurrent_gauge_current Method to
convert one currency to the other
application_convert_currency_concurrent_gauge_current{convert="custom"} 0
# TYPE application_convert_currency_concurrent_gauge_min gauge
application_convert_currency_concurrent_gauge_min{convert="custom"} 0
# TYPE application_convert_currency_concurrent_gauge_max gauge
application_convert_currency_concurrent_gauge_max{convert="custom"} 1
```

@Gauge

The @Gauge metric is used to sample the return value of a method. This method is mostly a business method that returns some form of meaningful, business context value for analysis. The method will be invoked by the Metrics runtime and the return value assigned as the value of the metric. @Gauge can be used for only methods.

As an example, if we want to sample the number of currency conversions in jwallet, @Gauge is the perfect metric for that. The return value of the method is the value of the metric. This metric can only be used with @ApplicationScoped or @Singleton CDI beans because using it with other non-singleton beans will not be clear as to which instance of the bean to use for obtaining the gauge value. Listing 9-5 shows the RateService @ApplicationScoped bean with a countConversions gauge method.

Listing 9-5. showing @Gauge usage

```
@ApplicationScoped
public class RateService {

    @Gauge(name = "convert_currency_gauge_count", unit = MetricUnits.
    NONE, absolute = true)
    public int countConversions() {
        return ThreadLocalRandom.current().nextInt(250, 500 + 1);
    }
}
```

Listing 9-5 shows the RateService singleton with countConversions method that returns an int. When this metric is queried, the runtime will call this method and use the returned method value as the value of the metric. With the name, this metric can be directly accessed from the path /metrics/application/convert_currency_gauge_count. A sample invocation return data is shown in Listing 9-6.

Listing 9-6. showing sample return data for the @Gauge metric

```
# TYPE application_convert_currency_gauge_count gauge
application_convert_currency_gauge_count 474
```

@Metered

The @Metered annotation is a metric that tracks the frequency of invocations of the annotated method or constructor or class instantiation. It tracks the mean throughput and one-, five-, and fifteen-minute exponentially weighted moving average throughput. The default MetricUnit is seconds. @Metered can be used on a class, method, or constructor.

Listing 9-7. shows the convertCurrency method with the @Metered annotation

```
@Consumes(MediaType.APPLICATION_JSON)
@Produces(MediaType.APPLICATION_JSON)
@Path("rates")
public class RateResourceImpl implements RateResource {

    @Inject
```

```
    RateService rateService;

    @Path("convert")
    @POST
    @Override
    @Metered(name = "convert_currency_meter", absolute = true)
    public ConvertCurrencyResponse convertCurrency(ConvertCurrencyRequest
    convertCurrencyRequest) {
           return rateService.convertCurrency(convertCurrencyRequest);
    }

}
```

Listing 9-7 shows the @Metered annotation of the convertCurrency method. With the passed absolute name, the metric can be queried from the path /metrics/application/convert_currency_meter, with a sample returned data shown in Listing 9-8.

Listing 9-8. shows the @Metered sample returned data for the convertCurrency method

```
# TYPE application_convert_currency_meter_total counter
application_convert_currency_meter_total 5
# TYPE application_convert_currency_meter_rate_per_second gauge
application_convert_currency_meter_rate_per_second 0.017981750828888407
# TYPE application_convert_currency_meter_one_min_rate_per_second gauge
application_convert_currency_meter_one_min_rate_per_second
0.009080280587651975
# TYPE application_convert_currency_meter_five_min_rate_per_second gauge
application_convert_currency_meter_five_min_rate_per_second
0.3266223165978052
# TYPE application_convert_currency_meter_fifteen_min_rate_per_second gauge
application_convert_currency_meter_fifteen_min_rate_per_second
0.5934799986177786
```

@SimplyTimed

The @SimplyTimed annotation is a metric for marking a method, constructor, or class as simply timed. By simply timed, it means a timer to track elapsed time duration and count. It measures duration in nanoseconds. Listing 9-9 shows the convertCurrency method of RateResourceImpl simply timed with @SimplyTimed.

Listing 9-9. showing the @SimplyTimed annotation on convertCurrency

```
@Consumes(MediaType.APPLICATION_JSON)
@Produces(MediaType.APPLICATION_JSON)
@Path("rates")
public class RateResourceImpl implements RateResource {
    @Inject
    RateService rateService;

    @Path("convert")
    @POST
    @Override
    @SimplyTimed(name = "convert_currency_simple_timer", absolute = true)
    public ConvertCurrencyResponse convertCurrency(ConvertCurrencyRequest
    convertCurrencyRequest) {
        return rateService.convertCurrency(convertCurrencyRequest);
    }

}
```

Listing 9-9 shows the @SimplyTimed metric, passed the absolute name convert_currency_simple_timer, making this metric directly accessible from /metrics/application/convert_currency_simple_timer. A call to that endpoint returns the sample data shown in Listing 9-10.

Listing 9-10. showing the result for the @SimplyTimed metric on convertCurrency

```
# TYPE application_convert_currency_simple_timer_total counter
application_convert_currency_simple_timer_total 45
# TYPE application_convert_currency_simple_timer_elapsedTime_seconds gauge
```

```
application_convert_currency_simple_timer_elapsedTime_seconds
33.18222481900005
# TYPE application_convert_currency_simple_timer_maxTimeDuration_
seconds gauge
application_convert_currency_simple_timer_maxTimeDuration_seconds
1.587411011000001
# TYPE application_convert_currency_simple_timer_minTimeDuration_
seconds gauge
application_convert_currency_simple_timer_minTimeDuration_seconds
0.586819599
```

@Timed

The @Timed metric is used to track how frequently a class, constructor, or method is invoked and tracks how long it took the invocations to complete. @Timed aggregates timing durations to provide duration and throughput statistics for the annotated object. It is a much more detailed metric relative to @SimplyTimed that only tracks elapsed time duration and count. Listing 9-11 shows the convertCurrency method annotated @Timed.

Listing 9-11. showing usage of @Timed

```
@Consumes(MediaType.APPLICATION_JSON)
@Produces(MediaType.APPLICATION_JSON)
@Path("rates")
public class RateResourceImpl implements RateResource {

    @Inject
    RateService rateService;

    @Path("convert")
    @POST
    @Override
    @Timed(name = "convert_currency_timer", absolute = true)
    public ConvertCurrencyResponse convertCurrency(ConvertCurrencyRequest
    convertCurrencyRequest) {
        return rateService.convertCurrency(convertCurrencyRequest);
    }

}
```

Listing 9-11 shows the @Timed metric on the convertCurrency method. With the absolute name, the metric can be accessed directly from /metrics/application/convert_currency_timer. A sample call returns the metric data shown in Listing 9-12.

Listing 9-12. showing the @Timed metric data

```
# TYPE application_convert_currency_timer_rate_per_second gauge
application_convert_currency_timer_rate_per_second 0.07333255542294032
# TYPE application_convert_currency_timer_one_min_rate_per_second gauge
application_convert_currency_timer_one_min_rate_per_second
3.0039512838912655E-4
# TYPE application_convert_currency_timer_five_min_rate_per_second gauge
application_convert_currency_timer_five_min_rate_per_second
0.02560887973769466
# TYPE application_convert_currency_timer_fifteen_min_rate_per_second gauge
application_convert_currency_timer_fifteen_min_rate_per_second
0.02345612678178861
# TYPE application_convert_currency_timer_mean_seconds gauge
application_convert_currency_timer_mean_seconds 0.9913156544019269
# TYPE application_convert_currency_timer_max_seconds gauge
application_convert_currency_timer_max_seconds 4.622333082
# TYPE application_convert_currency_timer_min_seconds gauge
application_convert_currency_timer_min_seconds 0.375723652
# TYPE application_convert_currency_timer_stddev_seconds gauge
application_convert_currency_timer_stddev_seconds 0.8967743131501213
# TYPE application_convert_currency_timer_seconds summary
application_convert_currency_timer_seconds_count 35
application_convert_currency_timer_seconds_sum 34.812993443
application_convert_currency_timer_seconds{quantile="0.5"} 0.687353305
application_convert_currency_timer_seconds{quantile="0.75"} 1.037883712
application_convert_currency_timer_seconds{quantile="0.95"}
4.261452175000005
application_convert_currency_timer_seconds{quantile="0.98"} 4.622333082
application_convert_currency_timer_seconds{quantile="0.99"} 4.622333082
application_convert_currency_timer_seconds{quantile="0.999"} 4.622333082
```

As you can see from the returned data, the @Timed metric returns a lot more detailed information about the method invocation relative to the @SimplyTimed metric. These two complement each other for when you need lightweight and heavyweight timing metrics.

Injecting Metrics

Apart from the use of annotations, you can also directly inject metrics of type meter, timer, counter, and histogram in your applications. You can inject metrics into fields, methods, and parameters using the @Metric annotation in combination with @Inject. The @Metric annotation supports all the metadata that the respective metrics support, such as name, description, and absolute values.

Using Histogram Metric

One metric that does not have an annotation equivalent is the histogram. This is a complex metric that measures the min, max, mean, standard deviation, and quartiles like the median or 95th percentile. To use this metric, we can inject it as shown in Listing 9-13 in the RateService bean.

Listing 9-13. shows the use of a histogram metric through injection

```
@ApplicationScoped
public class RateService {

    @Inject
    @Metric(name = "count_conversions_histogram",
                absolute = true,
                description = "A histogram for the count of conversions",
                tags = { "count=histogram", "metric=histogram" })
    Histogram histogram;

    @Gauge(name = "convert_currency_gauge_count", unit = MetricUnits.
    NONE, absolute = true)
    public int countConversions() {
    int conversionCount = ThreadLocalRandom.current().nextInt(250,
    500 + 1);
        histogram.update(conversionCount);
```

```
            return conversionCount;
        }
}
```

Listing 9-13 shows the use of @Inject in combination with @Metric to inject the Histogram metric. This metric takes a long or int for its update methods to update the internal data. The @Metric annotation is used to pass in the name, description, and absolute metadata values to the metric. Within the countConversions method, the returned count is passed to the update method for the computation. With the name set to absolute, the metric can be queried from the path /metrics/application/count_conversions_histogram. Listing 9-14 shows the sample returned data for the invocation.

Listing 9-14. showing the data returned for the Histogram metric

```
# TYPE application_count_conversions_histogram_mean gauge
application_count_conversions_histogram_mean{count="histogram",metric="hist
ogram"} 417.7099758660769
# TYPE application_count_conversions_histogram_max gauge
application_count_conversions_histogram_max{count="histogram",metric="histo
gram"} 500.0
# TYPE application_count_conversions_histogram_min gauge
application_count_conversions_histogram_min{count="histogram",metric="histo
gram"} 253.0
# TYPE application_count_conversions_histogram_stddev gauge
application_count_conversions_histogram_stddev{count="histogram",metric="hi
stogram"} 82.50134125075685
# TYPE application_count_conversions_histogram summary
# HELP application_count_conversions_histogram A histogram for the count of
conversions
application_count_conversions_histogram_count{count="histogram",metric="his
togram"} 21
application_count_conversions_histogram_sum{count="histogram",metric="histo
gram"} 8541
application_count_conversions_histogram{count="histogram",metric="histogram
",quantile="0.5"} 462.0
```

```
application_count_conversions_histogram{count="histogram",metric="histogram
",quantile="0.75"} 490.0
application_count_conversions_histogram{count="histogram",metric="histogram
",quantile="0.95"} 500.0
application_count_conversions_histogram{count="histogram",metric="histogram
",quantile="0.98"} 500.0
application_count_conversions_histogram{count="histogram",metric="histogram
",quantile="0.99"} 500.0
application_count_conversions_histogram{count="histogram",metric="histogram
",quantile="0.999"} 500.0
```

As shown in Listing 9-14, the Histogram metric returns statistical data for a given object that you want to track. Unlike the other metrics, you will need to inject the histogram as done in Listing 9-13 to have it automatically registered in the registry or manually register it.

Manual Registration of Metrics

The histogram metric can equally be manually instantiated and registered in the metrics registry by first injecting the MetricRegistry through CDI, then building the metadata through the MetaData interface, and finally calling the histogram method on the injected MetricRegistry instance to register and get a Histogram instance. Listing 9-15 shows these steps in code in the RateService bean.

Listing 9-15. showing manual instantiation of the histogram metric

```
@ApplicationScoped
public class RateService {

      @Inject
      MetricRegistry registry;

      @Gauge(name = "convert_currency_gauge_count", unit = MetricUnits.
      NONE, absolute = true)
      public int countConversions() {
            int conversionCount = ThreadLocalRandom.current().nextInt(250,
            500 + 1);

      Metadata metadata = Metadata.builder()
```

```
                                .withName("count_conversions_histogram")
                                .withDescription("A histogram for the count of
                                conversions")
                                .withDisplayName("A histogram")
                                .build();
        Histogram manualHistogram = registry.histogram(metadata);
        manualHistogram.update(conversionCount);

        return conversionCount;
    }
}
```

Listing 9-15 shows the histogram metric manually instantiated in the RateService bean. The MetricRegistry is injected with @Inject. Then the builder pattern is used to build a Metadata object. This Metadata is exactly the same details you would have passed to the @Metric annotation. Then the histogram method is called on the MetricRegistry object, passing in the just built metadata object. This invocation returns a Histogram instance that can then be used to create histograms. The Histogram functionality will be the same no matter which construct is used to instantiate it.

Metrics Metadata

Metadata is all the information that helps describe a given metric. You can retrieve metadata about an individual metric or that of a given scope or the entire set of metrics by making an HTTP OPTIONS call to /metric or any of its variations. The Accept header of the OPTIONS call should be application/json because the metadata is returned as JSON. For instance, we can get all the metadata for all the metrics covered in this chapter by making an HTTP OPTIONS call to /metrics/application. The sample call shown in Listing 9-16 returns the metadata shown in Listing 9-17.

Listing 9-16. showing a sample metadata call

```
OPTIONS http://localhost:3001/metrics/application/base
Accept: application/json
```

Listing 9-17. showing metadata for the application metric scope


```
{
      "convert_currency_simple_timer": {
            "unit": "nanoseconds",
            "displayName": "convert_currency_simple_timer",
            "name": "convert_currency_simple_timer",
            "description": "",
            "type": "simple timer",
            "tags": []
      },
      "convert_currency_counted": {
            "unit": "none",
            "displayName": "Convert currency method",
            "name": "convert_currency_counted",
            "description": "Method to convert one currency to the other",
            "type": "counter",
            "tags": [
                  [
                        "info=conversions",
                        "type=meta"
                  ]
            ]
      },
      "convert_currency_timer": {
            "unit": "nanoseconds",
            "displayName": "convert_currency_timer",
            "name": "convert_currency_timer",
            "description": "",
            "type": "timer",
            "tags": []
      },
      "convert_currency_meter": {
            "unit": "per_second",
            "displayName": "convert_currency_meter",
            "name": "convert_currency_meter",
```

```
        "description": "",
        "type": "meter",
        "tags": []
    },
    "count_conversions_histogram": {
        "unit": "none",
        "displayName": "count_conversions_histogram",
        "name": "count_conversions_histogram",
        "description": "A histogram for the count of conversions",
        "type": "histogram",
        "tags": [
            [
                "count=histogram",
                "metric=histogram"
            ]
        ]
    },
    "convert_currency_concurrent_gauge": {
        "unit": "none",
        "displayName": "convert_currency_concurrent_gauge",
        "name": "convert_currency_concurrent_gauge",
        "description": "Method to convert one currency to the other",
        "type": "concurrent gauge",
        "tags": [
            [
                "convert=custom"
            ]
        ]
    }
}
```

Other MicroProfile Spec Metrics

As a suite of tightly integrated specifications, using the Fault Tolerance API in an application automatically exposes related metrics under the /metrics/base scope. As a developer, all you have to do is use the Fault Tolerance API, and you will have these metrics exposed for you. As an example, a call to the /metrics/base endpoint returns all the Fault Tolerance metrics, a sample of which is shown in Listing 9-18.

Listing 9-18. showing a sample of the Fault Tolerance metrics

```
# TYPE base_ft_bulkhead_runningDuration_mean_seconds gauge
base_ft_bulkhead_runningDuration_mean_seconds{method="com.example.jwallet.
rate.rate.control.RateService.convertCurrency"} 0.6664609707678424
# TYPE base_ft_bulkhead_runningDuration_max_seconds gauge
base_ft_bulkhead_runningDuration_max_seconds{method="com.example.jwallet.
rate.rate.control.RateService.convertCurrency"} 7.678077344
# TYPE base_ft_bulkhead_runningDuration_min_seconds gauge
base_ft_bulkhead_runningDuration_min_seconds{method="com.example.jwallet.
rate.rate.control.RateService.convertCurrency"} 0.28274852300000003
# TYPE base_ft_bulkhead_runningDuration_stddev_seconds gauge
base_ft_bulkhead_runningDuration_stddev_seconds{method="com.example.
jwallet.rate.rate.control.RateService.convertCurrency"} 1.504029612722161
# TYPE base_ft_bulkhead_runningDuration_seconds summary
base_ft_bulkhead_runningDuration_seconds_count{method="com.example.jwallet.
rate.rate.control.RateService.convertCurrency"} 20
base_ft_bulkhead_runningDuration_seconds_sum{method="com.example.jwallet.
rate.rate.control.RateService.convertCurrency"} 14199386249
base_ft_bulkhead_runningDuration_seconds{method="com.example.jwallet.rate.
rate.control.RateService.convertCurrency",quantile="0.5"} 0.308184634
base_ft_bulkhead_runningDuration_seconds{method="com.example.jwallet.
rate.rate.control.RateService.convertCurrency",quantile="0.75"}
0.39874514600000005
base_ft_bulkhead_runningDuration_seconds{method="com.example.jwallet.
rate.rate.control.RateService.convertCurrency",quantile="0.95"}
0.48290750400000004
```

```
base_ft_bulkhead_runningDuration_seconds{method="com.example.jwallet.rate.
rate.control.RateService.convertCurrency",quantile="0.98"} 7.678077344
base_ft_bulkhead_runningDuration_seconds{method="com.example.jwallet.rate.
rate.control.RateService.convertCurrency",quantile="0.99"} 7.678077344
base_ft_bulkhead_runningDuration_seconds{method="com.example.jwallet.rate.
rate.control.RateService.convertCurrency",quantile="0.999"} 7.678077344
```

CDI Stereotypes and Metrics

As discussed in the chapter on Jakarta Contexts and Dependency Injection, CDI stereotypes are a way to group common infrastructure annotations together under one annotation. Using the resulting stereotype on a bean is as if all the annotations that make up the stereotype are used individually on the bean.

Consequently, when you annotate a stereotype with any of the Metrics annotations, the resulting bean will be treated by the Metrics runtime as if the metrics annotation was applied directly to the bean. The resulting names of the metrics are computed relative to the name and package of the bean itself, not of the stereotype.

As an example, the @Action stereotype, developed in Chapter 4, is reproduced in Listing 9-19, annotated with @Counted and @SimplyTimed. These annotations will cause all beans that are annotated @Action to have their constructor and method invocations counted and simply timed, respectively.

Listing 9-19. showing the @Action stereotype with @Counted and @SimplyTimed

```
@Stereotype
@RequestScoped
@Counted
@SimplyTimed
@Transactional
@Logged
@Retention(RetentionPolicy.RUNTIME)
@Target(ElementType.TYPE)
public @interface Action {

}
```

Summary

This chapter discussed the Eclipse MicroProfile Metrics specification for use on the Jakarta EE platform. We looked at the metrics scopes, data format, and how to use metrics through annotations, CDI injection, or manual instantiation. All through, you learned how to retrieve metrics information from the provided /metrics endpoint of a MicroProfile-enabled application.

CHAPTER 10

Taking a Pulse with Heal Check

Applications packaged as container images and deployed to the cloud are mostly managed by automated scheduling and deployment systems like Kubernetes. These systems will kill unhealthy containers, spawn new ones, and route requests to the requisite containers, all automatically. To help achieve these, the deployment manager will need to be able to probe the application instance for some health-related information.

A kubelet (the Kubernetes "agent") will probe a container to check if it's live and ready to accept requests. The response will determine if traffic gets routed to that deployed container instance or it gets killed and replaced with a healthy one. Cloud-native applications therefore should be able to answer three simple questions in a cloud environment:

- Have you started?
- Are you live?
- Are you ready to accept requests?

The Eclipse MicroProfile Health specification provides the API constructs for adding machine-to-machine health checks to applications so they can answer these questions. This specification is similar and compatible with existing such specifications like the Kubernetes[1] Liveness, Readiness, and Startup Probes. This chapter discusses the Health API and how to add it to your application.

[1] Configure Liveness, Readiness and Startup Probes | Kubernetes

L. Saeed and G. Abdallah, *Pro Cloud Native Java EE Apps*, https://doi.org/10.1007/978-1-4842-8900-6_10

Health vs. Metrics

The Health and Metrics APIs are both APIs that generate application performance information. However, the similarity between both ends there. The Health API is primarily designed to generate machine-to-machine-level information. In a typical cloud cluster where everything about application deployment is automated, the Health API provides the construct for enabling an application to respond to simple machine queries about its status and readiness to accept requests.

The Metrics API (discussed in Chapter 9), on the other hand, is designed primarily for generating detailed application performance data. For instance, the Metrics API can be used to query how long a given method takes to execute, what the maximum number of concurrent connections to the method is, what the mean response time is, and other such detailed, fine-grained information. These two APIs complement each other in the design of modern cloud-native applications.

Health API Structure

The Health API revolves around two types: the HealthCheck interface and the HealthCheckResponse class. All health check procedures can be queried from the / health context path. An HTTP GET request to this path returns call health checks in that particular application in the JSON format. Successful health check probes will return the HTTP 200 status code. A failed health check will return HTTP status code 503. In this case, the application implementation of the HealthCheck returns a DOWN status.

The HealthCheck Interface

The HealthCheck interface is a functional interface with the single method call() that returns a HealthCheckResponse. This interface is the entry point to the Health API. A class that wants to respond to health check probes will extend the HealthCheck interface, implementing the call() method in an application-specific way, eventually returning a HealthCheckResponse.

The HealthCheckResponse

The HealthCheckResponse is a class that encapsulates the response that a health check probe returns. It has three simple fields, namely, name, status, and data. The first two fields are of type String and the last one is an Optional< Map<String, Object>> type. The data field can be used to return free-form additional data that a health check implementation would like to return to a calling client. It has a convenient builder method for building the response. The name field is mandatory and must be provided for every instance of the HealthCheckResponse.

After a health check component performs some kind of application-specific check, it can then build the HealthCheckResponse and return an instance that tells the caller if the particular health check is up or down and also pass some optional data.

Health and CDI

The Health API is built on the Jakarta Contexts and Dependency Injection specification (Chapter 4). What this implies is that all health check components are CDI beans. As health check components are required to implement the HealthCheck interface, all health check components are bean types of at least HealthCheck.

However, as mentioned in the opening section, the Health API allows an application to respond to two simple questions. As there can be more than one bean type of HealthCheck, the API comes with three CDI qualifiers to distinguish HealthCheck beans from each other.

Health Check Qualifiers

The three health check qualifiers for identifying which beans respond to which health probe are

- @Readiness
- @Liveness
- @Startup

@Readiness

The @Readiness qualifier, used on a HealthCheck bean, creates a readiness health check procedure. This health check allows the caller to know if the application is ready to accept requests. Readiness health checks can be queried from the resource /health/ready. To create a readiness health check, annotate a bean of type HealthCheck with @Readiness as shown in Listing 10-1.

Listing 10-1. shows a @Readiness health check

```
@ApplicationScoped
@Readiness
public class HelloReadiness implements HealthCheck {

    CountDownLatch countDownLatch = new CountDownLatch(2);

    @Override
    public HealthCheckResponse call() {
        countDownLatch.countDown();
        return countDownLatch.getCount() == 0
                    ? HealthCheckResponse.up("rate-readiness")
                    : HealthCheckResponse.down("rate-readiness");
    }
}
```

Listing 10-1 shows the HelloReadiness bean implementing the HealthCheck interface. This bean is an @ApplicationScoped bean that bears the @Readiness qualifier. Since a health check probe covers the entire application, a single application-scoped instance of the HealthCheck implementation suffices. We don't need to create a new contextual instance for each probe. The @Readiness annotation marks this bean as a readiness health check and will be called by the Health runtime if the /health root health resource is queried or the specific /health/ready endpoint.

For this example, the call method implementation uses a simple CountDownLatch to simulate some form of countdown. As the bean is a CDI bean, you can inject any dependency into and carry out any custom, application-specific task to determine the readiness of the application. The only requirement is to return the HealthCheckResponse object.

A sample readiness probe to the path /health/ready returns the health data as shown in Listing 10-2.

Listing 10-2. shows the response from a call to /health/ready

```
{
    "checks": [
        {
            "data": {},
            "name": "rate-readiness",
            "status": "UP"
        }
    ],
    "status": "UP"
}
```

Listing 10-2 shows the JSON representation of the HealthCheckResponse object. For the @Readiness probe, the health check procedure reports that it is UP and ready. This means the rate module of jwallet is up and ready to accept requests.

@Liveness

The @Liveness qualifier on a HealthCheck bean creates a health check to determine if the application is running. In a cloud environment, if this call fails with a DOWN status, for instance, a kubelet could then use this information to discard that container instance and replace it with a healthier one. To create @Liveness health check, annotate a HealthCheck bean with @Liveness as shown in Listing 10-3.

Listing 10-3. shows a @Liveness health check implementation

```
@ApplicationScoped
@Liveness
public class HelloLiveness implements HealthCheck {

    LocalDateTime init = LocalDateTime.now(ZoneOffset.UTC);

    @Override
    public HealthCheckResponse call() {
        LocalDateTime now = LocalDateTime.now(ZoneOffset.UTC);
```

```
        Duration upDuration = Duration.between(init, now);

        return HealthCheckResponse.builder()
                .up()
                .name("rate_service_live")
                .withData("up_since", upDuration.toMinutes())
                .build();
    }
}
```

Listing 10-3 shows @Liveness health check implementation in the HelloLiveness bean. This implementation simply returns the UP status and a free-form data showing the number of minutes that the service has been live. The free-form data can be anything the health check implementation would like to return to the client. A sample call to this @Liveness implementation returns the data shown in Listing 10-4.

Listing 10-4. shows a liveness health check response

```
{
    "checks": [
        {
            "data": {
                "up_since": 2
            },
            "name": "rate_service_live",
            "status": "UP"
        }
    ],
    "status": "UP"
}
```

Listing 10-4 shows the HealthCheckResponse JSON representation from the @Liveness check. With this information and the HTTP status code 200, a kubelet will know that the application instance is up and running.

@Startup

@Startup is a health check that allows applications to create custom startup health checks that can be used for some form of application-specific verification before the liveness probe takes over. This health check procedure, in a cloud environment will be mapped to the startup Kubernetes probes. @Startup is suitable for situations where your application depends on an external service. In such cases, you might want to ensure the external service is up and running before your application is put into service. Listing 10-5 shows a startup health check implementation in the HelloStartup bean.

Listing 10-5. shows a @Startup health check implementation

```
@ApplicationScoped
@Startup
public class HelloStartup implements HealthCheck {
      CountDownLatch countDownLatch = new CountDownLatch(5);
      LocalDateTime upSince = LocalDateTime.now(ZoneOffset.UTC);

      @Override
      public HealthCheckResponse call() {

            countDownLatch.countDown();
            return countDownLatch.getCount() == 0
                        ? HealthCheckResponse.named("rate-startup")
                        .withData("up_since", upSince.toString())
                        .up()
                        .build()
                        : HealthCheckResponse.down("rate-startup");

      }

}
```

Listing 10-5 shows a @Startup health check implementation that simply counts down to five and returns UP after. A sample call to the /health/started endpoint returns the data shown in Listing 10-6.

Listing 10-6. shows the returned data for the startup health probe

```
{
    "checks": [
        {
            "data": {
                "up_since": "2022-08-14T17:26:33.363745328"
            },
            "name": "rate-startup",
            "status": "UP"
        }
    ],
    "status": "UP"
}
```

Combining Health Checks

The health checks seen so far have all been implemented by separate beans. However, they can all be combined and implemented by a single bean. In this case, the single HealthCheck bean will be annotated with all the required health check qualifiers. Such a HealthCheck implementation will be used to resolve all health checks for which it is annotated. Listing 10-7 shows a single health check implementation for @Liveness, @Readiness, and @Startup.

Listing 10-7. shows a single health check implementation

```
@ApplicationScoped
@Liveness
@Readiness
@Startup
public class HelloHealth implements HealthCheck {
    LocalDateTime upSince = LocalDateTime.now(ZoneOffset.UTC);
    @Inject
    ApiLayer apiLayer;

    @Override
```

```
    public HealthCheckResponse call() {
        JsonObject currencySymbols = apiLayer.getCurrencySymbols();
        boolean success = currencySymbols.getBoolean("success", false);
        return success
                    ? HealthCheckResponse.named("rate-service")
                    .withData("up_since", upSince.toString())
                    .withData("rate_api_provider", "up")
                    .up()
                    .build()
                    : HealthCheckResponse.down("rate-service");
    }
}
```

Listing 10-7 shows a single health check implementation for liveness, readiness, and startup. For this implementation, an external call is made to the rate service provider for the application. The only time we want to return an UP health check response is when the external service provider is available. Since we delegate rate conversion to that service, there is not much point in putting our application into service when the external provider we depend on is down. A call to /health, /health/live, /health/ready, and health/started will all be routed to this single implementation. A sample call to /health returns the data shown in Listing 10-8.

Listing 10-8. shows data for the single health check implementation


```
{
    "checks": [
        {
            "data": {
                "up_since": "2022-08-14T17:59:26.592292658",
                "rate_api_provider": "up"
            },
            "name": "rate-service",
            "status": "UP"
        }
    ],
    "status": "UP"
}
```

Producing Health Checks

As discussed in the chapter on Jakarta Contexts and Dependency Injection (Chapter 4), producers are a construct for creating CDI beans. As HealthChecks are CDI beans, they can be produced using the CDI producer method construct. Listing 10-9 shows the WalletHealthCheckProducer bean with three producer methods, each with a qualifier for the three health checks of liveness, readiness, and startup.

Listing 10-9. shows HealthCheck creation with producer methods

```
@ApplicationScoped
public class WalletHealthCheckProducer {
      CountDownLatch readinessCountdown = new CountDownLatch(2);
      CountDownLatch startupCountdown = new CountDownLatch(5);
      @Inject
      @ConfigProperty(name = "free.memory.limit")
      Integer freeMemoryLimit;
      @Produces
      @Liveness
      HealthCheck livenessCheck() {
            String healthCheckName = "wallet-liveness-health-check";
            return () -> {
                  long totalMemory = Runtime.getRuntime().totalMemory();
                  long freeMemory = Runtime.getRuntime().freeMemory();
                  boolean adequateMemory = (((float) freeMemory /
                  totalMemory) * 100) > freeMemoryLimit;
                  return adequateMemory ?
                              HealthCheckResponse
                                          .builder()
                                          .name(healthCheckName)
                                          .up()
                                          .build() :
                              HealthCheckResponse
                                          .named(healthCheckName)
                                          .down()
```

```
                    .build();
        };
    }

    @Produces
    @Readiness
    HealthCheck readinessCheck() {
        return () -> {
            readinessCountdown.countDown();
            return readinessCountdown.getCount() == 0 ?
                    HealthCheckResponse
                            .up("wallet-liveness") :
                    HealthCheckResponse
                            .down("wallet-liveness");
        };
    }

    @Produces
    @Startup
    HealthCheck startupCheck() {
        return () -> {
            startupCountdown.countDown();
            return startupCountdown.getCount() == 0 ?
                    HealthCheckResponse
                            .up("wallet-started") :
                    HealthCheckResponse
                            .down("wallet-startup-failed");
        };
    }
}
```

Listing 10-9 shows the @ApplicationScoped WalletHealthCheckProducer with three methods. Each method is annotated with the CDI @Produces and a health check qualifier. The first method is a @Liveness check that returns a status if the free memory relative to the total memory available in the JVM is more than the passed configured value. In the sample code, the MicroProfile config value passed in the microprofile-config.properties is 40. So if the free memory in the JVM is more than 40%, then the liveness check returns a HealthCheckResponse object with status up. Otherwise, it returns a down status.

The second method is a @Readiness check that simply counts down to two and returns an up status. The third method is a @Startup check that also counts down to five and then returns an up status. Listing 10-10 shows the returned data for a sample call to the /health endpoint for this module.

Listing 10-10. showing the returned health check data for the produced health checks

```
{
        "checks": [
                {
                        "data": {},
                        "name": "wallet-readiness",
                        "status": "UP"
                },
                {
                        "data": {},
                        "name": "wallet-liveness-health-check",
                        "status": "DOWN"
                },
                {
                        "data": {},
                        "name": "wallet-started",
                        "status": "UP"
                }
        ],
        "status": "DOWN"
}
```

Listing 10-10 shows the response for the /health probe for the wallet module of jwallet. In the sample call, the JVM reports the available free memory to be less than 40% of total memory, resulting in the @Liveness check returning a down status. It is important to note that the response isn't necessarily returned in any given order. Even though in the code the liveness call is declared before the readiness check, the call to the base /health endpoint returns the result of the readiness check first before the liveness check.

Summary

This chapter discussed the Eclipse MicroProfile Health specification. We looked at the difference between this specification and Metrics specification. The discussion then looked at the structure of the Health API. We then looked at using it within the context of the CDI API. You should be able to create custom health check procedures for your cloud-native applications using the Health API.

CHAPTER 11

Security with JWT

Security is one of the most important aspects of application development. There are so many things that can go wrong so fast with security. A rapidly evolving domain, there are constantly new threats, exploits, and breaches happening at all times. From the largest public-facing applications to the smallest, every application is at risk of security breaches.

Application security is a complex field that should be handled by security experts. This chapter discusses how to use the Eclipse MicroProfile JWT Propagation API to secure RESTful web services. This chapter is NOT about the how of security. But rather with the how of security in place, the goal of the chapter is to show how the MicroProfile JWT API can be used to make use of the security infrastructure to secure REST resources.

As application developers, we the authors trust the management of the entire process to security experts. As such, this chapter uses Keycloak[1] as the security framework, from which the MicroProfile JWT can be used to secure REST clients. Keycloak is an open source identity and access management (IAM) framework. It provides user federation, strong authentication, user management, fine-grained authorization, and more. This chapter delegates the process of creating users to Keycloak and focuses on using JWT to secure web resources.

Token-Based Authentication

RESTful web services are stateless by nature. This means every request is independent of the previous request. The server will need to be given the same security-related information with each request. The most efficient way to achieve this form of stateless security is through the use of tokens. A token is a long string that can be verified to ascertain the veracity of the claim of a calling client. It allows systems to authenticate,

[1] Keycloak

L. Saeed and G. Abdallah, *Pro Cloud Native Java EE Apps*, https://doi.org/10.1007/978-1-4842-8900-6_11

authorize, and verify the identity of a client. Token-based security does not rely on the HTTP session, making it much more scalable, performant, and reliable.

The token is mostly added to the request header. This will then be grabbed by the service and validated, introspective to extract information about the calling client and then create a security context that can then be propagated to all parts of the protected service. The MicroProfile JWT API is a token-based authentication, authorization, and role-based access control (RBAC) mechanism that can be used for token-based application security. JSON Web Token or JWT is a token-based standard[2] that has emerged as the most popular standard for creating lightweight security tokens.

A JWT token is usually signed so the service can verify the token. The information contained in a token is called claims. The claims can also be encrypted so they are not passed as plain text in the header. A typical JWT is made up of the header, the claims (or body), and the signature.

The Header

The JWT section of a JWT typically contains the type of algorithm used to sign the JWT (RS256, ES256, HS256, etc.), the type of the token (e.g., JWT), the key ID, and other metadata depending on the issuer of the token. Signing the JWT only enables receiving service to verify that the information has not been tampered with. It does not make the token unreadable. For that, a token will need to be encrypted, in addition to the signing.

The Claims (or Body)

The claims or body of the JWT is all the information that the client would like to pass to the server. A lot of the time, the body contains the roles that a given client is assigned. Roles determine the extent to which a client can carry out different operations in an application.

The Signature

The signature is optional by highly recommended information that allows the service to verify that the token has not changed or been tampered with along the way.

[2] JSON Web Token (JWT)

A JWT is a base64 encoded string of the header, claims, and signature information. Listing 11-1 shows a sample JWT token.

Listing 11-1. Sample JWT


```
eyJhbGciOiJSUzI1NiIsInR5cCIgOiAiSldUIiwia2lkIiA6ICJEMkdxYmxJU3YzY1Jpdmh2
ZFROYmpaVDg2VkFGeUFpT29wZGlvZHYtQllJIn0.eyJleHAiOjE2NjE2MzY5MDksImlhdCI6
MTY2MTYzNjYwOSwianRpIjoiOTAxOGVlZmEtZDc2NiooODI4LTgwMmUtYjFkNjMwO
TQ5ODUxIiwiaXNzIjoiaHROcDovL2xvY2FsaG9zdDo1MDUwL3JlYWxtcy9qd2FsbGVOIi
wiYXVkIjoiYWNjb3VudCIsInN1YiI6ImY2OTUOYTRkLTFmZmEtNGNkMCO5YmRhLTM4NmVk
OWQwNzQ3ZCIsInR5cCI6IkJlYXJlciIsImF6cCI6Imp3YWxsZXQtc2VydmljZSIsInNlc3Npb
25fc3RhdGUiOiJlOTY1ZWQ3YSOOOTI3LTQ5MzItODQyOS1jNWNhMjNmYzQ5NzMiLCJhY3IiOi
IxIiwicmVhbG1fYWNjZXNzIjp7InJvbGVzIjpbIm9mZmxpbmVfYWNjZXNzIiwiZGVmYXVsdC
1yb2xlcy1qd2FsbGVOIiwidGVsbGVyIiwidW1hX2F1dGhvcml6YXRpb24iXXOsInJlc291cm
NlX2FjY2VzcyI6eyJhY2NvdW5OIjp7InJvbGVzIjpbIm1hbmFnZS1hY2NvdW5OIiwibWFuYW
dlLWFjY291bnQtbGlua3MiLCJ2aWV3LXByb2ZpbGUiXX19LCJzY29wZSI6InByb2ZpbG
UgZW1haWwiLCJzaWQiOiJlOTY1ZWQ3YSOOOTI3LTQ5MzItODQyOS1jNWNhMjNmYzQ5NzMi
LCJ1cG4iOiJtYXgiLCJlbWFpbF92ZXJpZmllZCI6ZmFsc2UsImdyb3VwcyI6WyJvZmZsaW5l
X2FjY2VzcyIsImRlZmF1bHQtcm9sZXMtandhbGxldCIsInRlbGxlciIsInVtYV9hdXRob3Jp
emFOaW9uIl0sInByZWZlcnJlZF91c2VybmFtZSI6Im1heCJ9.lG6zEr-BEMQwyEUsw
IgCM5InWAH4ljAu8JK6ZcOnaHD8kcaGAssxsXHzf315n--cysYJzeAQBfDmzsJr_RoeOio2
nN4CZ61T6Vz4YnE_5_RRn9n6cl2rG_1oIsLknqKVseNQ4itZZjKfIGVUYxURxKmO6gsCH8FC
HN1hu7rmq4jwPCOaO7Ypvjg2IpExsIociprXk7_1iyflIZ4XnlHYBADOpkNOduJgMyojQwBgTz
-xa-9sBb-eoKys1gBD3nbV8STNbKAGzOUiQaq28T4x3pIn6JNfw2JbBu6_cxKXhzghoPukboLh
n2C_MYJt4OiycxuprsbDRKoxAIjus_9yoA
```


Listing 11-2 shows the decoded JWT. It shows the three parts, namely, header, claims, and signature.

Listing 11-2. Decoded JWT

```
{
  "alg": "RS256",
  "typ": "JWT",
  "kid": "D2GqblISv3cRivhvdTtbjZT86VAFyAiOopdiodv-BYI"
}
```

```
{
  "exp": 1661636909,
  "iat": 1661636609,
  "jti": "9018eefa-d766-4828-802e-b1d630949851",
  "iss": "http://localhost:5050/realms/jwallet",
  "aud": "account",
  "sub": "f6954a4d-1ffa-4cd0-9bda-386ed9d0747d",
  "typ": "Bearer",
  "azp": "jwallet-service",
  "session_state": "e965ed7a-4927-4932-8429-c5ca23fc4973",
  "acr": "1",
  "realm_access": {
    "roles": [
      "offline_access",
      "default-roles-jwallet",
      "teller",
      "uma_authorization"
    ]
  },
  "resource_access": {
    "account": {
      "roles": [
        "manage-account",
        "manage-account-links",
        "view-profile"
      ]
    }
  },
  "scope": "profile email",
  "sid": "e965ed7a-4927-4932-8429-c5ca23fc4973",
  "upn": "max",
  "email_verified": false,
  "groups": [
    "offline_access",
    "default-roles-jwallet",
```

```
    "teller",
    "uma_authorization"
  ],
  "preferred_username": "max"
}

{
  "e": "AQAB",
  "kty": "RSA",
  "n": "3buUZWrOFp9Rm85GPIAoYfiqNapj2DxW8gjMWOjPEgg4KUqg3tSC6GOkAzPJ7OzMm
  fe-b3CWBQvmNXWIUZCXPlnBuVKyWcowBQk7QRnEkOuw5vL6bYU5I2DA_1CPIn4v3g4oxOGmjO
  wDflrlb2vlPw76BpHIKd-EUI-mkm-Yv6H6OBZmo7iRyVF7TNGVYgIgOxrVFPIvTDV2yvZKO4q
  G6qYWk2khMPqXm-725QBp2wgWDhowibjuoOCW1S5BCr5qc3N-uaPej7Nbcub8Ov1XGJ7feHq
  g4TXtNDCSikTAGCaOgeW3eP1wRoE_9QYzKlN45LI8Lxhnc
  Ul58WpdulgblQ"
}
```

The MicroProfile JWT

The MicroProfile JWT API provides a standard, mostly opinionated way of verifying a JWT token, authorizing the client and propagating the resulting security context to the rest of the application. It achieves these objectives by requiring that JWTs be signed with RSA-based digital signature algorithms. All that the JWT runtime needs is the public key of the authorizing server which creates the JWT to verify the token. It also mandates certain information to be available within the claims of the JWT. These are as follows:

- exp – The expiration of the JWT. This ensures old, expired tokens are rejected.
- iss – The issuer of the token.
- iat – The issued at, identifies when the token was issued.
- upn – This is the user principal or the preferred username of the currently logged in user.

It also has recommended claims as follows:

- sub – Who is being represented by this token?
- jti – A unique identifier for this claim.
- aud – Identifies the MP JWT endpoint(s) which can be accessed by JWT.

These requirements allow a Jakarta EE application to be fully stateless. The sub claim will be mapped to a java.security.Principal instance. The groups will be used to determine if the Principal is in a given role required by a given resource method. The client will send the token with each request; the JWT runtime will validate and propagate the security context with each call.

MicroProfile JWT Security Process

MicroProfile JWT allows the creation of stateless microservices by delegating the session information about users to the client. Each call by the client contains all the information needed to construct a security context. This security context is then plugged into existing Jakarta EE infrastructure that is available to all parts of the application. There are three steps in the MicroProfile JWT security process.

Authenticate the Client

The MicroProfile JWT runtime automatically validates the passed JWT token on the request header using the available public key of the issuing server or authority. This is where Keycloak comes in in our context. We use Keycloak as the issuing authority to issue the JWT tokens on our behalf.

A typical enterprise application will have two tiers: the client or UI tier, which can be written in, for instance, Angular or Vue, and the server or resource tier, which is what we have seen so far in this book. The client tier is the "user" or client of the server or resource tier. An end user will typically interact with the UI tier. When the end user clicks a button in the UI to, for instance, make a currency conversion, the UI sends a request to the back end or server. This request by the UI to the server is what will contain the JWT token. But how does the UI get the token?

When an application uses Keycloak like we are doing (and recommending), when a user clicks to sign up through the UI, that user creation process will be delegated to Keycloak. So the user credentials will be stored in Keycloak. When the user logs in through the UI, the UI redirects the user to Keycloak to log in. Keycloak authenticates the user and redirects them back to the UI. From this point, any operation made by the logged in user that entails calling the back-end server, the UI can go to Keycloak for a JWT token, which will be forwarded to the server with each request that the logged in user performs.

This architecture fully decouples the back-end server, or in this case our Jakarta EE application, from knowing anything about the user. Our resources simply require a valid token, and respective methods will require the currently executing user to have certain roles. All of this will be sent to the server with each call. This way, the UI tier and the back-end server tier are fully decoupled and stateless. There is no state sharing between them. Every security information needed by the server is sent with each client request.

The bundled Keycloak has a sample user called max with the password max that can be used to obtain JWTs. The sample cURL call in Listing 11-3 can be made to the open-id/connect endpoint in Keycloak to obtain a JWT token. This is the call that was used to generate the JWT shown in Listing 11-1.

Listing 11-3. Sample Keycloak call

```
curl --request POST --url http://localhost:5050/realms/jwallet/protocol/
openid-connect/token \
  --header 'Content-Type: application/x-www-form-urlencoded' \
  --data realm=jwallet \
  --data grant_type=password \
  --data client_id=jwallet-service \
  --data username=max \
  --data password=max
```

Providing the Public Key

The MicroProfile JWT runtime will validate and authenticate the passed JWT automatically by using the public key of the issuing server, in this case Keycloak. The MicroProfile JWT spec requires the provision of the public key or a URL for getting the public key. The specification defines two MicroProfile Config properties for passing the public key of the issuing authority or server to the MicroProfile JWT runtime. These properties are mp.jwt.verify.publickey and mp.jwt.verify.publickey.location.

The first property allows the passing of the public key text itself as the value of the property. The second property allows specifying a URL from which the public keys can be downloaded. Specifying both properties results in a deployment exception. The mp.jwt.verify.issuer property is also used to verify the value of the iss or issuer claim. The passed value in the JWT must match the passed value in the property.

Listing 11-4 shows the public key and issuer properties as used in jwallet. Because Keycloak is bundled as a container with the application, we supply a URL to the Keycloak resource for loading the public keys.

Listing 11-4. Passing the public key URL

```
mp.jwt.verify.publickey.location=http://keycloak:5050/realms/jwallet/
protocol/openid-connect/certs
mp.jwt.verify.issuer=http://localhost:5050/realms/jwallet
```

A call to `http://localhost:5050/realms/jwallet/protocol/openid-connect/certs` returns the sample public keys shown in Listing 11-5.

Listing 11-5. Sample public keys


```
{
"keys": [
{
"kid": "D2GqblISv3cRivhvdTtbjZT86VAFyAiOopdiodv-BYI",
"kty": "RSA",
"alg": "RS256",
"use": "sig",
"n": "3buUZWrOFp9Rm85GPIAoYfiqNapj2DxW8gjMWOjPEgg4KUqg3tSC6GOkAzPJ7OzMmfe-
b3CWBQvmNXWIUZCXPlnBuVKyWcowBQk7QRnEkOuw5vL6bYU5I2DA_1CPIn4v3g4oxOGmjOwDfl
rlb2vlPw76BpHIKd-EUI-mkm-Yv6H6OBZmo7iRyVF7TNGVYgIgOxrVFPIvTDV2yvZKO4qG6qYWk
2khMPqXm-725QBp2wgWDhowibjuoOCW1S5BCr5qc3N-uaPej7Nbcub8Ov1XGJ7feHqg4TXtNDC
SikTAGCaOgeW3eP1wRoE_9QYzKlN45LI8LxhncUl58WpdulgblQ",
"e": "AQAB",
"x5c": [
"MIICnTCCAYUCBgGC2NIn1TANBgkqhkiG9wOBAQsFADASMRAwDgYDVQQDDAdqd2FsbGVOMB4
XDTIyMDgyNjA2MjIwN1oXDTMyMDgyNjA2MjMON1owEjEQMA4GA1UEAwwHandhbGxldDCCASI
wDQYJKoZIhvcNAQEBBQADggEPADCCAQoCggEBAN27lGVq9BafUZvORjyAKGH4qjWqY9g8Vv
```

```
IIzFjozxIIOClKoN7UguhtJAMzye9MzJn3vm9wlgUL5jV1iFGQlz5ZwblSslnKMAUJOOEZx
JDrsOby+m2FOSNgwP9QjyJ+L94OKMdBpozsA35a5W9r5T8O+gaRyCnfhFCPppJvmL+h+tAW
ZqO4kclReOzRlWICINMa1RTyLOw1dsr2SjuKhuqmFpNpITD6l5vu9uUAadsIFg4aMIm47qD
gltUuQQq+anNzfrmj3o+zW3Lm/NL9Vxie33h6oOE17TQwkopEwBgmtIHlt3j9cEaBP/
UGMypTeOSyPC8YZ3FJefFqXbpYG5UCAwEAATANBgkqhkiG9w0BAQsFAAOCAQEAuuo6yFAS
kSWDLh9kyMTZhhcfV87ZEoC4kmkNn/2N2dOgypqxxLWPDG7rk2QLqocNTOIP6wh+cr9TO/
oAUdIc1vAJuLWsw/XiGbPjTVmxw9r1eg3tMphrw+wG4CrRNsKTs1xgDDMnAyTA7zNZylSw
AJ2YBy/7WAb1DzPdpwxuERY3Bn1U9pTV6Tth+SY3nODVWYl9ik2eyv/UoTCLdf9gInxHxo
yl6moIH944UZXdVnZ9s+TONtVu278fQNUJMbvufN1+IQQkZLH5zehVd8IY/vX1q9ROjFea
HjYEYSoggo3tCT93KVFYGA6UCm2ADQfluMxNwkIIdvfRVzqIuCKZuw=="
],
"x5t": "uej9O_JH-rlIpJVQMTBiD6kf-1k",
"x5t#S256": "szj37ByL-T6Plrmzbgb7Bnq32KsYtGp_B_dDOYGEWcI"
},
{
"kid": "B5uP6pwSkS-wvKmh31ZeEmeXNKU_UaO9EfTOeutOONY",
"kty": "RSA",
"alg": "RSA-OAEP",
"use": "enc",
"n": "sR3wZR9t35zM_sftCb2EbX6_tZo1boubrmnuj8YZ1utCOl2pQGX7v3uz_YHGsAbp-
3J3iCt94KliRKA2yYCVi2Ozqd-EEz6GAYxF1HzYghWO-j9jMrNu1N-O8LXVEp21wPdIDsIu
CLkqYWZGgoOzY2yyWkVjiHcAu3_LokwufVu-BM9iRY2FZrvgYEHPGZOk5a8hTIHSIx6dXUc
U6oZOetiGdidrIWH5GFXLSZtpcuya-wO1_o1Khm97dCtGY3pVasnLgDK6Vguzul1MdpTQHw
FI7m3O7uQBOCRtqe8qPnNxVLal_Ow5b5N7YNw5fufEqvLk5Dz-au4TPuFwSSvVrw",
"e": "AQAB",
"x5c": [
"MIICnTCCAYUCBgGC2NIoXjANBgkqhkiG9w0BAQsFADASMRAwDgYDVQQDDAdqd2FsbGVOMB
4XDTIyMDgyNjA2MjIwN1oXDTMyMDgyNjA2MjMON1owEjEQMA4GA1UEAwwHandhbGxldDCCA
SIwDQYJKoZIhvcNAQEBBQADggEPADCCAQoCggEBALEd8GUfbd+czP7H7Qm9hG1+v7WaNW6L
m65p7o/GGdbrQjpdqUBl+797s/2BxrAG6ftyd4grfeCpYkSgNsmAlYtjs6nfhBM+hgGMRdR
82IIVjvo/YzKzbtTfjvC11RKdtcD3SA7CLgi5KmFmRoKDs2NsslpFY4h3ALt/
y6JMLn1bvgTPYkWNhWa74GBBzxmTpOWvIUyBOiMenV1HFOqGdHrYhnYnayFh+RhVyOmbaXL
smvsNNf6NSoZve3QrRmN6VWrJy4AyulYLs7pdTHaUOB8BSO5tzu7kAdAkbanvKj5zcVS2pf
zsOW+Te2DcOX7nxKry5OQ8/mruEz7hcEkr1a8CAwEAATANBgkqhkiG9w0BAQsFAAOCAQEAX
WOwtyu6Tmv6i9rEvly5jvNcsNsvHVpW9tSVOKVWFPOYgvQOdIQoRhygpvVfZMrlXW5EQOu
```

```
KnvZCbt/BzEPMl3G6DfsaTssw1GeaquMgw1osNqG7HCHGqQX8+EG5U3Neov4+
YsSCtYYCWsYqO8OYK6lqp8TQO+Ok6u9aTpFvH233Gd9ZmM72fN8omfR2X5dwlwL
6uNAKiGc6rqavklVOqK3/TpSbYXG8oPGuAFmJMGmSJ9Xr1+xOgr3ncsYQnHf7jjTx7y3BG
+AB2G7y3uez2fXDBktjBUiAV+31N4fh99WnbOPiVkhM2lWFMeuL1jg+vDgL/
+PDziAGo2R5tgJM1w=="
],
"x5t": "rU2BclI4blvOQgymzyXOGHmm_Tk",
"x5t#S256": "Vkv7YeizaqHS23BlvZCJwTSpjpvp55J1PCmE2LtREos"
}
]
}
```


With the provided keys, the MicroProfile JWT runtime will automatically validate and authenticate each REST call to all protected resources in the application. By default, the runtime will look for the key in the HTTP Authorization header. This can be configured to something else through the Config property mp.jwt.token.header. We recommend leaving the default unless you have a very specific architectural reason to change that.

Authorization

When the client is authenticated, the MicroProfile JWT then maps the passed groups in the claims of the JWT to client roles. For each protected resource, the runtime will automatically check if the currently executing client has the role declared by the server.

Security Context Propagation

With the token verified and client authenticated, the MicroProfile JWT API provides ways of getting the raw token which can then be passed to other back-end resources in the microservice cluster. For instance, when a client authenticates with Service A, and Service A depends on Service B, if both are secured with MicroProfile JWT, Service A can get the raw token passed by the client and use that to make a call to Service B, thereby propagating the JWT to Service B.

MicroProfile JWT Usage

The first step to protecting resources with MicroProfile JWT is through the use of the @LoginConfig on a Jakarta REST jakarta.ws.rs.core.Application class. Listing 11-6 shows the RootResourceConfiguration class, which extends Application, annotated with @LoginConfig with the MP-JWT auth method.

Listing 11-6. JWT configuration

```
@ApplicationPath("api")
@LoginConfig(authMethod = "MP-JWT")
public class RootResourceConfiguration extends Application {
}
```

The @LoginConfig annotation tells the runtime that all resources in the application should be protected, and thus all client requests will need to pass a valid JWT for verification and authentication. With the configuration in place, securing a web resource is as simple as annotating the resource class or methods with @RolesAllowed. Listing 11-7 shows the WalletResource requiring only authenticated users with the role teller. User roles are completely managed in Keycloak. In enterprise applications, the product owner together with the business team will determine the requisite role for each user of an application. All of this can be done fully in Keycloak. Our backed service is simply consuming what is configured in the security framework.

Listing 11-7. WalletResource secured

```
@Consumes(MediaType.APPLICATION_JSON)
@Produces(MediaType.APPLICATION_JSON)
@Path("wallets")
@RolesAllowed("teller")
public class WalletResource {
}
```

The @RolesAllowed annotation, from the jakarta.annotation.security.RolesAllowed package, will cause a 401 HTTP status code to be returned to clients that make calls to any resource in this class without a valid token. Listing 11-8 shows the response of a sample unsecured call.

Listing 11-8. Response from a call with no token

```
http://localhost:3001/wallet/api/wallets

HTTP/1.1 401 Unauthorized
WWW-Authenticate: Bearer realm="MP-JWT", error="invalid_token"
Content-Language: en-US
Content-Length: 0
Date: Sun, 28 Aug 2022 00:13:24 GMT
```

Getting Information from Tokens

When a user successfully verified and authenticated, the application might want to get hold of some information contained in the claims of the token. The API provides two primary ways of accessing the claims in the body of the JWT. These are the JsonWebToken bean and the injection of claims value using the @Claim qualifier.

JsonWebToken

The JsonWebToken interface extends the java.security.Principal and contains methods for getting the claims in the JWT. It also has a method for getting the raw token. This can be used to get the raw token for onward propagation to other services. This is our recommended approach to consuming the claims of the JWT because the JsonWebToken instance does not require the bean into which it is injected to be @RequestScoped. Listing 11-9 shows the injection of the JsonWebToken into the @ApplicationScoped WalletService.

Listing 11-9. Injection of JsonWebToken

```
@ApplicationScoped
public class WalletService {

      @Inject
      JsonWebToken jsonWebToken;

      public BalanceResponse createWallet(CreateWalletRequest request){
            Wallet wallet = new Wallet();
            wallet.setBalance(BigDecimal.ZERO);
```

```
        wallet.setCurrency(request.getCurrency());
        wallet.setAuthUserId(jsonWebToken.getSubject());
        wallet = walletRepository.save(wallet);

        return getBalance(wallet.getId());
    }
}
```

The WalletService is an application-scoped bean that has the JsonWebToken injected into it. The MicroProfile JWT runtime will provide an implementation of the interface for us. The injected JsonWebToken can be used to obtain the claims of the token. The createUser method calls the getSubject method on the jsonWebToken to get the subject of the token. The subject of the token returned by Keycloak is the IAM ID of the user.

This way, we link wallet database records to the users in Keycloak without both services knowing anything about each other. The WalletService is not a Jakarta REST artifact. It is a plain CDI bean, but through the MicroProfile JWT API, we are able to access the claims in the token passed through the HTTP header in the service layer of our application. We believe this is the cleanest way to access claims from the JWT and thus recommend this approach. Even if an endpoint is not secured, resulting in no token passed, an empty instance of the JsonWebToken will be created. All method invocations on the empty instance will return null.

With this, we can also refactor the AbstractEntityListener to finally set the createdBy audit field for persisted entities. Listing 11-10 shows the updated AbstractEntityListener using the JsonWebToken to set the createdBy and updatedBy fields.

Listing 11-10. Using the JsonWebToken

```
@ApplicationScoped
public class AbstractEntityEntityListener {

  @Inject
  JsonWebToken jsonWebToken;

  @PrePersist
  void init(final Object entity) {
    final AbstractEntity abstractEntity = (AbstractEntity) entity;
    abstractEntity.setCreated(LocalDateTime.now(ZoneOffset.UTC));
```

```
    abstractEntity.setCreatedBy(jsonWebToken.getClaim(Claims.upn));
  }

  @PreUpdate
  void update(final Object entity) {
    final AbstractEntity abstractEntity = (AbstractEntity) entity;
    abstractEntity.setUpdated(LocalDateTime.now(ZoneOffset.UTC));
    abstractEntity.setEditedBy(jsonWebToken.getClaim(Claims.upn));
  }

}
```

The @PrePersist and @PreUpdate Jakarta Persistence callback methods use the getClaim method of the JsonWebToken to get a specific claim. The org.eclipse.microprofile.jwt.Claims enum contains constants of all claims in the JWT.

Injecting into Raw Types and ClaimValue

JWT claims can also be injected into simple Java types through @Inject and the use of the @Claims qualifier. We generally do not recommend this way of getting the tokens because some of the field types into which claims can be injected require the beans into which they're being injected to be @RequestScoped. Effectively, to be able to fully utilize injecting claim values this way, the bean should be @RequestScoped. Listing 11-11 shows the injection of claims using these two constructs.

Listing 11-11. Injecting into simple types

```
@Action
public class WalletService {

      @Inject
      @Claim(standard = Claims.sub)
      private String subject;

      @Inject
      @Claim(standard = Claims.raw_token)
      private ClaimValue<String> rawToken;

}
```

The subject field is a simple String type annotated @Inject and the qualifier @Claim. The standard parameter of the @Claim qualifier is passed the name of the claim to inject into this field. The Claims enum is used to pass the sub or subject claim as the claim of interest. The org.eclipse.microprofile.jwt.ClaimValue is an interface that extends the Principal interface. It has two methods, getName and getValue. getName returns the name of the claim, and getValue returns the value of the claim in the token.

MicroProfile JWT and the SecurityContext

The jakarta.ws.rs.core.SecurityContext interface is a Jakarta REST artifact that can be injected into resource artifacts through the @Context annotation. It has methods for getting the Principal, checking if the currently logged in user is in a given role, if the request was made through an HTTPS connection and the authentication scheme. In a MicroProfile JWT application, the isUserInRole method will map the role set to the passed groups of the claims in the token. The getPrincipal method will also return a Principal, which is also an instance of JsonWebToken. Effectively, the MicroProfile JWT propagates all the information passed through the token to all parts of the application and existing security infrastructure within Jakarta EE. Listing 11-12 shows injecting the SecurityContext into the Wallet Resource.

Listing 11-12. Injecting SecurityContext

```
@Consumes(MediaType.APPLICATION_JSON)
@Produces(MediaType.APPLICATION_JSON)
@Path("wallets")
@RolesAllowed("teller")
public class WalletResource {

    @Context
    SecurityContext securityContext;

}
```

Summary

This chapter covered the use of the MicroProfile JWT API for securing Jakarta EE REST resources. Given the complex nature of application security, this chapter followed best practices by offloading the handling of user credentials to an external service, in this case Keycloak. You learned how to activate the MicroProfile JWT in an application with the @LoginConfig annotation, then how individual resources can be secured either at the class or resource method level through the use of @RolesAllowed.

You also learned about how to access claims in a token through the JsonWebToken interface. You also learned that JWT claims are automatically propagated and available in existing Jakarta EE security infrastructure like the Principal and SecurityContext interfaces. We would like to reiterate again that security is a very complex and fast-changing domain, with new exploit breaches every day. As such, a hybrid security approach as discussed in this chapter, where the more complicated aspect like user credential handling is delegated to a specialist application like Keycloak, leaving our application to only consume the token generated is one way to mitigate security risks.

CHAPTER 12

Testing with TestContainers

Testing is an important aspect of application development. Whether it's a monolith of microservices applications being developed, testing must and should form a core part of the entire application development cycle. Even though testing is universally acknowledged as important, there is no one "right" way of doing it. The kind, type, and mode of testing chosen are mostly application and domain dependent.

A lot of the time, the application development platform will determine the testing options available to the application developers. On the Jakarta EE platform, which has the Java SE as its base, there is a vast array of testing options available. Picking the most optimal combination of the available testing options will mostly boil down to the application domain. This chapter will explore testing Jakarta EE applications using the venerable JUnit and TestContainers libraries.

The chapter starts off by exploring some basic testing theories, then takes a look at unit-testing Jakarta EE components, and then finally shows writing integration tests with TestContainers.[1] By the end of the chapter, you will have a good understanding of how to craft and write tests for your enterprise application.

The Theory of Application Testing

Testing can be defined as the process of establishing the general correctness and reliability of an application through a combination of different test types. The term "general" is important because testing does not guarantee that an application has no defects. It only surfaces possible defects in the application. There are two broad categories of tests, namely, manual and automated tests. Then there are different types

[1] Testcontainers

L. Saeed and G. Abdallah, *Pro Cloud Native Java EE Apps*, https://doi.org/10.1007/978-1-4842-8900-6_12

of tests that can be run under each of these categories. Some test types transcend both categories. The following is a list of the general types of application tests.

Types of Tests

Unit Tests

A unit test is an automated test that tests a single component in isolation to verify if the component is working as expected. Unit tests are the most atomic tests in any test suite. Depending on the particular component being unit-tested, its dependencies might be mocked in order to be able to unit-test just that component in isolation. Unit tests are generally very fast to run because of their isolated nature.

Integration Tests

An integration test is a test for asserting that different components of the application that together carry out a specific function work correctly. Integration tests span more than one component or microservice. For example, an integration test to assert the successful creation of a wallet can first assert the creation of a user before asserting for the creation of a wallet. In this case, an actual call will be made to both modules. Integration tests tend to be much more time consuming to run because they can span several components and most likely include several network calls. Integration tests are also automated.

Functional Tests

A functional test focuses on the business aspect of an application. Functional tests will normally verify the results of the operation under test. There is a slim difference between functional and integration tests because both tests will cause different components of the application to be invoked. In some organizations, functional and integration tests are one and the same. However, technically, functional tests assert the output of an operation to verify that it equals a preset, expected value. Integration tests, however, generally check if the components are working. Functional tests can be manual or automated.

Performance Tests

A performance test checks how the application behaves when subjected to different workloads. Performance tests can help unearth bottlenecks because they measure things like the speed of the application, the reliability of a site, and how scalable a component is, among others. This kind of test can help optimize applications based on the data gathered from the tests. Performance tests are automated.

Smoke Tests

A smoke test is mostly a manual test that checks if the basic functionality of an application is working as expected. Smoke tests generally follow a new build or release of the application and precede other types of checks.

Other Tests

There are other tests like end-to-end and acceptance testing that are different variations of integration and functional tests. In the end, every organization will have a mix of different test types and modes based on the domain. The test types enumerated earlier are in no way an exhaustive list of all the test types out there. But these are the most common that cut across all types of organizations.

Principles of Testing

As important as software application testing is, there is no universal criteria for determining what comprises good testing practices. The plethora of programming languages and application development frameworks out there mean testing is a highly heterogeneous activity that differs from one platform to the other and from one application to the other. The American Software Testing Qualifications Board (ASTQB) has identified seven principles[2] that can help guide the creation of an effective testing regime. These principles are as follows.

[2] Seven Testing Principles | ISTQB Foundation Level

Testing Shows the Presence of Defects, Not Their Absence

Tests can help surface bugs in an application. However, tests cannot guarantee that an application is bug-free. All the tests in a test suite passing does not mean there are no defects that can be unearthed. This notwithstanding, having extensive tests can give reasonable assurance that the application will not fail under conditions that have been tested.

Exhaustive Testing Is Impossible

Enterprise applications are very large and complicated. It is not possible to have tests that cover every possible permutation of an application. Attempting any such activity will prove expensive. An analysis of different core features should be made and test efforts focused on critical areas.

Early Testing Saves Time and Money

A quick smoke test of a new application release can help identify showstopper bugs that could have required the running of the entire test suite to unearth. This also applies to implementing test-driven development as much as possible.

Defects Cluster

A small number of components in an application will be responsible for the majority of bugs. Testing should then focus on these components that are responsible for the majority of the bugs. This is essentially applying the Pareto principle to testing application components.

Beware of the Pesticide Principle

The same set of tests repeated over a long period of time may end up not catching new defects. This principle is a simile to the ineffectiveness of pesticide applied to the same area over a long period in killing insects. Tests will need to be updated and refactored with new input data and permutations to keep them effective at identifying application defects.

Testing Is Contextual

Testing is a highly context-dependent activity. The tests applied to a business application will differ from the tests applied to an aerospace computer control application. This is important to keep in mind when taking inspiration for creating testing systems.

Absence of Errors Is a Fallacy

As elucidated in the first principle, tests do not guarantee the absence of errors. As such, it is a mistaken notion to assume an application is free of defects if tests do not unearth any. Also, identifying and fixing defects does not guarantee the system cannot fail.

Testing in Jakarta EE

Jakarta EE as an application development platform does not have a testing specification or API of its own. However, as it is built on Java SE, the gamut of testing libraries and frameworks available on Java SE can be used to test Jakarta EE applications. However, testing a Jakarta EE application presents some challenges.

A modern Jakarta EE application, like the one discussed so far in this book, makes heavy use of the Jakarta Contexts and Dependency Injection API. Almost all components are managed by one runtime or the other. For instance, a CDI bean might declare a dependency on another bean that in turn has a dependency on a JPA-managed artifact like the EntityManager.

Unit-Testing Jakarta EE Components

Unit-testing Jakarta EE components can be achieved with a little bit of refactoring of the component under test. A component under test that uses field injection can be refactored to use constructor injection for its dependencies. This way, the component under test can have its dependencies passed to it by CDI during application runtime and manually instantiated during testing through its constructor, passing in mocked instances of its dependencies.

JUnit

JUnit is a Java testing library for making assertions on test artifacts. It has a number of callbacks for setting up and tearing down test data. It also has an extension API that other testing libraries have built on top of to extend testing for different purposes. JUnit is arguably the most popular testing library in enterprise Java.

Mockito

Mockito is a Java library for creating mocked objects in unit tests. A component under test that has dependencies on other components will have those dependencies mocked. Mocking allows predictable values on the mocked objects to be returned and later asserted.

To test the WalletService CDI bean of jwallet, we first refactor it to use constructor injection for its two CDI-managed application components. This way, in a unit test, the WalletService can easily pass mocked objects. Listing 12-1 shows the refactored WalletService.

Listing 12-1. Refactored WalletService

```
@Action
@NoArgsConstructor
public class WalletService {

      WalletRepository walletRepository;
      TransactionRepository transactionRepository;
      RateService rateService;

      @Inject
      public WalletService(WalletRepository wallet,
            TransactionRepository txn,
            RateService rate) {

            this.walletRepository = wallet;
            this.transactionRepository = txn;
            this.rateService = rate;
      }
}
```

The WalletService has a dependency on the WalletRepository, TransactionRepository, and RateService. It has been refactored out to use constructor injection, with a single constructor annotated @Inject, passing in the three dependencies and initializing the class field with those. With this simple refactor, the WalletService is now ready to be unit-tested. Listing 12-2 shows the WalletService unit test class, WalletServiceTest.

Listing 12-2. WalletServiceTest

```
@ExtendWith(MockitoExtension.class)
public class WalletServiceTest {
    @Mock
    WalletRepository walletRepository;
    WalletService walletService;

    static String walletCurrency;
    static BigDecimal balance;
    @BeforeAll
    public static void initAll() {
        walletCurrency = "GHS";
        balance = new BigDecimal("50");
    }
    @BeforeEach
    void init() {

        walletService = new WalletService(walletRepository,
        null, null);
        when(walletRepository.findById(anyLong())).thenAnswer(i -> {
            Wallet wallet = new Wallet();
            wallet.setId(i.getArgument(0));
            wallet.setCurrency(walletCurrency);
            wallet.setBalance(balance);
            return wallet;

        });
```

```
    }

    @Test
    void shouldFindWallet() {
        BalanceResponse response = walletService.getBalance(1L);
        assertNotNull(response);
        assertEquals(1L, response.getData().getWalletId());

        assertEquals(balance, response.getData().getBalance());
        assertEquals(walletCurrency, response.getData().getCurrency());
    }
}
```

The class is annotated by @ExtendWith and passed the MockitoExtension.class. This registers the MockitoExtension with the JUnit runtime. The @Mock annotation is used to mock the WalletRepository. The @BeforeAll callback method sets up some expected data that the component under test, in this case the WalletService method to be tested, should return. The WalletService object is instantiated, passing in the mocked WalletRepository and null for the other two parameters. We could equally have mocked the two other parameters of the WalletService constructor.

The static Mockito *when* method is called to mock a call to the WalletRepository. findById method. The mock simply captures the passed ID and constructs a Wallet with it. We now have everything in place to unit-test the getBalance method of the WalletService.

The shouldFindWallet test method calls the getBalance method on the WalletService and proceeds to use the JUnit assertion methods to assert the expected data. This is generally how you craft unit tests in Jakarta EE for application components. Note that nothing significantly different was needed apart from the small refactoring of the component under test to use constructor injection to initialize dependent fields.

This kind of test is incredibly fast and can be run multiple times on the CI/CD pipeline. It is important to note that the WalletServiceTest is tested as a POJO that has nothing to do with Jakarta EE. Its method is tested and asserted to be acting as expected. As much as possible, you should unit-test core components of your application.

Integration Testing in Jakarta EE

Unlike unit testing, integration testing requires different components to talk to each other. This requires having a running instance of the application within the test context. Jakarta EE integration testing, depending on the application, entails making a call to an entry point in the application that will then result in the call to all constituent units of interest. This entry point is mostly a REST endpoint.

Deploying a running application in the test context had always been a little cumbersome in Jakarta EE. Frameworks like Arquillian helped in this regard. But even that was difficult to set up and required significant plumbing for the various compatible runtimes. As more and more applications are being developed to be cloud native first, the use of containers means a given environment can be replicated in different contexts as long as there is support for containers within that context.

TestContainers is a library for deploying applications as docker containers in a test environment. As jwallet is packaged as docker containers, spawning a running instance for integration testing requires only a docker-compose file. This docker-compose file will be used by the TestContainers library to create a running application instance in the test. With a running application instance, we can then proceed to fire REST calls to the application.

With TestContainers, there is no difference between the application running in the test and the deployed one because they are both created from the same docker containers. TestContainers have different modules for different stacks. The DockerComposeContainer module is for running containers from docker-compose files. Listing 12-3 shows the setup of DockerComposeContainer to create containers from the wallet module's docker-compose file.

Listing 12-3. DockerComposeContainer

```
try (DockerComposeContainer composeContainer = new
DockerComposeContainer(new File("docker-compose.yaml")).
withExposedService("wallet", 3001)) {
                composeContainer.start();

                walletServiceUrl = String.format(walletService
                UrlTemplate,
```

```
                            composeContainer.getServiceHost
                            ("wallet", 3001),
                            composeContainer.getServicePort
                            ("wallet", 3001));
                client = ClientBuilder.newClient();
                target = client.target(walletServiceUrl);
        }
```

The DockerComposeContainer is instantiated in a try-with-resources block so it can be auto-closed for us (it is AutoClosable). It is passed the docker-compose file and the service to expose from it, along with the port. The start method is called on the instance. The getServiceHost and getServicePort methods are called to get the host and port of the service as created in the running container. This is then passed to the target method of the Jakarta REST Client object. With this setup in place, we have a full running instance of the wallet module against which REST calls can be made and test assertions carried out on the responses. Listing 12-4 shows the createWallet JUnit test in the WalletResourceIT class.

Listing 12-4. createWalletTest

```
class WalletResourceIT extends AbstractWalletIT {

    @Test
    void createWallet() {
        CreateWalletRequest createWalletRequest = new
        CreateWalletRequest();
        createWalletRequest.setCurrency("USD");

        BalanceResponse balanceResponse = target.path("wallets").request()
                .post(Entity.json(createWalletRequest),
                BalanceResponse.class);

        assertEquals("0", balanceResponse.getResponse().getResponseCode());
        assertEquals("OK", balanceResponse.getResponse().
        getResponseMessage());

      assertEquals(createWalletRequest.getCurrency(), balanceResponse.
      getData().getCurrency());
```

```
        assertEquals(BigDecimal.ZERO, balanceResponse.getData().
        getBalance());

    }
}
```

The WalletResourceIT class extends AbstractWalletIT, which contains the TestContainers instantiation code. The createWallet method is a JUnit test that fires a REST call to the wallet resource to create a wallet and then makes some assertions on the returned data. Unlike the unit test, this test could take some time because the wallet creation process involves a call to the database. With just a few lines of code, we have a fully containerized application runtime from which we can make calls to create integration tests. We highly recommend you take a look at TestContainers for your Jakarta EE testing.

Summary

This chapter started with theories about software application testing, then looked at how to create unit and integration JUnit tests for Jakarta EE applications. The process of creating unit tests entailed isolating the component to test by mocking its dependencies of interest. We looked at using TestContainers to create a fully containerized Jakarta EE runtime to create integration tests.

As stated in the chapter, testing is a very domain-dependent activity that requires business analysis to identify what combination of the various test types to use and where testing resources should be concentrated. This chapter showed you the most efficient and straightforward options available for creating the two most popular types of tests – unit and integration tests.

CHAPTER 13

Jakarta EE Application Deployment Considerations

This book has covered the core APIs on the Jakarta EE platform for building applications. We have extensively looked at developing the various aspects of an application using the different APIs from a code perspective. As a general-purpose platform, the Jakarta EE specifications allow you to build all kinds of applications. This chapter covers the general theory of getting an application ready for production.

The chapter starts off by discussing what to look out for in preparing for production, options, and considerations for deploying a Jakarta EE application and how to structure an application for easy feature additions and bug fixes and general considerations. By the end of the chapter, you should have a firm theoretical foundation of getting an application ready for production deployment and maintenance afterward.

Production Readiness

Determining the readiness of an application for deployment is a combination of both technical and business considerations. The following are some factors to consider in readying an application for production.

L. Saeed and G. Abdallah, *Pro Cloud Native Java EE Apps*, https://doi.org/10.1007/978-1-4842-8900-6_13

Business Requirements Met?

Has the application met the business requirements for which it was developed? This will mostly be something for the business analysts to decide. A comprehensive requirements checklist will need to be compared to the application to determine that. Flowing from that checklist will be the testing requirements.

Test Requirements

A decision on what combination of tests to employ for the application will need to be made. What proportion of the tests should be automated? Manual? Of course, during the application process, a combination of unit and integration test sets would have been created. But a test strategy is needed to test application releases.

This test suite is independent of the tests in the application itself. These are mostly from the business perspectives, covering different aspects of the functional requirements of the application. This set of tests should have varying combinations of manual and automated tests, with the automated tests made up of a healthy balance of integration and performance tests.

CI/CD Pipelines

The continuous integration/development pipeline to ship bug fixes and new features from development to production will need to be considered. Of course, ideally there should be one in place as part of the development process right from the start.

Further Development Strategy

An application being deployed is the first step to a continuous process of refinements and bug fixing. There will be new feature requirements and bug fixes needed as long as the application is in use. Unlike in development where it's easy to break things, a deployed application requires careful consideration to not bring down the production instance. Mitigation strategies like database migrations should be employed to have a clear path to extending existing data. How often new releases get deployed to production should also be considered and standardized.

Security

Security is the single most important consideration for an application about to be deployed. Irrespective of the type of application being deployed, an end-to-end security consideration spanning user creation, authentication, authorization, access control, and revocation among other security processes will need to be considered.

More importantly is if security will be handled internally or outsourced to a security service. As nonsecurity experts, we recommend the Keycloak IAM framework to manage application security. Unless there are in-house dedicated security experts, we do not recommend rolling out custom security implementations.

These are by no means all the considerations that should be made in determining the readiness of an application. Every business domain will have its own checklist of readiness checks. In the end, an application is never completed. It only gets put into use while being perpetually worked on. With the readiness checks done, deployment options will need to be considered.

Jakarta EE Deployment

Jakarta EE applications are mostly packaged as web archive (WAR) files. These files are mostly dropped into the deployment folders of compatible runtimes, and the runtimes will then deploy the application. Thus, the basic unit of a Jakarta EE application deployment is the runtime. The runtime can be packaged as a docker container, as is done with the sample code seen so far, or stand-alone.

We recommend the adoption of containers throughout the application development process because it provides uniformity and predictability across teams and between team members. The problem of "but it was running on my machine" is largely done away with by the use of containers.

The runtime chosen for application development is almost always the runtime used for production deployment. Whichever option it is, choosing a runtime is the first step to deploying a Jakarta EE application.

Choosing a Runtime

Choosing a Jakarta EE–compatible runtime requires some considerations on the part of an organization. Some of these considerations are as follows.

Popularity of the Runtime

How popular a runtime is is an important consideration to make. A popular runtime will mean a much larger user base, and that consequently implies stronger momentum in the development of the runtime, whether closed or open source.

License Considerations

Is the runtime an open source, a closed source, or a hybrid license? An organization will need to determine if the license of the runtime fits into its overall application development strategy.

Support

What is the support model of the runtime? If it is open source, is there enough of a community around it from which community support can be expected? If it is closed source, what is the support structure and cost relative to the organization's budget?

Additional Features

One of the selling points of Jakarta EE is that it is an open platform on which implementation vendors can compete through the addition of add-on features above the base platform. The choice of an implementation should consider what other features beyond the platform base the runtime has.

Existing Knowledge

Picking a runtime should also consider the existing knowledge of people that will be working with it. How familiar is the team with the runtime? This will help reduce the time it takes for the team to get productive with the runtime.

Other Considerations

There will always be business domain–specific considerations that should be carried out when picking an application runtime. Jakarta EE has a healthy ecosystem of implementation runtimes and vendors that give an organization an abundance of choice to select.

Containerization

The rise of containers has made the packaging and deployment of applications much easier. For instance, the sample code for this book is packaged with docker and ready to run in any docker/kubernetes-managed infrastructure. The ease of use, universal availability, and platform-agnostic nature of containers mean every application development process should be containerized by default. There are different ways of using containers to run and package applications.

When incorporating containers into application development, it is important to create predictable images. Predictable images mean the container should generally act the same when given the same input data at all times and across all machines. This means the use of tags when pulling images from a registry. Tagging ensures the same image will be pulled in at all times.

Cloud Deployment

Deploying an application to the cloud entails picking a cloud option. Will the application be deployed to an in-house on-premise hosted set of servers or a hybrid or full cloud? These are decisions that will be made based on the existing infrastructure, knowledge, experience, and budget of the organization. With the use of containers, whichever option that is chosen will eventually come down to the organizational preference based on the aforementioned factors.

There is an abundance of choice when it comes to picking a cloud provider. Almost all cloud providers have support for docker and kubernetes. This means a modern Jakarta EE application can easily be deployed to any cloud provider. This is why we recommend the adoption of containers as part of the Jakarta EE application development cycle.

Database

Every application will need a durable data storage. The choice of database will be based on business and technical considerations. In the end, a choice between using a managed database service from a cloud provider or bundling one with the application as part of the set of containers will be made. We recommend using all the datasource management features of the chosen runtime. Jakarta EE runtimes traditionally have provided ways to define datasources that can then be passed to the application.

Security

Touching on security here as well since the deployment option, whether on-premise, hybrid, or fully cloud, will all have security implications. It is important to keep security in mind when weighing all available options for deployment.

Deploying a Monolith

Deploying a monolithic application is, in theory, easier than a suite of microservices. This is primarily because a monolith comprises a single unit. This single unit, when packaged into a WAR, is all of the application. There is nothing special to be done with regard to the actual deployment process. All the points discussed earlier should apply to deploying any Java application. And deploying a Jakarta EE application is deploying a pure Java application.

Application Maintenance

Once an application is deployed, maintaining it becomes an important aspect of its longevity. However, application maintenance starts right from when application development starts. No matter the application domain, incorporating best practices into the application development process will lead to much easier application maintenance and improve the longevity of an application and its codebase. The following are general guidelines to developing long-lived applications and making working on the application code a productive experience.

Use the Platform

The Jakarta EE platform, augmented with the MicroProfile project, provides a fairly rich collection of APIs for building general-purpose enterprise applications. Almost all core functional requirements will have corresponding APIs in the platform. For instance, there's an API for dependency injection, data persistence, REST web services, WebSockets, configuration, and fault tolerance, among others.

Your first choice of API should always be what is available on the platform. The use of third-party libraries should be carefully considered and adopted only when there is no API in the platform for that function.

Have a Package Standard

Having a standardized package structure means all applications, modules, and libraries of the organization will have the same structure and thus be easy to navigate for new joiners. A natural reality of every organization is that people will come and go. Having a standardized way of structuring applications means irrespective of who is doing the development, the structure of the application stays the same.

Choose a Runtime Carefully

Choosing the application runtime should be done carefully because the runtime can impact developer productivity. A runtime that is easy to spawn as a container, fast, easy to learn, and adopt is much preferable to one that does not have these characteristics. Since the runtime chosen for development is what eventually will be used to deploy the application, having a runtime that developers are familiar with and makes them productive is important.

Avoid Excessive Use of Third-Party Libraries

The Java ecosystem has a massive array of third-party libraries for solving almost all application development tasks. It can get tempting to want to adopt some of these libraries because they may look attractive. But it's important to keep in mind that every extra library that gets drawn in becomes a part of the maintenance overhead of the application. Thus, the use of the third-party libraries should be minimized and used only as a last resort.

Keep Things Simple

Application development is very much an art. Finding the right balance between complexity and simplicity is something that will take some trial and error. However, simplicity should be a theme that runs through the codebase. Keeping things simple allows for relatively easy extensions, feature additions, and bug fixes. It also helps other developers settle in much faster with the codebase. These are all intrinsic benefits that add up over a long period of time. Simplicity, as the adage goes, is the ultimate sophistication.

Have a Convention

Having an application development process convention is important to maintaining a system that supports productivity. How new joiners are onboarded, what the standard operating procedure is for creating new features, how production bugs are handled are all normal parts of the application development process that should be standardized. Systems like SCRUM and Kanban help create a system that gives participants a routine. Whichever system that is chosen should support structures that automate as much of the work process as possible.

Document Excessively

Documentation, right from the code level (in-line, Javadocs) to the API level to the business level, should be a part and parcel of the application development process. Documentation first of all serves as an extended memory to the application developers. Having documentation covering as much of the codebase as possible helps different developers work on different aspects of the application. It also helps new developers get familiar with the codebase much faster. Whether the application is a consumer application with a UI-facing tier, or an API application, documentation for the client should be an important aspect of the entire process.

Build and Dependency Management

Every enterprise Jakarta EE application will most likely use one of two dominant build and dependency management tools - Maven or Gradle. These two tools allow the automation of a lot of common application development tasks like management of transitive dependencies and building of application artifacts. Whichever tool that is chosen should be standardized upon. All services should use the chosen build tool. As a lot of Jakarta EE applications are built with Maven, we recommend it over Gradle solely because of user adoption in the space. However, Gradle is equally a capable build tool that can do everything Maven can. Whichever tool that is chosen should be done based on which one will produce the maximum business returns.

There are a number of ways to automate some of the documentation process. For instance, the MicroProfile OpenAPI specification[1] provides declarative ways of documenting Jakarta REST resources, much similar to the Swagger API.[2] The documentation can be published in a central place for easy access to end users. Whichever form that is chosen, a culture of excessive code documentation should be encouraged and nurtured because documenting the whys of the various parts of the application to the hows of its usage is an investment that will compound over the life of the application.

Summary

This chapter discussed general considerations that should be taken into account before an application is deployed. We discussed some guidelines to determine if an application is ready for production and looked at deployment guidelines and finally some pointers to creating a long-lived, maintainable application.

[1] MicroProfile OpenAPI 3.0 Specification Release

[2] Swagger

CHAPTER 14

Cloud-Native Jakarta EE Monoliths to Microservices

Microservices software architecture is increasingly becoming the dominant choice for creating enterprise, cloud-native applications. The Jakarta EE platform, augmented by the Eclipse MicroProfile project, even though originally designed for large monolithic applications, has evolved to become a capable platform for developing microservice applications.

This chapter explores general guidelines for breaking down a monolithic application to a set of microservices. It starts off by first exploring the pros and cons of monoliths, then explores the need, if any, for microservices, and finally offers strategies for migrating a monolith to microservices that is cloud-ready for deployment to a kubernetes cluster.

Monoliths

A monolithic application is one that has all the constituent parts bundled together as a single unit. A large number of enterprise applications out there are monolithic. Even before the rise in popularity of the microservices architecture, Jakarta EE, or then Java EE, applications have always been more of modular monoliths. A modular monolith is an architecture where core parts of the application are broken down into submodules within the application. So, for instance, a typical Jakarta EE application would have the UI layer, which could be written with Jakarta Faces or any JavaScript framework, then you have the services layer, which is typically made up of a combination of CDI beans

L. Saeed and G. Abdallah, *Pro Cloud Native Java EE Apps*, https://doi.org/10.1007/978-1-4842-8900-6_14

and EJB session beans (EJBs are being supplanted by CDI) for managing database connections and application logic.

Such an application might not necessarily have a REST component because the UI layer (if using Jakarta Faces) makes direct calls to the service layer. During packaging, this kind of application will be packaged as a single WAR file. But in actual sense, it's much of a modular monolith, lending itself to easy migration to microservices if the need arises. The sample code of this book so far has been a cross between a pure microservices and a pure monolith.

Pros of the Monolith Architecture

Even though the microservices architecture has taken off in recent years, monoliths still have their place because as with all things technology, they have some unique advantages over microservices in some contexts. The following are some of the strong parts of the monolith architecture.

Simple to Develop

Because a monolith is a single-unit application, it is generally much more easy to develop. With all parts in the same codebase, developing, adding features, refactoring, and extending the application are relatively easy. It is also easy to onboard new developers to the project since there is a single point of reference.

Easier to Test

As a single unit, it is relatively easy to write full end-to-end tests for a monolith. Because all the constituent parts of the application are in a single package, writing automated integration tests is much more easy and straightforward.

Easier to Deploy

As the whole application is packaged as a single WAR file, deployment entails dropping this war file into the deployment folder of a runtime. Whether packaged as a docker container or using the traditional deployment methods, deploying a single WAR file is generally straightforward.

Easier to Debug

Debugging a monolith is relatively easy since the entire application is available within the debugging context. Following the flow of execution to different parts of the application to identify the source of a bug is easy and straightforward.

Reusability

A lot of common functionality like cross-cutting concerns are developed and used over and over again. There is also less duplication of code since everything is in one place.

Easy to Add New Developers

Developers will always come and go. A monolith allows for relatively easy onboarding of new developers to the application development team. With everything in one place, there is less cognitive overhead in getting comfortable with the codebase.

Easier Application Evolution

With a unified codebase and a relative ease in onboarding new developers, a monolith is easy to evolve with the addition of new features.

Easy to Scale

Horizontally scaling a monolith generally entails multiple copies of the same deployment artifact behind different load balancers. In that regard, it is easy and cheaper to scale when the need arises.

Challenges of the Monolith

Even though a monolith has these and other advantages, it also comes with some challenges, especially as the complexity of the application grows. The following are some challenges that can arise from the use of the monolith architecture.

Single Point of Failure

As the entire application runs as a single instance, a problem in one component can bring down the whole application. For instance, an out-of-memory error resulting from an unclosed file reader could cause the whole instance to crash.

Slow to Adopt New Technologies

As the entire application is in a single unit, it is much slower to adopt new versions of libraries and APIs because careful thoughts need to go into impact assessment of every single change. This takes time and can be quite expensive.

Full Redeployment

Any change in the application, irrespective of the size, generally requires a redeployment of the full artifact.

Grown Complexity

At some point, a monolith might become too large and complex to be fully understood by any single person. This could result in impaired change impact assessments, resulting in changes that may not be fully understood.

Microservices

Considerations for Adoption or Migration

Despite its shortcomings, the monolithic architecture has worked well for the vast majority of applications. As with all other things, there is always a need to take the business domain and context into consideration when deciding whether to use the microservices architecture or not. The following are some guidelines to help determine the need for the use of the microservices architecture.

Application Insights

The first factor to consider when thinking about microservices is if there are enough application insights for the currently running application. This could entail detailed knowledge of the different possible bottleneck areas, application performance under different conditions, which components have caused the most failures over a given period of time, and other such metrics. This is important to ascertain if there really is a need to split the application up into different microservices. These insights will help to know what constituent microservices the application should be split into. It will also help to know which (if any) part of the application needs scaling independent of the other parts.

Availability of Technical Knowledge

The availability of the engineering knowledge to maintain a set of microservices needs to be considered. Since every microservice is a "mini application," consideration will need to be given to whether there is the engineering knowledge to keep each unit running.

Onboarding New Developers

Unlike a monolith, a microservice application will be made up of different services, each acting as a self-contained application. Consideration will need to be given to how new developers get onboarded onto the development team. How to get new joiners to become as productive as possible is something that merits consideration.

Deployment Costs

Unlike a monolith, microservices might require different deployment servers and platforms. This merits consideration from both the engineering and the finance perspective to determine if any marginal costs of deployment relative to the monolith are worth it.

Keeping the End Goal in Mind

Microservices should be understood to be a means to an end. This end could vary from organization to organization, but in the end, it always involves the use of an application to provide some form of value to its users. As such, microservices are just one means of attaining such a goal and should not become a focus in and of itself. Unless the marginal benefit of developing with microservices architecture outweighs the benefit, it should not be adopted for its own sake.

Migrating a Monolith

The process of migrating a monolith to a microservices architecture is a very domain-dependent exercise. However, the following sections give general guidelines that can be adopted and customized for different domains.

Single Responsibility Principle

Every microservice should be responsible for a single core function of the application. The function of each service should be simple to understand based on its name and REST interfaces. Since each microservice will be exposed to other modules through REST endpoints, it should be clear, on the face of these endpoints, what each service does.

Organize Around the Business Domain

Each service should be organized around the business domain. For instance, a restaurant application should be broken down into the different core aspects of running a restaurant - order placement service, billing service, kitchen service, and such. The bounded context of the various services should be the business domain.

Create Libraries for Common Functionality

Commonly used cross-cutting functionality should be abstracted into a library, packaged as a JAR file that can then be depended upon by services that need those functions. Code duplication should be minimized through abstractions.

Deployable Unit

Each microservice should be a single deployable unit. Consequently, each service should be an application on its own, complete with its own suite of tests. Each service should have its own pipeline and CI/CD infrastructure. By deployable unit we mean each service should have its own build tool files (pom.xml, build.gradle files), ideally inheriting from a parent file that contains common libraries if applicable, and have its own runtime packaging files (Containerfile, Dockerfile, docker-compose.yaml, and a kubernetes manifest descriptor). This is because each unit should be independently deployable as a container instance, manageable as a pod in a cluster.

Communicate via REST

All the services should be exposed for consumption through HTTP REST endpoints. Each application should separate the boundaries from the actual implementations of the REST endpoints. The client of each service should only know about the artifacts of the service exposed through the REST infrastructure of the service. No implementation detail should be exposed to consuming clients of a service. The default data exchange format should largely be based on JSON. Each REST resource should be secured, ideally through the MicroProfile JWT runtime.

Separate Security Contexts

Each service should have a separate security context. In Keycloak, each service should be a separate client in the application realm.[1] Each service should have its own set of roles and permissions.

Sample Migrated Application

With these and other guidelines, let us take a look at the wallet microservice of the project code for this book. The full application was originally a monolith that allows users to create a wallet of different currencies and get exchange rates for each wallet, with each transaction stored for each wallet.

The wallet service handles a wallet and its transactions. The rate service handles the external call to the rate service using the MicroProfile REST Client. There are two external rate services configured, with one being a fallback service that should be automatically invoked should the primary service fail.

This fallback feature is configured with the MicroProfile Fault Tolerance API. The account service layer handles the user account. It has a REST endpoint for creating accounts that will be invoked by a callback in Keycloak when a user creates an account. Breaking this application down in microservices, using the guidelines in the previous section, entails having at least three services - account, rate, and wallet.

The wallet service is going to be the focal point of discussion for the migration. However, everything discussed about it pertains to the other two services. The root entry point is the pom.xml shown in Listing 14-1.

[1] Server Administration Guide

Listing 14-1. Wallet pom.xml

```
<?xml version="1.0" encoding="UTF-8" ?>
<project xmlns="http://maven.apache.org/POM/4.0.0"
   xmlns:xsi="http://www.w3.org/2001/XMLSchema-instance"
   xsi:schemaLocation="http://maven.apache.org/POM/4.0.0 http://maven.
   apache.org/xsd/maven-4.0.0.xsd">
   <modelVersion>4.0.0</modelVersion>

     <parent>
       <groupId>com.example</groupId>
       <artifactId>jwallet</artifactId>
       <version>1.0-SNAPSHOT</version>
   </parent>

   <artifactId>jwallet.wallet</artifactId>
   <packaging>war</packaging>

   <dependencies>
       <dependency>
           <groupId>${project.groupId}</groupId>
           <artifactId>jwallet.core</artifactId>
           <version>${project.version}</version>
       </dependency>
   </dependencies>

   <build><finalName>wallet</finalName></build>

</project>
```

The wallet service is one of three distinct microservices that showcase the breakdown of a monolith to constituent parts. The root pom file of the wallet service, as shown in Listing 14-1, declares a parent pom file. This parent pom file that is partly shown in Listing 14-1 declares all common dependencies for all microservices in the application. For instance, it declares the Jakarta EE and MicroProfile dependencies.

The parent pom file is packaged as a maven pom file that can be consumed or inherited by its children. The wallet root pom makes use of the parent to pull in the common dependencies. The use of the parent/child inheritance feature of the Maven build management tool allows us to keep the root pom file simple. Only a single dependency is declared here, which is to the core module.

The core module allows us to abstract artifacts and functions that are common across all services into a single service. For instance, the AbstractEntity Jakarta Persistence parent entity class, the AbstractEntityListener class, and the CDI @Action stereotype are all declared in the core module. The abovementioned artifacts are all discussed in detail in their respective chapters. The wallet service is created as a single-unit maven web application. As such, it has all the structures of a maven project as shown in Figure 14-1.

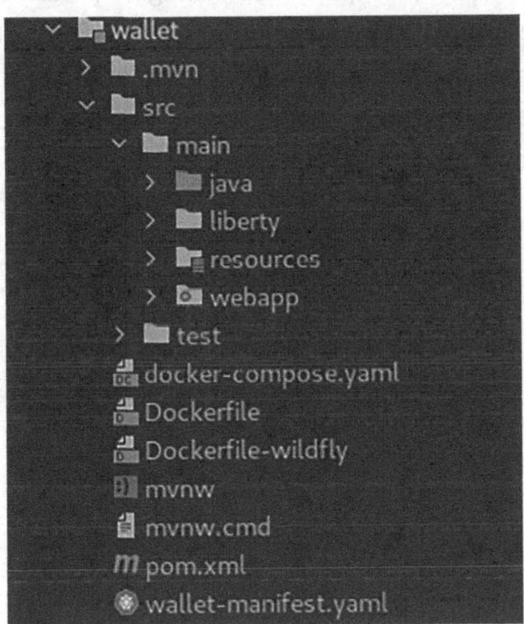

Figure 14-1. *Wallet service structure*

As a single-unit, packageable service, it has a Dockerfile, docker-compose.yaml file, and Kubernetes descriptor. The Dockerfile allows us to build this service as a docker image that can be pushed to any docker registry. Listing 14-2 shows the Dockerfile.

Listing 14-2. Wallet service Dockerfile

```
FROM icr.io/appcafe/open-liberty:22.0.0.3-full-java11-openj9-ubi

COPY --chown=1001:0 src/main/liberty/config /config
COPY --chown=1001:0 src/main/liberty/*.jar /opt/ol/wlp/usr/shared/
resources/
COPY --chown=1001:0 target/*.war /config/apps

EXPOSE 3001

RUN configure.sh
CMD ["/opt/ol/wlp/bin/server", "debug", "defaultServer"]
```

The Dockerfile depends on the OpenLiberty image. OpenLiberty is the Jakarta EE runtime used to run the application. The OpenLiberty configs, database driver file, and the application war files are copied with the COPY command to the container. This is essentially all that is needed to run the wallet service as a docker container. The docker-compose.yaml file is shown in Listing 14-3.

Listing 14-3. Wallet docker-compose.yaml file

```
version: "3"

services:

  postgres:
    image: postgres:12.3
    #    ports:
    #      - "5432:5432"
    environment:
      POSTGRES_USER: jwallet
      POSTGRES_PASSWORD: jwallet

  wallet:
    image: jwallet/wallet:latest
    ports:
      - "3001:3001"
    build:
      context: .
      dockerfile: Dockerfile
```

The docker-compose file composes a fully running set of container instances by pulling in the Postgres version 12.3 image and building the wallet image through the bundled Dockerfile. With these files, the wallet module can be packaged and run as a cloud-native, self-contained Jakarta EE application. The wallet service is exposed to clients through HTTP REST resources in the WalletResource class shown in Listing 14-4.

Listing 14-4. WalletResource

```
@RegisterRestClient(baseUri = "http://wallet:3001/wallet/api")
@Consumes(MediaType.APPLICATION_JSON)
@Produces(MediaType.APPLICATION_JSON)
@Path("wallets")
@RolesAllowed("teller")
public interface WalletResource {

    @POST
    @Traced(operationName = "create-wallet")
    @SimplyTimed(name = "create_wallet_timer")
    BalanceResponse createWallet(CreateWalletRequest
    createWalletRequest);
    @GET
    @Path("{walletId}/balance")
    @Traced(operationName = "get-wallet-balance")
    @SimplyTimed(name = "get_wallet_balance_timer")
    BalanceResponse getBalance(@PathParam("walletId") long walletId);

    @GET
    @Path("{walletId}/transactions")
    @Traced(operationName = "get-wallet-transactions")
    @SimplyTimed(name = "get_wallet_transactions_timer")
    TransactionsResponse getTransactions(@PathParam("walletId")
    long walletId);

    @POST
    @Path("{walletId}/transactions/debit")
    @Traced(operationName = "debit-wallet")
    @SimplyTimed(name = "debit_wallet_timer")
```

```
    TransactionResponse debit(@PathParam("walletId") long walletId,
    TransactionRequest transactionsRequest);

    @POST
    @Path("{walletId}/transactions/credit")
    @Traced(operationName = "credit-wallet")
    @SimplyTimed(name = "credit_wallet_timer")
    TransactionResponse credit(@PathParam("walletId") long walletId,
    TransactionRequest transactionsRequest);

}
```

The WalletResource is a Jakarta REST resource that can also be used as a MicroProfile REST Client with the @RegisterRestClient. It consumes and produces JSON and requires the executing client to have the role teller. MicroProfile JWT is used to validate and propagate JWT tokens passed by the client. It also declares some metrics using the MicroProfile Metrics API. The module also has its own unit and integration tests.

The implementation of these resource methods can and, in general, should reuse the existing logic from the monolith. Migrating from a monolith to microservices will mostly center around the boundary and packaging of the application. Existing business logic should be reused as much as possible.

This resource, on the face of it, gives a description of the functions of the wallet service. As an HTTP service, we can deploy it in a cloud cluster and let Kubernetes manage its deployment, scaling, and updating. The wallet-manifest.yaml file creates a Kubernetes-managed object. Listing 14-5 shows the manifest file.

Listing 14-5. Wallet manifest file

```
apiVersion: networking.k8s.io/v1
kind: Ingress
metadata:
  name: wallet
  labels:
    app: wallet
spec:
  rules:
    - host: "*.wallet.sslip.io"
```

```
      http:
        paths:
          - path: /
            pathType: Prefix
            backend:
              service:
                name: wallet
                port:
                  name: wallet-port
---
apiVersion: v1
kind: Service
metadata:
  name: wallet
  labels:
    app: wallet
spec:
  ports:
  - name: wallet-port
    port: 3001
    targetPort: 3001
  selector:
    app: wallet
---
apiVersion: apps/v1
kind: Deployment
metadata:
  name: wallet
  labels:
    app: wallet
spec:
  replicas: 1
  selector:
    matchLabels:
      app: wallet
```

```
  template:
    metadata:
      labels:
        app: wallet
    spec:
      containers:
      - name: wallet
        image: k3d-registry.localhost:12345/jwallet/wallet:latest
        resources:
          limits:
            memory: "512Mi"
            cpu: "500m"
        ports:
        - containerPort: 9080
        env:
          - name: JAEGER_AGENT_HOST
            value: jaeger
          - name: JAEGER_AGENT_PORT
            value: "6831"
          - name: JAEGER_SAMPLER_TYPE
            value: const
          - name: JAEGER_SAMPLER_PARAM
            value: "1"
        livenessProbe:
          httpGet:
            path: /health/live
            port: 3001
          initialDelaySeconds: 60
          periodSeconds: 60
          timeoutSeconds: 10
          failureThreshold: 10
        readinessProbe:
          httpGet:
            path: /health/ready
            port: 3001
```

```
initialDelaySeconds: 60
periodSeconds: 60
timeoutSeconds: 10
failureThreshold: 10
```

With these file descriptors in place, we have transformed the wallet microservice into a cloud-native Jakarta EE application. The rate and account services have a similar structure to the wallet service. Using the guidelines in the previous section, we are able to decompose the monolith into business-bounded contexts. Each service is a single deployable unit, complete with its own tests.

The sample code contains a shell script that has commands to package and run the application as docker containers deployed to a Kubernetes-managed cluster. The Readme file contains all the needed information to run the application or individual microservices. Each service can be run stand-alone or together as a single unit. With the application packaged as containers and with the requisite descriptors, deploying to a cloud provider is as simple as pushing the generated images to a docker registry (most cloud providers have their own registry) and choosing the pushed image to deploy. The Microsoft Azure Kubernetes Service[2] (AKS) is a good starting point for your own experimenting.

Summary

This chapter looked at monoliths and their pros and cons, then proceeded to discuss the considerations to keep in mind when adopting or migrating to a microservices architecture. The chapter then moved to take a look at one of three microservices and the general parts that will need changing when migrating an application from a monolith to microservices. As stated in the chapter, migrating an application is a domain-dependent task; however, we have attempted to provide broad guidelines and considerations that should help clarify the process and task of migrating.

[2] Azure Kubernetes Service (AKS)

Index

A

B

C

L. Saeed and G. Abdallah, *Pro Cloud Native Java EE Apps*, https://doi.org/10.1007/978-1-4842-8900-6

D

E

I

J

K

L

M

Q

R

S

Printed in the United States
by Baker & Taylor Publisher Services

Printed in the United States
by Baker & Taylor Publisher Services